CU00704390

STRATEGIC LEADERSHIP

ADRIAN H. T. DAVIES

STRATEGIC LEADERSHIP

Making corporate plans work

Published in association with
The Institute of Directors
and
The Institute of Chartered Secretaries and Administrators

WOODHEAD-FAULKNER
NEW YORK   LONDON   TORONTO   SYDNEY   TOKYO   SINGAPORE

Published by Woodhead-Faulkner (Publishers) Limited,
Simon & Schuster International Group,
Fitzwilliam House, 32 Trumpington Street,
Cambridge CB2 1QY, England

First published 1991

© Woodhead-Faulkner (Publishers) Limited

Conditions of sale
All rights reserved. No part of this publication may be reproduced, stored in
a retrieval system or transmitted, in any form or by any means, electronic,
mechanical, photocopying, recording or otherwise, without the prior permission
of the publisher.

British Library Cataloguing in Publication Data
Davies, Adrian H. T.
Strategic Leadership
1. Business enterprise. Long-range planning
I. Title   II. Institute of Directors   III. Institute of
Chartered Secretaries and Administrators
658.4012
ISBN 0-85941-724-7

Designed by Geoff Green
Typeset by Cambridge Composing (UK) Ltd, Cambridge
Printed in Great Britain by BPCC Wheatons Ltd, Exeter

CONTENTS

FOREWORD

For many years in my business career I have been a director of a number of companies of varying sizes and the current popular phrase 'corporate governance' has become progressively more meaningful to me as the manner in which the affairs of corporations are directed.

Whether it is by 'mission statements' or by 'business strategies' the need for the visionary long-term overview, against the background of increasingly unpredictable and rapid and dramatic discontinuities, becomes progressively more powerful.

And who should provide these overviews in the first instance? It is the board of directors endowing the organisation with effective far-sighted leadership.

The potential benefits to be obtained from the presence of non-executive directors took a long time to be appreciated in the United Kingdom and we lagged behind our competitor nations for many years in inviting 'outsiders' to become part of the hierarchical structure of our companies. But momentum, once established, is gaining speed and the need to exhort companies to appoint a fair proportion of these outsiders to their boards is less urgent. Nevertheless, there remains a need to select non-executive directors with a view to building boards capable of effective team-work and to use their talents more extensively to the benefit of their company.

But having established them on our boards what do we expect of them? The answer is, 'quite a lot' as they bring their experience and personal qualities to the board table. But, in my view, of the wide-ranging contributions they make to corporate governance nothing is more important than their involvement in the development of the company's strategy.

Interest in improving corporate governance was very much stimulated by the wave of takeovers in the 1980s and by the prospect of unfettered European competition in the 1990s. The ongoing debate on short-termism has alerted companies to the need to look beyond the next annual report and to build a defensible future.

The Strategic Planning Society has concentrated on improving awareness of, and the practical use of, strategy throughout companies. As responsibility for achieving results is progressively devolving to those nearest the customer, the need to improve strategic planning down the line has grown and the Society has helped to meet this challenge. This process is, however, ineffective unless it takes place within a strategic framework provided by the board. It is in providing this framework and in continually reviewing it in the light of changed and competitive pressure that the board provides leadership. Prior to the publication of this book, the methodology for doing this has not previously been made readily available for directors to examine and adapt to their own businesses.

I commend this book to your attention.

Sir John Hedley Greenborough
President, The Strategic Planning Society
Former President, Confederation of British Industry

PREFACE

This is not primarily a textbook of corporate planning of which there are already many, ranging from Ansoff to Argenti. I have written this book in order to demystify planning and hopefully make it accessible to those who have to set a sustainable strategic direction for line executives to follow, with assistance from the limited planning staff now left in most companies. Planning has for too long been the realm of the planners, just as management has been usurped by managers. I hope that this book will help restore the balance on both accounts and bring the boardroom back into the pivotal role which it seems to have lost in too many companies.

Much of the content of this book relates to the experience and practice of larger companies. This is because strategic planning was nurtured and developed in larger companies and, as a result, the available evidence and best practice is mainly in the large-business area. Numerous surveys in many countries have shown that the use of strategic planning enables smaller companies to achieve improved results, but specific examples are difficult to identify. As far as possible smaller-company experience is quoted in this book, but the value of effective strategy is as great for smaller companies as for the larger ones into which they aspire to grow.

Strategy is the major ongoing responsibility of the board. The survival and growing prosperity of their company is, or should be, the primary concern of shareholders. Loyalty of employees to their company has suffered in recent years from waves of redundancy; directors' loyalty has suffered from short term pressures for performance; and the loyalty of shareholders (with institutions holding most of the shares on average) has been diverted from ownership to the maximisation of short term gain. Without commitment from its stakeholders, it is difficult to sustain a long-term strategy enabling the company to prosper and reward its shareholders, its directors and its employees with growing and compounding wealth.

How can this commitment be won? If we look at companies which have prospered over an extended period (for example, Stora Kopparbergs, St Gobain, Dupont, Cadbury Schweppes, and others) their performance seems to have been sustained by a powerful mixture of corporate culture and leadership. The 'idea of the business' has been clear over the years, even though some like Stora have changed products, and those running the company have shown skill, determination and consistency in pursuing the goals of the business, and in winning support from employees, shareholders and others in so doing. If Stora has done this for 600 years, it must be possible to set other companies on the virtuous road to sustained prosperity.

The leadership to do this must come initially from the boardroom. The directors are appointed by the shareholders to manage their company and, despite denials and grumbling, most employees want to be given a framework of objectives and policies within which they can develop and exploit their talents. They want to be part of a winning team, and the teams that win usually have clear objectives and the will to succeed. To create a winning team the board must not only establish and sell a challenging strategy, but also deploy its resources with skill over the time needed to achieve that strategy.

This book is about the process of equipping and motivating the board to undertake, sustain and achieve its strategic task. This is not something that the board does in isolation from stakeholders both inside and outside the company. Stakeholders have a part to play in the strategic task and need to be committed to their parts through ownership of them, but the board remains accountable to shareholders for its stewardship and must initiate, renew and bring the process to fruition. This is a task requiring professional skill and dedication – and some of the luck of Napoleon's favourite marshals – in order to succeed. I hope this book will stimulate interest in, and commitment to, creative strategic planning. As for luck, remember Pasteur's saying that chance favours the prepared mind!

Strategic planning is a technical subject, although I have striven to avoid unnecessary detail and have quoted only key passages of important texts. These I have listed in a reference section intended for those who wish to pursue particular issues in more depth. References to articles in journals and occasional papers are also given.

I am grateful to Woodhead-Faulkner for their invitation to write this book, and to the Institute of Directors and the Institute of Chartered Secretaries and Administrators for their association with it. A debt of thanks is due also to the Strategic Planning Society for their recommendation of my work – in particular to Bruce Lloyd and Christopher Clarke who have patiently and thoroughly read the draft. Particular thanks are due to Philip Sadler, lately Chief Executive of Ashridge Management College, for his thoughtful contribution on education for future directors.

1

STRATEGY IN A COMPETITIVE
WORLD

1.1. The changing environment

The environment in which all boards will have to operate in the foreseeable future is characterised by turbulence, change, uncertainty, risk and the search for survival.

Turbulence and the growing pace of change

In his book *Future Shock*, Alvin Toffler (1971) describes the growing pace of change in the early 1970s and its effects on society and individual human beings. His theme is the capacity of humanity to adapt to change and the future he describes envelops us today. Permanence never existed in reality, as the ruins of countless empires testify with brutal clarity. There was, however, an illusion of permanence in the ordered societies of the past. Life in a feudal village might not change perceptibly in a hundred years, and even in the Age of Enlightenment men believed that the rule of Reason would bring a steady and ordered improvement in the lot of mankind.

Since the late eighteenth century the old order has been subjected to successive waves of turbulence and has virtually disappeared. Its few vestiges, such as a modified British monarchy, serve only to emphasise the change that has occurred, and to show the increasing speed with which everything else is altering, most recently in Eastern Europe and the Middle East.

Uncertainty and risk

Given that turbulence is increasing, that change is accelerating and that there is no discernible pattern in the process, uncertainty will progressively increase and risk will take new and more menacing forms.

Risk comes in many shapes, but those affecting business mainly comprise commercial, political and social risks. Commercial risks are those affecting the capital, cash flow or profits of a company as a result of its normal trading activities, its development decisions and its investment moves. These might include bad debts, property losses or abortive research work. Political risks are essentially extraneous to the business and are concentrated in areas of governmental fiat both at home and overseas, and on the wider hazards of trading internationally (payment problems, exchange losses, and so on). Social risks are often linked to political risk but are worth identifying separately, since unlike commercial and many political risks most of them are in practice uninsurable. Such risks include fashion and habit changes, social attitudes, environmental issues and many aspects of human relations or employment.

Survival and beyond

In 1978 Reginald Jones, Chairman of General Electric Corporation speculated that the business corporation might not survive into the twenty-first century due to the pressure of change. Such a devastating threat is now less readily accepted, though the survival of every individual business has still to be fought for.

As Peter Drucker says, 'In a competitive economy, above all the quality and performance of its managers determine the success of a business, indeed they determine its survival' (1967). Drucker sees survival as the central purpose of the firm in his article 'Business Objectives and Survival Needs' (1958) and establishes a set of survival objectives needed for maintaining a business in existence. This philosophy may be seen in the objectives of many businesses today where survival is the fundamental plank in the structure.

Survival in itself is sterile, but is an essential prerequisite for achieving results which will build the long-term future of the company in the business in which it has chosen to compete.

1.2. Short term and long term

The concept of short and long periods in economics was developed by Alfred Marshall in a search for a stable equilibrium between supply and demand. A later economist W. W. Rostow has attacked the validity of separating the short and long periods as follows:

At any given moment of time the economy is in fact being shaped by the long run flow of demographic and technological change, as well as by short period movements along fixed supply and demand curves or by short term shifts in effective demand and supply. Contrary to Keynes' famous dictum 'in the long run we are all dead' – the long run is with us every day of our lives. (Rostow, 1980)

In his book *Megatrends* John Naisbitt (1984) attacks the short-term focus of American management, with its emphasis on the next quarter's earnings per share and its annual reward system. This he contrasts with Japanese business philosophy and with the growing concern about protecting the environment among thinking people. 'Short-termism' has been attacked in the United Kingdom also and was the subject of a CBI survey a few years ago which found that the problem had been exaggerated. Soon after came the crash of October 1987.

It is revealing to list Naisbitt's ten megatrends, as follows:

1. Movement from an industrial society to an information society.
2. From forced technology to high tech/high touch (balancing material wonders with spiritual demands).
3. From a national economy to a world economy.
4. From short term to long term (avoiding domination by numbers).
5. From centralisation to decentralisation (rebuilding bottom-up).
6. From institutional help to self-help.
7. From representative democracy to participatory democracy (consumerism, outside board members, shareholder activism, employee participation).
8. From hierarchies to networking.
9. From north to south (shift of polarity in the United States).
10. From either/or to multiple options.

Most of these trends will have a very significant effect on the plans of any perceptive business today, and the identification of such fundamental movements is of immense value in the search for order and meaning among the chaos of change which envelops every firm. It is the perception of such order and meaning, coupled to a strategic vision of what the business should become over time, that makes it possible to plan realistically for the long term.

Definitions of short and long term abound and differ from business to business. Ansoff (1979) speaks of a 'proximate period' (three to ten years) which extends to the 'planning horizon' of the firm. Beyond that lies the long-term period for which accurate forecasts cannot be made. Most modern practitioners would see the short term as much closer to the present, and make the distinction less in terms of the ability to forecast as in terms of strategic relevance. Strategies need to be timely to be successful and need time to achieve success. Ohmae points out that more strategies fail because they are overripe than because they are premature; he warns word-processor manufacturers of their failure to recognise the threat of personal computers to their market. Of the time needed to achieve success he says,

Successful companies pace their strategies. They realise that steady step by step progress is a much surer way of winning than an all-or-nothing dash that could end in exhaustion far short of the goal. The history of Japanese corporate casualties is studded with companies that overreached themselves in this way, mainly through ill-calculated speculations. (Ohmae, 1983).

The accelerating rate of change in the markets served by most businesses not only threatens to shorten their planning horizon but puts increasing pressure on them to speed up the development and marketing of new products. Tom Peters (1989) talks of 'time-based' competition, involving flexible manufacturing systems and computer-integrated manufacturing, electronic data interchange, just-in-time stock management and other techniques aimed at maximising market responsiveness. This time-based competition is linked to a rapid shrinking of product life cycles, making rapid market penetration and high market share crucial for profitability. This will intensify the pressure of competition in most markets and raise the stakes for corporate survival.

1.3. The all-pervading impact of competition

Michael Porter (1985) identifies five basic forces driving competition in a typical industry – entry, threat of substitution, bargaining power of buyers, bargaining power of suppliers, and rivalry among current competitors. Entry is achieved either by diversification or by acquisition (not strictly a new entity but likely to create more competitive pressure); substitute products are particularly threatening when they have a better price-performance balance than the established product; the bargaining power of buyers reduces the overall profitability of the supplying industry; the bargaining power of suppliers to the industry also reduces its overall profitability; and rivalry among current competitors also leads to reduced profitability for the industry unless the price elasticity of demand can match lower unit revenues. In many industries, therefore, competition is at best a zero-sum game and often will lead to a net loss, unless the market for the product can be widened significantly by competitive action.

Examples abound of markets which have been popularised by competition, ranging from cars, through household equipment, to airline tickets, package holidays and some financial products. Cars were originally sold exclusively to the rich, and the market took off only when mass production, mass marketing and hire purchase were orchestrated successfully by Ford and General Motors.

Businessmen have constantly striven to limit or control competition. The big trusts which sought to dominate the railways, oil and other industries in the nineteenth century were succeeded by the cartels which have sought to manage trade in the earlier years of this century. The steel, textile and some other industries remain 'managed' today despite the present emphasis on market forces in the major free-world economies. In his book *The New Industrial State*, J. K. Galbraith (1967) paints a picture of ordered and manipulated markets behind a facade of liberal economic appearances. In a recent lecture to the Strategic Planning Society (1989) he emphasised that Ronald Reagan had not restored classical free enterprise in the United States and drew attention to the bureaucratic ossification of much of large-scale industry in the capitalist world. This contrasts with the increasing mobility of technology, capital and know-how which enables entrepreneurs and firms in lesser-developed countries to steal its markets.

Despite continued attempts to control markets and impose fair trading regulations the world economy is increasingly open and effective competition is reaching into more and more of its markets, although this process is threatened by the risk that the Uraguay Round of trade negotiations may fail. In his book *Innovation and Entrepreneurship*, Peter Drucker (1986) demonstrates how the United States has moved from a 'managerial' to an 'entrepreneurial' economy in the last twenty years. In that period America was subject to deindustrialisation and at least five million jobs were lost in the traditional employing institutions. Yet total employment grew by thirty-five million, so that forty million new jobs must have been created, many of them for married women. Few of these jobs are 'hightech'; 'hightech' merely replaced the five million jobs lost from 'smokestack' industry. What Drucker sees is an entrepreneurial revolution, subsequently reflected in many other countries, in which systematic innovation takes over as the driving force of the economy.

Since competition cannot effectively be tamed over time, and since there is burgeoning activity in new ventures, franchises and other entrepreneurial activities, it would seem that competition is no barrier to enterprise, but rather that enterprise is well able to cope with it and may, in some cases, thrive on it.

This phenomenon has been recognised by Michael Porter. In his book *Competitive Advantage* he seeks to codify the rules for success against competitors:

Competition is at the core of the success or failure of firms. Competition determines the appropriateness of a firm's activities that can contribute to its performance such as innovations, a cohesive culture or good implementation. Competitive strategy is the search for a favourable competitive position in an industry, the fundamental arena in which competition occurs. Competitive strategy aims to establish a profitable and sustainable position against the forces that determine industry competition.

Competitive advantage grows fundamentally out of value a firm is able to create for its buyers that exceeds the firm's cost of creating it. Value is what buyers are willing to pay, and superior value stems from offering lower prices than competitors for equivalent benefits or providing unique benefits that more than offset a higher price. There are two basic types of competitive advantage: cost leadership and differentiation. (Porter, 1985)

We shall meet these strategies and others later in this book.

Strategy is the key weapon to be used to ensure the survival and to further the growth of a business in a hostile and turbulent environment, in which lurk enemies both known and unknown. The quality of strategy depends critically on the exercise of strategic thinking. This process requires total objectivity, the widest possible scope of vision, the abandonment of prejudices and constraints, and rigorous critical honesty. Strategic thinking starts with analysis – identifying all the issues and factors which may effect the business over time, dissecting them into their basic elements, and evaluating them individually and in their interrelationships. The process then relies crucially on the strategic thinker's ability to identify new interrelationships or to discern gaps and weaknesses in the pattern revealed which can be used to his advantage. This stage relies on identifying the critical issue(s) underlying the situation and is as crucial for success as the diagnosis made by a physician for an effective cure. The differences between strategic thinking, intuition and systematic thinking are well illustrated by Ohmae (1983) in his book *The Mind of the Strategist*. From Figure 1.1 it can be seen that the greater the attention paid to analysis (the more the parts are broken up), the larger the number of options derived in the process of synthesis. The generation of options is critical for successful strategic thinking; the solution achieved by mechanical systems thinking is linear, that achieved by intuition is singular. By generating options, strategic thinking avoids the dangers of obvious solutions, but also opens the door to eccentric possibilities which, when tested, may yield better potential results.

Edward de Bono (1982) contrasts the potential of 'vertical thinking' and 'lateral thinking'. The former is a closed procedure which promises at least a minimal result; the latter makes no promises but may yield a maximal result. Lateral thinking is open-ended and, by giving scope for creativity, may lead to a brilliant solution. John Adair (1984) sees a third stage in the thinking process after analysis and synthesis – 'value thinking'. This is the process of relating means to ends, of assessing fitness for purpose. He cites man's survival as being due to judgments, such as the advantages of metal weapons over those made of stone, and suggests that value thinking is part of our genetic inheritance and has potential to enhance our decisions. Value thinking is not related to current fashions or established norms, but operates at a deeper level and may often challenge these norms; for example the continued use of stone weapons (*ibid.*). There is no doubt that the process of thinking is highly mysterious – John Adair likens thinking about thinking to trying to jump on your own shadow – but the importance of thinking in the decision-making process cannot be exaggerated. Ben Heirs (1989) in his book *The Professional Decision Thinker* challenges the primacy given by management to action rather than thinking. This might seem to attack the thesis of Peters and Waterman (1982) in their book *In Search of Excellence*, that a 'bias for action' is a factor of excellence. Further, Peters and Waterman place great emphasis on experimentation: 'Experimentation acts as a form of cheap learning for most of the excellent companies usually proving less costly – and more useful – than sophisticated market research and careful staff planning.' This concept evolves, in a later book by Peters (1989), *Thriving on Chaos*, into emphasis that a 'strategic mindset which

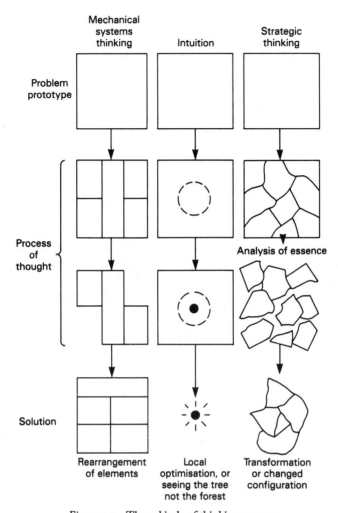

Figure 1.1   Three kinds of thinking process

focuses on skill/capability building (e.g. adding value to the work force via training to prepare it to respond more flexibly and be more quality-conscious) is more important than ever'. I believe that *In Search of Excellence* did not exclude strategic thinking but perhaps took it for granted. The denigration of staff planning in the first book is reinforced in the second, but emphasis is than placed on establishing a 'strategic mind set' in the line. It may be that the failure of some of the excellent companies in the earlier book to sustain their performance reinforced recognition in the later book of the key role of strategic thinking.

The value of strategic thinking is recognised by practitioners. Sir John Harvey-Jones (1989) states: 'One of the lessons I have learnt in life is that a bit more time thinking and planning will immeasurably increase the effectiveness of one's input.' The Vice-President, Corporate Business Development and Planning of General Electric Corporation, Michael Carpenter (1986) says, 'The goal of business strategy is to secure an enduring competitive advantage that leads to a high ROI (return on investment) relative to the industry as a whole', and goes on to reiterate his company's 'commitment to quality strategic thinking and management'.

1.4. Strategy as a means of coping with turbulence and competition

'Strategy is when you are out of ammunition but keep right on firing so that the enemy won't know' (unknown source quoted by Ansoff (1979) in *Corporate Strategy*).

The Oxford Dictionary defines strategy as: 'generalship, the art of war, management of an army or armies in a campaign, art of so moving or disposing troops or ships as to impose upon the enemy the place and time and conditions of fighting preferred by oneself.' Kenichi Ohmae (1983) develops the image: 'In business as on the battlefield, the object of strategy is to bring about the conditions most favourable to one's own side, judging precisely the right moment to attack or withdraw and always assessing the limits of compromise correctly.'

Strategy is not one dimensional. As John Grieve-Smith says in *Business Strategy*:

An important feature of business strategy is the need to consider the reactions of others to any initiative taken by the firm, particularly the reactions of its competitors, but also of such bodies as trades unions, national and local governments and regulating agencies. In this respect there is a close analogy with the need in military strategy to assess the possible reaction of the enemy; and neglect of this consideration is an important source of business failure. (Grieve-Smith, 1985)

Strategy is not unilateral. Use of the term implies a contest between at least two antagonists. Hofer and Schendel (1978) define strategy as 'the basic characteristics of the match an organisation achieves with its environment'. This I find too static as the word 'match' implies a state of balance which is never achievable in the real world. Ansoff (1979) sees strategy as being almost exclusively concerned with the relationship between the firm and its external environment with particular emphasis on product-mix and choice of markets. Ohmae (1983) defines a 'strategic triangle' involving the corporation, its customers and its competitors: 'In terms of these three key players, strategy is defined as the way to which a corporation endeavours to differentiate itself positively from its competitors, using its relative corporate strengths to better satisfy customer needs.' Porter describes 'competitive strategy' as:

taking offensive or defensive action to create a defendable position in an industry, to cope with the five competitive forces (entry, bargaining power of suppliers and buyers, substitution of products and rivalry between existing firms) and thereby yield a superior return on investment for the firm. (Porter, 1980)

Strategy must, therefore, involve conflict between two or more antagonists; a strategy which has no enemy is probably just a policy.

2

THE STRATEGIC TASK

2.1. Defining the company's environment

In defining strategy earlier it was seen that the concept involved the relationship between the company and its environment in conditions of competition. A key first task in developing a strategy is to make a strategic environmental appraisal, which is usually done, or led by, the corporate planning function.

The scope of such an appraisal may be very wide and a systematic approach to it is essential if the results are to be of use to the business. Basil Denning suggests the following questions are relevant:

1. Within what broad structure can events, trends and factors in the environment be considered?
2. How can a company determine which factors are relevant to its strategic problems?
3. What methods should be used for gathering relevant information?
4. What methods of forecasting would be helpful?
5. Can the cost of obtaining, processing and forecasting from this information be compared with the benefit obtained? (Denning 1987)

A study of firms engaged in environmental analysis, i.e. a systematic ongoing appraisal process, was published by Engelow and Lenz (1985). This suggests that sustained success in this area depends on the following factors:

1. Making a long-term commitment (as results will not be achieved in the short term).
2. Continually evaluating objectives (and relating them to current issues in the business).
3. Demanding linkages to present strategies and operations (involving line representatives in the process).
4. Fitting the style and culture of one's own organisation (custom built, not borrowed from elsewhere).

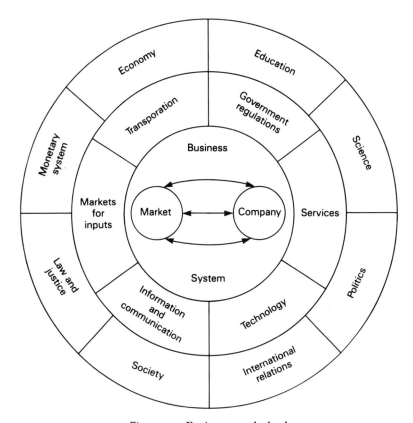

Figure 2.1   Environmental wheel

5.   Having design-flexible, versatile systems (possibly a core structure with spin-off activities as needed).

There are a number of systems of environmental analysis, many of which are very complex. Many of these systems involve the development of detailed scenarios, which attempt to picture the company's environment in a number of differing circumstances. More will be said about scenarios in Chapter 6, Section 6.2. Other systems involve Delphi techniques (explained in Chapter 6), or the building of sophisticated computer models.

A number of ways have evolved to present the model of the company and its environment schematically. One example is the 'environmental wheel' developed by Narchal, Kittappa and Bhattacharya (1987). This shows the business system at the hub of the wheel, with the primary areas of environmental interaction being in the inner circle and the wider environmental factors being in the outer circle. Changes in these factors are detected in the form of weak signals which have to be intercepted and interpreted by the system to give an early warning of impact on the business system.

This concept is part of a wider environmental scanning system the development of which comprises the following steps:

1. Identification of a company's environment and environmental areas.
2. Identification of the likely environmental descriptors in each of these environmental areas (i.e. those factors which affect the business system).
3. Identification of the environmental indicators in the planning system of the company which may be affected by the environment (i.e. the impact points in the business system of environmental descriptors).
4. Development of influence diagrams for the critical environmental indicators (showing the detailed interpretations of such environmental indicators within the business system).
5. Development of an environment data base, comprising an industry, a competitor and a general data base. The first comprises product, market and customer information with details of the key factors for success; the second contains all available information on competitors; and the third has economic, governmental, supplier, manpower and any other relevant information. Such information will be subject to an auditing process when first assembled.
6. Development of a structure of radars to monitor the environment and interpret the weak signals (radars are specially selected people working as an interactive group).
7. Generation of scenarios based on a set of assumptions about the environment. (The assumptions may be tuned to provide, for example, optimistic, most probable and pessimistic scenarios).

Such a system may be found to be daunting by many companies, and the cost of installing and maintaining it is considerable. Assuming that the options of ignoring the environment totally or of monitoring it in a random fashion are not acceptable, some systematic approach to the task is needed. Such an approach will need to embrace at least the following elements:

1. Establishing boundaries to the company's environment (what is/is not relevant).
2. Within those boundaries, identifying and ranking factors by their potential impact on the company's business.
3. Deciding how to obtain and update the information relevant to such factors (the effort being proportional to the potential impact).
4. Attempting to make forecasts or build scenarios based on the key factors for success.
5. Building the environmental appraisal and ongoing scanning into the company's planning system.

Boundaries

Boundaries are set partly for reasons of cost but also to ensure that the system is focused on data which is of actual or potential relevance to the company. For a local building firm data on the Japanese market is likely to be of academic interest until such time as its horizons can realistically be extended. Inability to control the situation is no reason to set it outside the boundary of the system. A firm may be affected by legislation in a foreign country blocking the supply of an essential material or product needed for its manufacturing process. Monitoring such a situation would be an essential part of its environmental scanning.

Boundary lines should be subject to regular review in order to ensure that they continue to encompass the company's environment realistically, allowing for established and predictable changes and also for the 'sleeping volcano' which may erupt sporadically.

Environmental factors

The range of factors contained in a company's environmental envelope may be vast and complex. It is therefore useful to break them down into a limited number of groups:

1. Political/societal.
2. Economic/industry/technology.
3. Competition/markets/suppliers.
4. The company itself.

This may be presented diagramatically as in Figure 2.2. This diagram shows that issues which may be remoter from the business are further from the core than those which are crucial to its day-to-day success. (Note, however, that issues may move; e.g. environmental issues are beginning to turn into industry issues as regulations are formulated.) While another approach to appraisal is to produce an atomic-style diagram, similar to that used by Shell UK which is shown in Figure 2.3.

Whatever the presentation the typical factors included are as follows:

1. *Political/societal factors*
   (a) Government impact on the company (policy, taxes, laws).
   (b) European Community effects.
   (c) International policy effects.
   (d) Demography (employment, labour market).
   (e) Sociological changes (expectations, life-style, social values, mobility).
   (f) Environmental issues.

2. *Economic/industry/technology factors*
   (a) Macroeconomic (balance of payments, inflation, GNP).
   (b) Microeconomic (investment, interest rates).
   (c) Present and future industry structure (dynamics of change).
   (d) Factors affecting entry/exit.

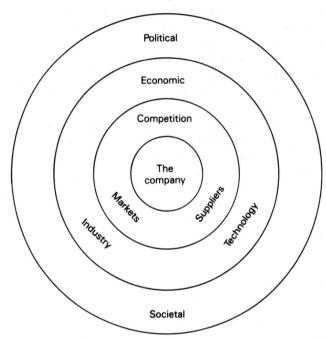

Figure 2.2   Environmental factors

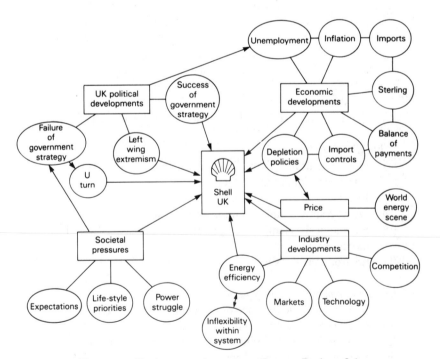

Figure 2.3   Environmental pressures (Source: Beck, 1982)

(e) Technologies likely to influence industry directly.

(f) Technologies which may have an indirect impact on industry.

3. *Competition/markets/suppliers*

(a) Known competitors.

(b) Potential competitors (also in potential markets).

(c) Present markets.

(d) Potential markets.

(e) Established suppliers.

(f) Potential suppliers.

4. *The company itself*

The posture of the company towards its environment is analysed in the Competitive Appraisal (see Section 2.2.).

Information

The information to flesh out the environmental appraisal may be obtained from a number of sources. The main ones are, for example:

1. Government information.

2. Commercial databases.

3. Desk research.

4. Industry sources.

5. Own research.

1. *Government information*

Most governments issue a regular flow of information, obtainable either from a central source (e.g. the UK Central Office of Information or from the relevant ministries). The quality of this data varies, although that provided by the United Kingdom and most OECD countries is tolerably reliable, though subject in the case of some economic information to retrospective adjustment. Government information provides a sound basic core for the environmental scanning system.

2. *Commercial databases*

There is a growing number of commercial databases in the major economies which provide an increasingly sophisticated source to their subscribers. Such databases are of value not so much for structuring environmental scanning systems but for obtaining information on specific matters at short notice. Much of the information is published elsewhere, in the public domain in many cases (e.g. Companies Registry). Nevertheless, products such as Infochech's Mergers and Acquisitions Database and DRI's Current Economic Indicators are increasingly used by companies who need to move quickly and confidently in making deals or assessing markets.

3. Desk research

This covers the traditional mode of using directories, handbooks and other library sources of data. Trade publications are useful in order to identify the major players in that industry and directories such as *Kompass* provide useful basic data on such players.

In finding information on wider issues such as the environment, greater creativity may be needed. Apart from the relevant ministries, environmental information may be sought from specialist bodies (Countryside Commission, Nature Conservancy Council, Rural Development Commission, etc.) and selectively from lobbyists (Friends of the Earth, Greenpeace, etc.).

Desk research needs a firm framework and systematic search. Judgements have to be made about the quality of data, and incompatibility of data from different sources has to be reconciled and recorded systematically. Desk research remains the core of any information system despite the growth of databases, because it is closely tailored to the specific needs of the individual company.

4. Industry sources

Information on a particular industry may be found in trade association publications, specific analyses made by brokers, *The Economist* and other specialist researchers and from industry itself. Another useful source of information is attendance at conferences and seminars dealing with industry issues. Attendance at such events provides contacts in the particular industry and may open up membership of an industry network of managers, industry watchers and consultants. As contacts in the industry come near to areas in which the company is directly competing, care will need to be exercised to avoid disinformation planted by competitors.

5. Own research

Although a great deal of data is available from public and published sources, the need for well-focused research, into areas not covered by available data or to elucidate that data in specific detail, remains critical. Such research can be done by appropriately qualified employees or, if confidentiality and/or objectivity are important, it may be preferable to commission outside researchers to do it. The key to good research is to formulate the right questions. This is not just an issue of clarity but of avoiding conditioned answers. Skill in this process is a major part of the researcher's stock in trade; his questions must not only elicit meaningful and unbiased answers but he must seek to find the insights which will give the research a competitive edge in the hands of the user. The official and public sources give the basic content of the environmental survey; the focused research gives it an internal life and leads to interactions within the planning system which enhance the results of the company.

Once the environmental appraisal has been completed it is important that the process is established on a sustainable basis to monitor the environment on a continuous basis. A possible monitoring system is described in Appendix 1.

2.2. Competitive appraisal

Competitive appraisal is the nexus of the strategic task. If it is done thoroughly, objectively and with imagination, it lays a firm foundation for the rest of the planning process. If it is trite, biased or mechanistic, it can lead to unthinkable disaster.

The archetypal approach to competitive appraisal is the SWOT analysis – a structured appraisal of a company's strengths and weaknesses and of the opportunities and threats facing it. To be successful such an exercise has to be comprehensive, and must be rooted in a thorough analysis and understanding of a firm's past from which comes the realistic assessment of how to shape its future. A full scale SWOT analysis usually requires outside help, both due to the work-load and to the need for rigorous objectivity. Such an analysis should also have input from all parts of the business, so that 'bottom up' sobriety can temper any illusions which may remain at the top.

The SWOT process involves a critical assessment of the company's strengths and weaknesses in relation to the markets which it seeks to serve, and in comparison with the known strengths and weaknesses of competitors. The analysis should not be carried out in a vacuum or in relation to unfocused ideals. The fact that no member of staff speaks Japanese is only a weakness if there is a realistic prospect of selling to Japan. The fact that the managing director is a scratch golfer may be a weakness not a strength if he is playing with customers and has to contrive not to embarrass them!

Lists of strengths and weaknesses are usually derived either separately and then brought together for discussion and refinement, or by discussion in a meeting guided by a member of management or an outside consultant and consolidated on to a flip-chart. It is important that the strengths and weaknesses are rigorously related to the competitive environment and that there is a broad consensus within the company about them. A typical SWOT analysis is shown in Appendix 2.

Once the strengths and weaknesses have been debated and codified, the task of identifying opportunities and threats becomes the logical corollary. The strengths will tend to feed the list of opportunities, tempered by competitive realities, and the weaknesses will point up many of the threats. There will, of course, be opportunities which do not relate to the company's strengths, and these will need to be placed in a separate listing since outside help or internal improvement will be needed to pursue them. There will also be threats which do not relate to company weaknesses, but these should be less menacing or should require action other than remedying weaknesses. A strong market leader will constantly be threatened by reanimated competitors or by potential new market entrants, but he will be able to develop counter-strategies from a position of strength.

Once the SWOT listings have been completed, an analysis of the interrelation between the factors listed needs to be carried out, which will identify the key issues emerging from the process and will set priorities for action. It is a basic rule that emphasis should be given to exploiting strengths rather than mitigating weaknesses (unless those are fundamental). As Drucker (1967) says, 'Results are obtained by exploiting opportunities not by solving problems.' Resources need to be devoted primarily to opportunities and to those which best match the company's strengths. Drucker defines the 'maximisation of opportunities' as the key entrepreneurial task.

Ansoff (1979) seeks to bring the concept of 'synergy' into the analytical process. Synergy he defines as an 'effect which can produce a combined return on the firm's resources greater than the sum of its parts', in shorthand, 2 + 2 = 5. To do this he uses profile comparisons. This involves creating a capability profile of the company, related to a reference level. A check list for this process is shown in Table 2.1. The reference level will be one appropriate to the firm and related preferably to its main markets.

This capability profile is then matched with a competitive profile structured on a similar basis and which is derived from the most successful competitors of the company. This process will highlight strengths and weaknesses relative to the present product–market posture. Ansoff then recommends an 'external appraisal' which maps the characteristics of other industries that can be related to the capability profile of the company in order to identify potential 'fit' and synergistic effect. The process then continues to narrow down the search for potential acquisitions. A similar technique developed by French consultants is the use of the 'morphological grid'.

John Grieve-Smith (1985) lays great emphasis on the 'corporate character', the underlying culture of the company. This concentrates on the factors which are distinctive about a company. An example is Marks and Spencer's outstanding capability in buying and merchandising. Although buyers and merchandisers trained by Marks and Spencer are active throughout the retail sector, no other company has been able to replicate the distinctive flair and professionalism of Marks and Spencer in these areas. The corporate character should ideally be geared to excellence in areas where the returns in terms of profit are above average.

This concept of excellence is explored in depth in *In Search of Excellence* by Peters and Waterman (1982). They start with the model of the McKinsey 7–S framework reproduced in Figure 2.4. This model introduces extra factors into the earlier Boston matrix approach to company positioning and shows the critical interrelationship between them all. From their analysis of

Table 2.1. Checklist for competitive and competence profiles

	Facilities and equipment	Personnel skills	Organisational capabilities	Management capabilities
General management and finance	Data processing equipment	Depth of general management Finance Industrial relations Legal Personnel recruitment and training Accounting Planning	Multidivisional structure Consumer financing Industrial financing Planning and control Automated business data processing	Investment management Centralised control Large systems management Decentralised control R and D intensive business Capital equipment intensive business Merchandising intensive business Cyclical business Many customers Few customers
Research and development	Special lab equipment General lab equipment Test facilities	Areas of specialisation Advanced research Applied research Product design: industrial consumer military specifications Systems design Industrial design: consumer industrial	Systems development Production development industrial consumer process Military specifications compliance	Utilisation of advanced state of the art Application of current state of the art Cost-performance optimisation
Operations	General machine shop Precision machinery Process equipment Automated production Large high-bay facilities Controlled environment	Machine operation Tool making Assembly Precision machinery Close tolerance work Process operation Product planning	Mass production Continuous flow process Batch process Job shop Large complex product assembly Subsystems integration Complex product control Quality control Purchasing	Operation under cyclic demand Military specifications quality Tight cost control Tight scheduling

Table 2.1. (Cont.)

	Facilities and equipment	Personnel skills	Organisational capabilities	Management capabilities
Marketing	Warehousing Retail outlets Sales offices Service offices Transportation equipment	Door-to-door selling Retail selling Wholesale selling Direct industry selling Department of Defense selling Cross-industry selling Applications engineering Advertising Sales promotion Servicing Contract administration Sales analysis	Direct sales Distributor chain Retail chain Consumer service organisation Industrial service organisation Department of Defense product support Inventory distribution and control	Industrial marketing Consumer merchandising Department of Defense marketing State and municipality marketing

a wide range of companies, Peters and Waterman identified eight attributes found in the distinctively excellent companies, as follows:

1. A bias for action.
2. Close to the customer.
3. Autonomy and entrepreneurship.
4. Productivity through people.
5. Hands-on, value driven.
6. Stick to the knitting.
7. Simple form, lean staff.
8. Simultaneous loose-tight properties.

1. *A bias for action*

This attribute manifests itself in a penchant for tackling problems head on, often using unstructured meetings to work through solutions involving all affected, rather than write structured reports and deal with the issues through the hierarchy. Task forces are symptomatic of the approach of companies with a bias for action, and so is a restlessness to get through to workable solutions. The growing complexity of modern business is too often an excuse for lethargy and inertia, which create complex analytical systems, mountains of paperwork and slow reactions. Action-biased companies fight complexity by setting priorities, identifying the key measures by which to judge the options generated by their task forces, and keeping their systems simple and subordinate to the management process.

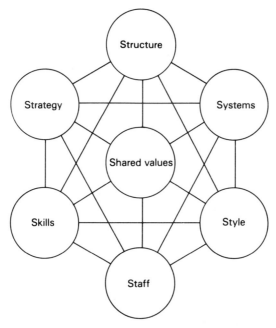

Figure 2.4 McKinsey 7–S framework

2. *Close to the customer*

In the words of Peter Drucker (1967) 'the purpose of a business is to create a customer'. Time and other pressures conspire to move the customer away from the centre stage in a company's preoccupations, whereas excellence is achieved by making the customer pervade every part of the company. In essence, being close to the customer involves a thorough understanding of his ambitions and problems, taking that understanding into the company's internal workings and making them responsive to it and the resultant needs, and delivering products or services which totally match those needs. Service, quality and reliability are the strategies which result from closeness to the customer, and revenue generation is enhanced by the loyalty generated by such intense commitment to the customer. Domino Printing is an example of a small company that has achieved a large global share in the market for date-labelling foodstuffs by intense concentration on this market.

3. *Autonomy and entrepreneurship*

Many of the 'excellent' companies identified by Peters and Waterman are large and at risk of sclerosis. This danger is countered by encouraging the benefits of smallness in their operations, largely by decentralisation. This drive to push autonomy down the line is aimed at releasing the entrepreneurial spirit in their employees. This involves a trade-off against tight control and coordination, but the prize of success is achieved by perpetual innovation. This can only be generated by highly motivated individuals and small teams. GE in the United States developed its engineered plastics business out of an off-line activity to $1 billion turnover in ten years. 3M creates venture teams to experiment with and develop new products. IBM encourages multiple team approaches to a common opportunity and then has a 'shoot out' to pick the best performer to carry the project into the marketplace. Success in this culture is encouraged by significant rewards and by understanding of heroic failure, but above all by sponsoring people with a sense of mission and by developing actual or potential competition to test them to the limit.

4. *Productivity through people*
It was in 1960 that Douglas McGregor (1987) challenged the traditional approach to managing people. He posited a 'Theory X' which detailed the traditional view that the average person (i) disliked work, (ii) needed to be coerced to work towards organisational objectives, and (iii) preferred to be directed rather than take responsibility. He then posited a 'Theory Y' which sought the integration of individual and company goals. This assumed that (a) work is as natural as play, (b) people will exercise self-direction towards objectives to which they are committed, (c) commitment is a function of reward for achievement, (d) people can learn to seek responsibility, (e) imagination, ingenuity and creativity are not narrowly distributed in the population, and (f) the intellectual potential of most people is only partially utilised.

McGregor's ideas are still far from widely practised and it is noted that most of the excellent companies succeed in part because of their willingness to trust and put faith in their employees. Thomas Watson Junior spoke of 'respect for the individual' as the most important belief in IBM's philosophy. Hewlett Packard practises 'management by wandering around'. Both companies have long sought to provide lifetime employment, though that ideal is no longer sustainable in the modern world.

Productivity is achieved by integrating the goals of individuals and the company. The excellent companies are performance-oriented and seek to set stretching targets. Given a results-driven culture and peer pressures, people in such companies set themselves ambitious targets and commit to them in exchange for company support and above-average rewards.

5. *Hands on, value driven*
John Gardner (1983a) wrote in *Morale*: 'Most contemporary writers are reluctant or embarrassed to write explicitly about values.' This reluctance has long been shared by businessmen preoccupied with 'hard' issues such as budgets, procedures and controls. Thomas Watson Junior (1945) wrote an entire book about values, and Peters and Waterman (1982) show how values are a key means of social integration in successful companies. According to Peters and Waterman (1982), the sort of values which emerge as basic to success are as follows:

1. A belief in being 'the best'.
2. A belief in the importance of the details of execution, the 'nuts and bolts' of doing the job well.
3. A belief in the importance of people as individuals.
4. A belief in superior quality and service.
5. A belief that most members of the organisation should be innovators, and its corollary, the willingness to support failure.
6. A belief in the importance of informality to enhance communication.
7. Explicit belief in, and recognition of, the importance of economic growth and profits.

Such beliefs are commonly built today into 'mission statements', which define the rationale for the company's existence, its purpose, objectives and beliefs, and lay the foundation for the strategic planning process. Mission statements will be discussed later in Section 3.5.

6. *Stick to the knitting*

Statistics show that most acquisitions are unsuccessful but that those which relate to the core business of the acquirer are more likely to be successful. 3M focuses on its core skill of coating and bonding technology. GE diversified successfully from turbines into gas turbine engines. Christopher Lorenz (1981) wrote: 'Pioneering European companies place more emphasis on specialisation than diversification and prefer internal expansion to mergers and takeovers.' Since that time Daimler Benz has expanded aggressively by acquisition at the same time that British Aerospace has positioned itself to compete in the same markets, and the results of both new strategies are not yet clear.

It is a matter of record that most of the conglomerate businesses built in the 1960s (ITT, LTV, Litton, etc.) have shrunk or disintegrated. Lord Weinstock has spoken of disaggregating GEC and some moves have been made to build partnerships in selected businesses rather than exercise total control. Paradoxically, some firms labelled as conglomerates have apparently prospered, for example, Hanson and BTR. Hanson has specialised in buying skilfully and in divesting businesses which do not relate to its core concept – investment in utility products with steady demand and limited need for innovation. BTR has kept more of its acquisitions but has built a core round rubber and plastics technology. Neither Hanson nor BTR is a true conglomerate – both have a clear concept of their business and stick closely to it.

7. *Simple form, lean staff*

As companies grow there is a tendency for structures to become more complex. To control such structures staff functions are expanded and systems are made more comprehensive. Companies quickly outgrow the basic functional structure and then find themselves in a multidimensional complex, with multiple products, markets and geographic areas to co-ordinate and control. As the functional structure is still relevant a four-dimensional matrix is indicated – logical but unworkable.

The excellent companies cope with this problem, first, by having one dimension with undisputed primacy, often the product dimension; secondly, they avoid the build up of staff functions to police the system; and thirdly, they encourage flexibility in changing structure to meet emergent needs, and the creation of task forces and project centres to accelerate progress where appropriate. Johnson and Johnson is a $5 billion company with 150 subsidiary product companies. They see the benefits of consolidation as very elusive compared with the control of his total business by a motivated manager.

Peters and Waterman's analysis leads to their 'rule of 100' in respect of corporate staffing. Despite wide variations in size, complexity and turnover they found that excellent companies had average corporate staff of about 100. This figure is reflected also in companies such as GEC and BTR in the United Kingdom.

8.   *Simultaneous loose-tight properties*
The excellent companies seem to reconcile at least three major paradoxes. The first is the ability to give maximum individual freedom to people while strengthening overall control of the company. The second is the use of soft concepts, like values, to produce improved hard results, profits. The third is the sharp focus and total commitment externally to the customer which achieves more effective and profitable internal operations than have normally been achieved by internally directed efficiency programmes and controls.

The core of the 'excellence' achieved by the companies reviewed by Peters and Waterman, and of many others with which they were not closely involved, is the working of shared values. It is no coincidence that 'shared values' is the core of the McKinsey 7–S framework referred to earlier in this chapter.

It will be seen that the process of competitive appraisal is very demanding, and that the company's attributes have to be analysed rigorously and without mercy if the appraisal is to form a sustainable basis for developing strategy. The best practice is rapidly overtaken by better practice, and all that is certain is that competition will intensify and the standards needed to succeed will constantly rise. A company's competitive appraisal will not only have to be traumatically challenging, but it will also need to be kept constantly under review to ensure that it remains firmly focused on an ever-changing reality.

2.3.   Developing and evaluating options

In *The Professional Decision Thinker* Ben Heirs (1989) states: 'People who need to work together as a team must first learn how to think together as a team.' Heirs suggests a four-stage process for decision thinking:

1. Defining the question and getting the relevant information.
2. Creating alternatives and tolerating waste.
3. Predicting the future consequences and planning for contingencies.
4. The decision – deciding on probabilities, risks and rewards.

This process is as relevant for strategic planning as for any operational decision. The importance of the second stage is underlined by Peter Drucker (1954): 'The understanding that underlies the right decision grows out of the clash and conflict of divergent opinions and out of the serious consideration of competing alternatives.' The development and evaluation of strategic options is, therefore, a critical stage in the development of strategy.

The process of developing options has been likened to Darwin's Theory of Natural Selection. There should be as wide a range of options developed as possible so that the process of natural selection is optimised. Heirs urges tolerance of such apparent waste and the importance of having the ability to persuade those involved to use the maximum of imagination, ingenuity and inspiration of which they are capable. The development of options is an essential prerequisite of a sound decision. As H. L. Meneken said, 'To every complex question there is an answer: direct, simple and usually wrong.' Lee Iacocca (1988) recalls, 'Robert McNamara taught me never to make a major decision without having a choice of at least vanilla or chocolate. And if more than a hundred million dollars were at stake it was a good idea to have strawberry too.'

Techniques for developing options vary from think-tank sessions to exercises in lateral thinking (see Edward de Bono (1982), *Lateral Thinking for Management*). Certainly options should not be generated by one person, since variety, creative conflict and a real consensus are lost thereby. Time has to be spent generating options which may initially seem remote, but those who have sponsored such an option will be its champion in the evaluation process, during which surprising insights may emerge.

In the context of developing strategy, the creation and evaluation of options arise from the environmental and competitive appraisals described earlier in this book. Having appraised the company in its environmental and competitive context, the strategic process moves on to decide the direction in which to proceed, how to progress in that direction and what resources are needed to do so. Strategic direction is critical for a company, since once launched in a particular direction it may be damaging, even fatal, to make an early change. If the appraisals show that there is a fundamental mismatch between a company and its operating context – too low a market share in a market with powerful competitors, or obsolescent products with no resources to innovate successfully, etc. – options for withdrawal, disposal, forming alliances, and retrenchment (among others) will need to be considered. If the appraisal shows an unexploited opportunity in the marketplace, the company will need to consider not only the implications of seizing it but also the implications of less obvious options. The irresistible offer may not be the best long-term choice for building the company's future, as British and Commonwealth discovered after buying Atlantic Computers.

Evaluating options requires not only the imagination needed to create them but also a variety of other qualities. Heirs postulates three rules for this process, as follows:

1. Stay young – avoid complacency, arrogance, inflexibility.
2. Do not force the pace – allow time for all the issues to surface.
3. Encourage debate, do not avoid it – debate stimulates the distillation of sound solutions.

Because the company is playing for high stakes in developing strategies on which its survival depends, the evaluation process has to be wide-ranging, creative, competitive, rigorous and, above all, realistic. No ideal solution will emerge from the process and any apparently ideal solution should be regarded with suspicion. In the words of Ohmae:

There is important common ground between the task of the military strategist on the one hand and the key strategic activities of middle and top management on the other: grasping the state of the market, objectively assessing the strengths and weaknesses of one's business, changing direction with flexibility when required, and calculating the amount of profit or loss likely to result from each management action. Both the business strategist and the military planner are prone to be trapped by perfectionism. (Ohmae, 1983)

Although operating managers often find the process of developing and evaluating strategic options to be wasteful and tedious, it is important that those who will have to deliver the strategies chosen by the company are involved in the process of selection. Much has been written of the 'not invented here' syndrome and wide ownership and commitment are essential if strategies are to be successful.

Evaluating options requires a systematic analysis of each one, recording the emerging advantages and disadvantages as they are identified, and referring back constantly to the environmental and competitive appraisals. A constant watch has to be kept on the limits of reality; strategies have to be stretching in order to have impact but the danger of going 'a bridge too far' is ever present, as WPP has recently discovered. A strategy nine-tenths delivered may be a major defect if the company is incapable of sustaining the inevitable counter-attack in the market place.

Resources have to be carefully assessed and not overcommitted. It is easy to underestimate the real call on resources made by challenging strategies. Care has to be taken to second-guess the reaction of competitors, customers and suppliers to these possible strategies in order to avoid being sucked into consequential situations which the company cannot handle. (Jaguar lost its independence in part by overreaching its effective resources in order to develop the US market.) Risk assessment is considered separately in the next chapter.

The process of evaluation should include the appraisal of each option against the key factors for success identified in the competitive appraisal. Unless the company can score highly against known competition in respect of these key factors, the option should be marked down. Some companies find it helpful to give numerical values to the key factors and to produce a score for each option. If this method gives comfort, it should not be resisted, but the evaluation process is largely judgemental, and scoring often gives a spurious sense of accuracy. What really matters is rigour, wide involvement of key employees and commitment to the outcome.

2.4. Assessing risks

We considered uncertainty and risk in Chapter 1, where it was recognised that risk was inherent in the business process. Risk cannot be avoided but must be managed. The assessment of risk is a critical part of the evaluation of options and merits special attention.

Peter Drucker identifies four types of risk:

1. The risk one must accept, i.e. the risk that is built into the nature of the business.
2. The risk one can afford to take.
3. The risk one cannot afford to take.
4. The risk one cannot afford not to take.

An example of a business built on risk is general insurance; another might be venture-capital lending. The risks inherent in such businesses are usually susceptible to actuarial calculation, based on past experience and the laws of probability. When an insurance company is assessing strategic options; for example, to increase market share by price cutting, it has to trade-off an increase in revenue against a reduction in unit margin. Inherent in that trade-off is an increase in risk, having written more business, and a lower risk premium following the cut in margin. Such a strategy has been followed by numerous car insurers, many of whom went out of business. The same strategy has been followed successfully by major insurers, particularly at the low end of the insurance cycle, and is necessary to maintain the critical mass required for their business. Success depends on a skilful risk evaluation combined with the ability to deliver the strategy in the market-place.

Businesses are built by identifying and exploiting opportunities. Each new opportunity will involve risks – the loss of the funds committed to it, the possibility of bad debts, the danger of claims on the company for loss or injury to customers, the loss of reputation, to name but a few – and risk evaluation needs to identify and quantify these risks relative to the prospective benefits to be obtained and to the maximum total risk the company can sustain. The sum of the risks must be significantly less than the benefits obtainable in the same time-frame to make the opportunity one worth pursuing. It must also be such that the worst outcome will not be fatal to the company.

In calculating the sum of risks it is important to make two calculations. One is the maximum exposure created for the company in respect of each identifiable risk totalled up. This may be a fearsome figure, as I know from experience in making such calculations to meet requirements in the public sector. In reality it is statistically most improbable that all risks will coincide, and the realistic calculation involves attaching probabilities to each risk, multiplying out the effective risk and calculating the sum of all such probabilities.

The risk one cannot afford to take is not only the reverse of the affordable risk but, more insidiously, is the risk of not being able to sustain the exploitation of a strategy to achieve total success. The first successful electronic body-scanner was developed by Thorn EMI well before that of any competitor and was launched into the market-place without adequate marketing planning or technical support. The product failed, partly due to timing and partly due to medical conservatism, but largely due to Thorn EMI being unable to sustain the promotion of the scanner long enough to succeed. This failure has left the company severely damaged and requiring a major restructuring in order to have any chance of long-term survival. American and Japanese companies now have a flourishing business in body-scanners.

The risk one cannot afford not to take can easily be confused with the type of risk taken by Thorn EMI. This is often the 'betting the company' type of risk, or is rationalised as such after it has proved successful. IBM claims to have 'bet the company' on the 370 series of machines, and similar claims have been made by aircraft and car manufacturers from time to time. In reality such risks are usually major long-term strategies which underpin the distant future of the company. Cable and Wireless has committed itself to a submarine and overland cable to circle the globe. At a time of great technical change, with increased use of satellite communications, this is a bold strategy. Without such a strategy, however, Cable and Wireless cannot be a world player in the communications business. Despite enormous difficulties with local governments and technical problems, this strategy seems to be steadily unfolding and moving towards success.

In assessing risk, consideration has to be given not only to the risks a company consciously incurs in order to exploit an advantage, but also to the risks that lie in wait for any business. These are the commercial, political and societal risks referred to in Chapter 1, Section 1. All of these need to be assessed relative to strategic options, and the possibility of hedging these risks has to be explored. Some companies hedge the risks inherent in their different businesses by developing a balanced portfolio of activities which have different market cycles, geographic profiles, cash-flow characteristics or customers. Such activities may be in a variety of industries, so that mature businesses can feed funds to nourish new enterprises and the portfolio can be changed by internal renewal as well as by acquisitions and disposals.

Other risks can be hedged. Exchange risks can be hedged by forward trading, by the purchase of options or by currency swaps. The risks attaching to short term loans, that is, that the lender will demand immediate repayment, can be hedged by limiting their ratio to total funds employed (equity, debentures, long-term loans, short-term loans or overdrafts) despite their lower real cost to the business. Many risks are insurable, including loss of assets, employee and third-party liability, and loss of profits. All such risks need to be assessed realistically and the extent of cover needed in practice ascertained. Given the high premiums attached to some risks, for example, product liability (especially in the United States), there is probably a need to insure the disaster spectrum of most risks and accept a limited excess at the lower end of the spectrum which the company will self-insure.

Once the risks attaching to each strategic option have been fully identified, assessed and, to the extent feasible, hedged, the resultant figure will need to be related to the probable cash flows and profits derived from the option. Before the option is fully evaluated it will be necessary to carry out a sensitivity analysis (see Chapter 5, Section 8).

2.5. Setting priorities

Having completed the environmental and competitive appraisals and evaluated strategic options for the company, it should be clear what are the shared values in the business, in what markets it can hope to operate and in which strategic directions it can choose to move. The strategic options now have to be related to the shared values of the business and a number of choices made. Peter Drucker (1967) perceives these to be as follows:

1. The idea of the business.
2. The specific excellence it needs.
3. The priorities.

The idea of the business

This is the quintessence of the appraisal and of the shared values identified. It is often easier to define negatively – 'This is not our kind of business' – but the need to define the idea of the business is essential to achieve clear focus and optimised results. The brothers Pereire said, 'our business is business development', and that concept spawned the entire investment banking industry. Such an idea might be too general to be sustainable in modern conditions, however, where businesses often need to specialise very narrowly (e.g. Sock Shop, Tie Rack, etc.). What is essential is that a definition is made and that it is adopted by all who work in the business.

The specific excellence it needs

In discussing competitive appraisal we examined different manifestations of excellence. Knowledge has to be an area of excellence for most businesses today, and if it is lacking there is a major weakness to be rectified. Excellence in innovation, systems, quality and service would seem to be essential for a business to prosper in the coming years. Defining the specific excellence needed not only draws out the business priorities, but also conditions the attributes of key staff and indicates the key areas for investment, training and research. Gary Hamel attributes much of the success of Japanese companies to their ability to identify 'core competences' needed to achieve competitive advantage and to the care taken to nurture and protect such core competences, particularly by insulating them from alliance partners.

The priorities

The opportunities identified by the appraisal process and evaluated in the strategic options will be more numerous than the firm's resources can realistically address. The company management will have to set priorities, based on the appraisals made earlier, reflecting the idea of the business and committing it to move in a specific direction. As Peter Drucker says, the difficulty lies in the options which are set aside and in the pain of that decision for the champions of such options.

The setting of priorities must therefore be a formal process, involving all the people who have contributed to the appraisals and developed the strategic options. All must be reconciled to the decisions taken, and these must limit the opportunities chosen to a number which will enable resources to be concentrated powerfully in order to give the best chances of success.

The outcome of this process is often distilled into a mission statement, which is, in effect, a charter for the management to run the business. Such mission statements are, therefore, sometimes communicated to shareholders and are normally transmitted within the company to all operating levels. A well-conceived and clearly written mission statement can be a powerful tool for concentrating company effort in the chosen strategic direction and for giving employees a clear vision of corporate purpose. Komatsu was able to distil its corporate purpose into the phrase 'encircle Caterpillar', and this unity of purpose played no small part in its competitive success.

2.6. Determining goals

In the 1960s much was made of management by objectives and King McCord (1962) developed the concept of the 'hierarchy of objectives'. This involves a pyramid of objectives, starting at the top with the mission statement or equivalent, moving down through strategic objectives, through financial objectives, down to operating objectives at all levels. All of these objectives must be interlinked and must be subject to personal commitment and achievement dates at all levels. This concept is of great importance for strategic management (see Chapter 7) although some of the rigidities of the original system have been discarded.

The setting of strategic objectives is now a more complex process than it was in the days of the 'robber barons' of the nineteenth century, when maximising profit was the sole, but tacit, objective. The trusts which controlled most major industries enabled the cost of investment to be quickly recovered by monopoly pricing. With the break-up of the trusts the trade-off between short-term profits and investment to achieve higher longer-term profits became a significant issue, and has remained so ever since.

Not only has the issue of profit objectives become more complex but the ownership and management of a business are now usually separate and other stakeholders, such as the employees, customers, suppliers, lenders of funds, government and others, may claim an input into the company's objectives. Pressure groups are increasingly active in seeking to influence companies and their stakeholders. Some companies reflect this change by seeking to establish social objectives. While this reflects the wider concerns of business in the modern world, such objectives are more in the nature of constraints on business objectives, like observing health and safety legislation, rather than true objectives of the company itself.

Ansoff proposes a system of objectives based on the following premises:

1. The firm has both a) 'economic' objectives aimed at optimising the efficiency of its total resource-conversion process and b) 'social' or non-economic objectives which are the result of interaction among individual objectives of the firm's participants ('stakeholders').
2. In most firms the economic objectives exert the primary influence on the firm's behaviour and form the main body of explicit goals used by management for guidance and control of the firm.
3. The central purpose of the firm is to maximise long-term return on the resources employed within the firm.
4. The social objectives exert a secondary modifying and constraining influence on management behaviour.
5. In addition to proper objectives two related types of influence are exerted on management behaviour: responsibilities and constraints. (Ansoff, 1979)

The major difficulty in determining long-term goals for a company is to calculate the passage of time. Ansoff differentiates between the 'proximate' and 'long-term periods', the former being the period over which detailed forecasts can be made, and the latter the period from the 'planning horizon', the end of the proximate period, and the 'time horizon' of the company, which may be infinity.

The other difficulty in establishing long-term goals is to allow for the unforeseen and to leave flexibility in the system to cope with it. As a result it is almost meaningless to say that the long-term return on investment

(ROI) should be × per cent. The rate will be meaningful only if it is higher than that achieved by competitors, and the minimum 'hurdle' rate will depend on the cost of funds at an indeterminate future point in time, increased by a factor to allow for the replacement of assets, research and development, and growth in working capital after payment of dividends. It has also to be recognised that new investment usually reduces ROI in the short term and that the theoretical ROI of old equipment is infinite!

It is therefore suggested that long-term goals cannot realistically be quantified. Long-term ROI can only be maximised at a level which provides the new investment needed to ensure the company's survival and continued prosperity. Goals can be set within the proximate period and should be quantified. In setting goals it is important to distinguish between ends and means. Only the ends are goals, the means may well be strategies. Many companies set a number of goals – profit, market share, new products, new markets, etc. Some goals may conflict. It is usual that a drive for market share will depress profits in the short term, so that multiple objectives are fraught with difficulty.

Ansoff suggests that both strategic objectives and goals should relate to the following ambitions:

1. Continuing growth of sales at least at the pace of the industry to enable the firm to maintain its share of the market.
2. Increase in relative market share to increase relative efficiency of the firm.
3. Growth in earnings to provide resources for reinvestment.
4. Growth in earnings per share to attract new capital to the firm.
5. Continuing addition of new products and product lines.
6. Continuing expansion of the firm's customer population.
7. Absence of excessive seasonal or cyclical fluctuations in sales and earnings and of consequent loss of competitive position through externally forced inefficiency in the use of the firm's resources. (Ansoff, 1979)

The following 'direct indicators of efficiency' are proposed by Ansoff:

(a) If turnover ratios are comparable to or better than those of competition, indications are strong that the firm is making good use of its resources. A key turnover ratio is return on sales; supporting ones are turnover of working capital, net worth, inventory, etc. Another key ratio is debt/equity, which indicates how well the firm is using its borrowing capacity.
(b) Depth of critical skills is a key indicator of future profitability. This may be measured by depth of management, of skilled personnel, and of research and development talent.
(c) Human and organisational assets must be backed up by modern physical assets. Among yardsticks are the age of plant, machinery and inventory. (Ansoff, 1979)

Ansoff develops this concept into a 'hierarchy of the long-term objective' (see Figure 2.5), but I would suggest that this should not be built into any rigid system but should be used as a check list to identify the key strategic

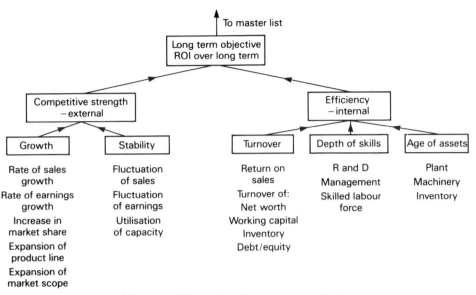

Figure 2.5 Hierarchy of the long-term objective

objectives and proximate goals of the company. As a working hypothesis the following factors may be considered:

1. *Overall profitability*
   - (a) Strategic objective: maximise return on total assets.
   - (b) Goal: return on total assets per cent.
   - (c) Comments: the modern equivalent of ROI.

2. *Shareholder profitability*
   - (a) Strategic objective: maximise earnings per share (allowing for dilution by rights issues).
   - (b) Goal: earnings per share (p).
   - (c) Comments: usual ratio in current use.

3. *Balance of equity: debt*
   - (a) Strategic objective: optimise use of debt.
   - (b) Goal: debt/equity ratio.
   - (c) Comments: danger of rise in interest rates.

4. *Turnover of capital*
   - (a) Strategic objective: maximise turnover of capital.
   - (b) Goal: sales/total assets ratio.
   - (c) Comments: measures use of capital.

5. *Benefit from internal efficiency*
   - (a) Strategic objective: maximise return on sales.
   - (b) Goal: return on sales per cent.
   - (c) Comments: shows benefit of volume where variable costs are low.

6. *Product renewal*
   - (a) Strategic objective: maximise efficiency of product renewal.
   - (b) Goal: new products (less than two years old)/ total products ratio.
   - (c) Comments: time factor should relate to industry.

7. *Innovation*
   - (a) Strategic objective: maximise efficiency of product renewal.
   - (b) Goal: expenditure on research and development/sales ratio.
   - (c) Comments: complements above.

8. *Employee productivity*
   - (a) Strategic objective: maximise pre-tax profit per employee.
   - (b) Goal: pre-tax profit/employee.
   - (c) Comments: basic measure compared with competition.

9. *Quality of service*
   - (a) Strategic objective: maximise sales relative to selling costs.
   - (b) Goal: sales and marketing costs/sales per cent.
   - (c) Comments: attempts to show dividend on service effort.

10. *Flexibility*
    - (a) Strategic objective: maintain appropriate level of free capital.
    - (b) Goal: fixed assets/equity per cent.
    - (c) Comments: Shows funding flexibility.

This list is far from exhaustive and may be adapted to suit the characteristics of individual companies. Experience has shown, however, that too many objectives lead to confusion and it may be helpful to rank them to avoid such confusion (for example, that overall profitability is more important than product renewal, even though neglect of product renewal will eventually undermine overall profitability). Even when established, the objectives/goals should not be 'set in concrete', but should be adapted to changing circumstances. Flexibility is important and will become increasingly so as change accelerates and uncertainty deepens.

Table 2.2. Calculating rents

1988/89 results	1 Operating profit £m	2 Return on all assets %	3 Return on sales %	4 Operating assets £m	5 Cost of operating* £m	6 Rents† £m	7 Input costs £m	8 Rents divided by inputs %
Sainsbury	369	21	7	2624	283	86	889	9.7
Tesco	274	23	6	1908	206	68	678	10.0
Gateway	205	21	5	1669	180	25	587	4.2
Asda	156	18	6	1508	163	−7	429	−1.6
Argyll	156	25	5	1081	117	39	487	8.1
Kwiksave	58	41	5	287	31	27	110	24.6

* Assuming a cost of capital of 10.8%, the average long-bond rate for April 1988–March 1989
† Rents = column 1 minus column 5.
Source: Davis and Kay. The Economist

A new approach to calculating company profits is shown in 'Assessing corporate performance', a paper by Evan Davis and John Kay (1990) of London Business School. This involves the calculation of economic rents, the return made after recovering the cost of capital employed. A table showing the economic rents of six supermarket groups in the UK is shown in a review of the LBS paper in The Economist of 28 July 1990 (Table 2.2).

Another interesting approach is to relate economic rents to input costs (labour and capital combined). If this ratio is compared with that for return on assets in respect of Sainsbury and Gateway, the weaker underlying performance of Gateway, of which return on sales is a symptom, emerges clearly. It may be useful for companies to use economic rents and the rents: inputs ratio as alternative bases for setting strategic objectives and goals.

2.7.   Elaborating the strategies to achieve the company's goals

Earlier we considered the development and evaluation of strategic options for building the company's business in competitive conditions. The choice of options depends, of course, on the company's strategic objectives and on the strategic direction it has set itself. It will depend also on the resources needed, and on the probability of success balanced against the consequences of failure.

Elaborating effective and sustainable strategies is second only to clarifying the company's goals in difficulty, and in importance for its future. Where the goals are the ends sought by the company, the strategies are the means by which those ends may best be achieved, allowing for uncertainty in the company's environment, for competitive action and reaction, for unforeseen opportunities and threats, and for changes in customer needs and tastes.

Ohmae (1983) believes that the only true strategies are those aimed at securing competitive advantage. This accords with our earlier finding that strategy implied two or more antagonists, and that plans of action without the search for competitive advantage were probably only policies. This does not mean that only marketing strategies are truly competitive – a strategy to improve management education and training is seeking competitive advantage, as is one to develop better management information systems. An interesting study into competitive advantage for small firms (STRATOS) is detailed in an article by Professor Bamberger (1989) of Limburg University.

In his book *Competitive Strategy* Porter (1980) identifies three 'generic' strategies which may be used individually, in combination or developed into more specific strategies, as follows:

1. Overall cost leadership.
2. Differentiation.
3. Focus.

1. *Overall cost leadership*

This is derived from the concept of the experience of learning curve, and is a co-ordinated drive through all business functions to achieve cost reductions through experience, improvements, control of overheads and customer selection. Low cost relative to competitors becomes the basic thrust of the business, although it must also provide quality, customer service and constant product improvement. A cost-leadership strategy pays off only where market share in the chosen market segment is significant, and it will probably require substantial initial capital investment to support it and ongoing investment in all areas of the business to sustain it.

2. *Differentiation*

This generic strategy requires the recognition by customers, competitors and suppliers that the company's product or service is, in some significant degree or particular, unique. Differentiation enables cost to be treated as a secondary issue (it must still be closely controlled), and enables a premium price to be earned and brand loyalty to be sustained. Differentiation may not achieve, or require, a large market share – Rolls Royce cars differentiate not only by quality but also by waiting lists. Coutts seeks individuals of high net worth to be its customers, and prices its services to discourage lesser mortals.

Considerable investment in building an image is required to achieve differentiation, and, when established, continuing effort and investment is needed to maintain and renew it. Morgan Cars is a small firm that has successfully consolidated its niche leadership in the traditional sports car market.

3. *Focus*

This strategy targets a selected buyer group or geographic market area, or offers a segmented range of products. By specialising, the company aims to offer a better service to targeted clients than its competitors who are more broadly positioned. This strategy is also termed a 'niche strategy', and is one particularly appropriate for companies which are not large enough to operate on a wide front. Focus enables the company to achieve cost leadership in its chosen niche and/or to differentiate itself as a specialist and achieve a premium price. Focus does, however, expose the company more to the risk of market changes than a company which has a broader base and which has the ability to offset difficulties in one market by its performance in another.

Porter (1980) emphasises that a company which does not adopt a competitive strategy based on one or a combination of his generic strategies is 'stuck in the middle' and at a growing competitive disadvantage. It 'lacks the market share, capital investment, and resolve to play the low-cost game, the industrywide differentiation necessary to obviate the need for a low-cost position, or the focus to create differentiation on a low-cost position in a more limited sphere.'

Having developed earlier a large number of strategic options and having reduced these to a number of priorities which best match the culture and ambitions of the company, these priorities now need to be attuned to the generic strategy or combination of generic strategies which are appropriate for achieving the company's long-term strategic objectives, and provide the sustainable strategic direction in the short term. It is unlikely that these will initially be a good fit and considerable work will need to be done to adapt and/or combine the chosen strategic options to ensure that they are internally consistent (e.g. so that if a cost leadership thrust is chosen, high advertising costs are not written in), and to ensure that they are focused on the company's strategic objectives.

This process will require patient iteration, and a realignment of priorities where strategies better attuned to the strategic objectives take over resources from others which are less focused. It will not usually be wise, however, to put all the company's resources into one strategy, as this will expose it to severe damage if a competitor succeeds in thwarting that strategy. Nor, as said earlier, should too many strategies be adopted, to avoid dissipating the company's resources. For smaller companies strategic alliances will often help to expand revenue without significant capital commitment. It is often advantageous to undertake the distribution of complementary products: this has been done, for example, by Cambridge Research Biochemicals.

Once the strategies best able to achieve the company's strategic objectives have been worked through and optimised, it is probable that the sum of the projected pre-tax profits will not equal the figures determined for the company's goals in the proximate period. This will require a further process to be undertaken – that of 'gap analysis'. Gap analyses will also need to be done for other chosen goals (return on total assets, earnings per share, etc.). Gap analysis is discussed in Chapter 5.

Where strategies are likely to take an extended period to deliver (e.g. the building of a major new factory or the development of a complex new product), it is essential for agreed milestones towards that achievement to be built into annual plans. The use of milestones enables firm control to be kept of strategies which require long periods to mature, especially where the timing of delivery is crucial.

In writing about strategy formulation it would be wrong to imply that only preformulated strategies are possible or valid. Particularly in times of great uncertainty and change it would be dangerous not to be able to respond to unforeseen opportunities or threats, and no amount of preformulated strategy can substitute for an ability to shape strategy incrementally or reactively. Henry Minzburg (1987) has studied this situation in depth and draws a clear distinction between 'intended' and 'emergent strategies'. Intended strategies are like the NASA strategy to put a man on the moon – carefully formulated and deliberately implemented. Emergent strategies are 'crafted':

craft evokes the notions of traditional skill, dedication, perfection through the mastery of detail. It is not so much thinking and reason that spring to mind as involvement, a sense of intimacy and harmony with the materials at hand, developed through long experience and commitment. Formulation and implementation merge into a simple fluid process of learning through which creative strategy evolves. (Minzburg, 1987)

It should be recognised, however, that reliance solely on emergent strategies militates against innovation, and the bold but calculated initiatives which are the real stuff of competitive strategy.

3

THE ROLE OF THE BOARD IN FORMULATING AND IMPLEMENTING STRATEGY

3.1. The traditional role of the board

It is in the concept of the 'corporation' that the differentiation between the individual and the 'body corporate' is founded. Corporations may either be 'corporations sole', where there is a permanent office and a succession of individuals hold office (e.g. The Crown), or 'corporations aggregate', in which a group of individuals is associated to form a separate legal persona (e.g. a town council). Incorporation for business purposes began historically with the grant of a royal charter to selected bodies, mainly to develop trade. Hence the Hudson's Bay Company of 1670 and the British South Africa Company of 1889, *inter alia.* Later it became more usual to incorporate bodies under a special Act of Parliament, and this was the habitual method of establishing public utilities such as canal, railway, water, gas, and electric light companies, and was needed to enable them to purchase land and exercise other powers which conflicted with private or other corporate rights.

The concept of limited liability became usual for such statutory companies, together with its corollary, the doctrine of *ultra vires* or specific limitation of powers. These concepts were included in the Joint Stock Companies Act 1856 and subsequent Companies Acts, and the differentiation between incorporated companies and partnerships, and other unincorporated business structures, became progressively more pronounced. Since corporations can only act through human agency the pivot on which the activity of joint stock companies turned was its board of directors. No specific definition exists of a board of directors although Table A (the standard form of Articles of Association in the 1948 Companies Act) does refer to 'board meetings'. It must be assumed the term has come down through usage, such as the 'Board of Admiralty' which itself was probably derived from the Scandinavian word *bord*, meaning table.

The role of the board is derived from the Articles of Association of the company and is subject to the powers defined in the Memorandum. The different Companies' Acts have said little about the style and content of board meetings and Table A of the 1948 Act is prescriptive only in key matters, as, for example, the quorum. The 1985 Companies Act is even less specific about the role of the board and no definition is given of the term 'director'.

As a result, the role of the board has evolved over time and has been shaped by companies to suit their individual culture and purposes. A pre-war picture of directors' meetings is given in Alfred Palmer's classic work *Company Secretarial Practice*:

As it is the board of directors which carries out the active management of the company it follows that it is at the directors' meetings that the real business is transacted. Board meetings are usually held frequently, the frequency depending on the policy of the directors and the nature of the business carried on by the company. A company owning a group of rubber plantations may find that a board meeting once a month is sufficient, whereas a company owning a chain of theatres or picturehouses may find it necessary to have weekly board meetings. The proceedings of board meetings are usually of an informal character and are almost invariably presided over by the person who acts as chairman of the company. (Palmer, 1953)

From this description it is evident that the traditional board of directors did not merely oversee the running of the business but was responsible and solely empowered to manage the business in detail. Only with the growth of businesses, and the resultant complexity and urgency that had to be faced, was the process begun of devolving responsibility and a minimal amount of authority which led to the growth of management below board level. The increasing range of technical expertise required by businesses also reinforced the expanding role of management, since boards remained largely proprietorial or custodial and were often more concerned to underpin their authority than to reflect the changing nature of the businesses which they directed.

In the present century the separation of proprietorship from control has evolved in most companies whose shares are quoted on the Stock Exchange, and in a large number of smaller and medium-sized companies also. As business has become more complex the need for specialist advice in the boardroom has become critical. It became necessary for the key functions (finance, sales, technology, manufacturing, etc.) to be represented by executive directors in most boardrooms, and subsequently the key operating divisions also had board representation. Where functions were not repre-sented in a balanced fashion the results were often disastrous; for example, Rolls-Royce had a preponderance of engineers and no finance director on the board when it had to be rescued by the Government in the early 1970s. As a result of the influx of executive directors and the effective transfer of control of the business to them, the activities of boards became more operations-driven. The main external concern was to project a positive image in the City of London and in particular to sustain the company's share price, and non-executive directors were often chosen for the contribution they could make to that end.

The role of the Board had by the 1960s changed from one of direct control to one in which control was beginning to move down into the business. Management committees were beginning to take over the direction of activity and the control of tactics, and functional executives dealt with the detailed working out and implementation of policy.

While the United Kingdom has maintained a unitary board system, with the frequent addition of a management committee comprising executive directors and key managers who can contribute to operational decision-making, Germany and some continental countries have adopted a two-tier board structure for major corporations. This comprises the supervisory board (*Aufsichtsrat*) and the management board (*Vorstand*). The supervisory board typically comprises a non-executive chairman and directors representing main shareholders (including banks and foundations) other outside interests and the workforce, reflecting the European view of industry as a partnership between capital and labour. Its role is to establish the mandate of the management board to manage the company in detail and to oversee the performance of that management board. It is advisory and not executive. The link between the two boards is sometimes only the chairman of the management board, effectively the chief executive officer of the company, though German law prohibits election of executive officers to the *Aufsichtsrat*.

It may be significant that the presence of worker directors on many supervisory boards makes the two-tier board the obvious model for possible European Community legislation on worker participation. Whether such a model would be helpful to UK business is a matter for debate, and an improvement in the effectiveness of British and American boards is urgently needed to defuse any uninformed enthusiasm for the German model in the European Commission and elsewhere.

3.2. The changing role of the board

When boards were conceived ... nobody envisioned the world in which they misfunction today. (Drucker, 1981)

The role of the board has evolved from one of executive proprietorship, through a phase in which directors held significant powers (technically in trust for shareholders) to one of overseeing the exercise of real power by the executive management of the company. In the last twenty years there has been considerable debate about the role of the Board and *Controlling Companies* by Geoffrey Mills (1989a) is one of the most significant British contributions to that debate. Much of the argument has taken place in the United States, largely among academics but involving H. M. Williams of the SEC and the famous poacher-turned-game-keeper, Harold Geneen, among others. The issues at stake are not so much the need to justify the continued existence of the board (though that is not unimportant) but to explain the poor performance of British and American business in recent years and to try to bring the board's role and performance back into focus.

The legal position of the board is less than satisfactory for the role it faces in modern conditions. Shareholders are protected by limited liability; directors are exposed to the full force of the civil and criminal law jointly, and severally in certain instances, and hold office in some cases at the whim of a powerful shareholder. The temptation to avoid taking initiatives and to seek to maintain a steady growth of earnings and dividends without undue exposure to risk must be enormous. With the ability to manage in detail having moved in most larger businesses down into functional and/or divisional management, the board must find it tempting to leave the direction of the company to executive management, subject only to constraints and procedures to protect the position of the directors! In such a situation, however, the board is not 'adding value' to the company's operations. It becomes almost a legal fiction, and the meaningful processes of the company take place outside the boardroom.

Assuming, however, the will to show leadership and to steer the company, and allowing for the reasonable protection of directors through insurance, what should be the role of the board today and for the foreseeable future? Given the power of information technology systems it is theoretically possible for boards to recentralise control of a company's operations and to imitate the nineteenth-century style of direct management. Businesses such as Marks and Spencer are run successfully with a highly centralised management, but this operates below board level and pivots on the buying and merchandising functions. The banks use information technology to operate on a real-time basis, but, again, this does not directly affect the operation of their boards. It would seem that direct management is unlikely to be part of the future role of boards which have already devolved operations to a level in their business where they can be effectively managed. To seek to take back the prerogative of managing in detail would put effective performance at risk, alienate the key staff who have had that prerogative, and burden the board with day-to-day matters at the expense of attention to other issues. Except in the case of smaller companies and apart from situations of crisis it is, therefore, unrealistic for boards to be involved in direct management.

In present and foreseeable circumstances, therefore, the role of the board is likely to comprise the following major elements:

1. Defining the business or businesses in which the company shall engage.
2. Establishing and maintaining the values by which the company shall be managed.
3. Setting the long-term objectives of the company.
4. Evaluating the strategies to deliver those objectives.

5. Electing, monitoring the performance of (and, if necessary, dismissing) the managing director or chief executive.
6. Ensuring that senior appointments are properly made and management succession is planned.
7. Overseeing the process of management development and training.
8. Evaluating internal controls to ensure protection of shareholders' assets and to validate financial statements issued by the company.

1. *Defining the business*

Perceptive and precise definition of the business(es) in which the company is engaged is a basic task of the board. Unless this definition is clear, and related to the skills, experience and reputation of the company, there is no concept against which new opportunities can be evaluated. Definition has to be perceptive because of the impact of change; in his article 'Marketing myopia', Theodore Levitt cited the example of Canadian Pacific which redefined its business as being in the 'transportation' business instead of the 'railway business' and created a successful airline. Properly focused and supported by the necessary resources the idea of the business is fundamental to sustained success and must be subject to constant review and evaluation by the board.

2. *Values*

The values by which a company is run are also a crucial factor for success and they also need to be defined and communicated effectively by the board. As the custodian of values the board is able to set standards which serve to sustain the growth of the company and to which parties inside and outside the business can relate. Values set the tone of the company, and the board makes itself responsible for seeing that values are not put at risk in the pressure of daily operations in a way which places the long-term prosperity of the company in jeopardy.

3. *Long-term objectives*

The company's long-term objectives are derived from the business(es) in which it engages and its system of values. They must, therefore, be defined and constantly kept under review by the board. The nature of these long-term objectives was examined earlier in this book and the practical difficulties of quantifying such objectives explained. This lack of precise quantification, and the need for perceptiveness and flexibility in defining long-term objectives, make the task one which requires considerable experience and a deep knowledge of the company's business in order to find the wellhead of excellence appropriate to the company.

4. *Evaluating strategies*

Strategies are the means of achieving company objectives and goals. The choice of strategies and the commitment of resources to support them are matters which closely involve the board. Geoffrey Mills' definition of the board's role does not mention strategy, though it does require the board to allocate resources. Many companies (e.g. GEC, BTR and Hanson) push the responsibility for strategy into operating companies or divisions, yet many more see a key strategic role for the board, particularly in smaller companies. Even in conglomerate businesses, such as those mentioned above, there are strategic issues of innovation, acquisition and divestment which may not relate to existing businesses (or in the case of divestment may not result from local initiatives). ICI has pushed operating responsibilities firmly into the divisions but the board retains responsibility for strategic direction, reinforcing the divisions technically, commercially, financially and with skilled people. The ICI board takes an overview of its operating divisions and evaluates plans and performance, being able to move in on a deteriorating situation by stages to head off disaster. There are a number of styles of corporate parenting which will be discussed later in this book. Although the degrees of board involvement in strategy vary, no sound model exists for the board to be totally uninvolved in strategy, if only in the evaluation of strategies proposed by the chief executive.

5. *Managing director/chief executive*
The election of the managing director by the board is usually required by the Articles of Association. This election is crucially important as the managing director, often nowadays called the chief executive in line with supposed US practice, is the key link between the board and the management structure of the company. As the board is placing very great, sometimes total, reliance on one individual to produce the results which it requires, the election, supporting, monitoring and, if necessary, dismissal of the managing director is a key part of the board's role.

6. *Senior appointments and succession*
In part this element of the board's role complements the interface with the managing director. It is, however, not solely at the managing director's behest that this function is carried out, since it is crucial to the company's ongoing prosperity, and patronage belongs to the company not to any one of its officers. To deal with the salary and perquisites of executive directors, a board committee is often formed, comprising the chairman and the non-executive directors. This ensures that the issue is dealt with objectively and with the benefit of outside experience. Succession is an issue which will usually be handled personally by the chairman, involving fellow directors as he sees fit; the process is, however, part of the role of the board, and the board must be involved in it and approve specific moves when the time comes to show its hand.

7. *Management development and training*
This part of the board's role feeds into the process of selection and succession planning referred to above. It is, however, more overt in its operation and will be a key element in the job of the personnel director. The role of the board in this area is to ensure that management development and training is shaped by the company's strategic ambitions, and relates closely to the resource requirements identified as necessary by the strategic planning process.

8. *Internal controls/validating financial statements*
The directors are responsible legally for financial statements issued in the company's name (annual accounts, prospectuses, etc.). It is, therefore, a key part of the board's role to ensure that such statements are correct in accordance with the accounting standards currently in operation. As the auditors are appointed to ensure that the company's accounts show a true and fair picture of the financial situation at the time of reporting, it is important that they have access to the board and vice-versa. The directors also have a common-law duty to protect the company's assets, and are therefore concerned to ensure that systems and procedures and other internal controls are working effectively. These requirements are often met by establishing an audit committee in which non-executive directors have access to the auditors, the company internal auditor and other officials as needed.

In carrying out its role as described above, the board has to equip itself to be well informed and prepared for foreseeable eventualities. In most larger and medium-sized companies the bulk of company resources will be under the control of executive management and devoted to delivering established strategic plans. Not only is it unwise for the board to need to borrow resources, it makes the board less able to carry out its role effectively. A small staff should be available to provide information to the board, particularly in the form of external intelligence. Constant scanning of the external environment will provide insights not available from the company's dedicated research efforts, and will identify potential threats and opportunities not captured by the more focused commercial intelligence system used to support company operations. Part of this 'third ear' intelligence should come from non-executive directors and their networks, from directors' external contacts (many not directly involved in company business) and from the network of lenders, advisers and others.

Growing awareness of the need to improve board performance and to link its role into the total company activity has led to an increase in the use of mission statements for boards. A recent survey by IMI in Geneva (Demb *et al*, 1989) showed that of the thirty-six companies replying (out of seventy canvassed), fifteen had board mission statements or working procedures. Half of these were in North America and none had turnovers in excess of

$50 billion per annum. Most of the positive replies lay in the turnover range from $5–20 billion/year. On analysis, only one mission statement was found to be comprehensive and there was concern that many boards were working on implicit missions rather than explicit ones.

The recommendations made by the IMI survey team are:

1. The development of a clear and shared understanding of its mission should be a primary goal for the board and top management of a company.
2. The process should be explicit.
3. As a minimum, the mission discussion should address: the overall mandate or intent of the board; an expression of values relating to the various roles; a definition of to whom and for what the company board should be held accountable; and an expression of expectations about the quality of the preparation for and the process of conducting board business.
4. Monitoring the performance of the board in fulfilling its mission should be a regular and scheduled part of the board agenda.

The expression of values will include issues such as the courage to ask difficult questions or ones which might reveal ignorance, the use of constructive controversy, business ethics, conflicts of interest, environmental issues and relationships outside the company (local community, etc.).

3.3. Executive and non-executive directors

The law does not distinguish between executive and non-executive directors and both have the same legal rights and obligations. These rights and obligations are very well documented in the Institute of Directors' (1985) publication *Guidelines for Directors* which has become the bible for company directors in the United Kingdom.

The roles of the chairman and of the managing director

Before examining the separate roles of executive and non-executive directors, it is useful to focus on the roles of the chairman and of the managing director, both appointments recognised and distinguished in the Companies Acts, who are the prime members of the board. To quote from *Guidelines for Directors*:

The Chairman
The Chairman is appointed by the board to preside over the board and will normally, under a provision in the company's Articles, also take the chair at general meetings of the company. In practice, however, the Chairman is not only seen as being the chairman of the board, but is also expected to act as the company's leading representative, presenting the collective views of the board to the outside world.
    What are the distinctive features of the Chairman's role? First, obviously, to take

the chair at meetings of the board, including in this function not only the orderly conduct of meetings, so that everyone who should have a say does have a say of an appropriate length, but also the allocation of time to different items, the determining of the order of the agenda, directing discussion towards the emergence of a consensus view, and adequately summing up decisions so that everyone understands clearly what has been agreed on policy and on action.

Second, as suggested above, to act as the company's leading representative in its dealings with the outside world.

Third, to play a leading role in determining the composition of the board and any sub-structure of committees, so as to make the board an effective team, working with a high degree of harmony.

Fourth, to take whatever decisions are delegated by the board to him to take between meetings of the board.

Managing Director

Most companies' Articles (if they follow Table A [of the 1948 Companies' Act]) contain a provision permitting directors to appoint one or more Managing Directors to whom any necessary powers may be delegated and to remunerate them for their services in that capacity. In practice, the Managing Director is the pinnacle of the management structure, including any executive directors. The Managing Director has personal responsibility for the success of the company's operations within the strategy determined by the board of which he, unlike a general manager, is a member.

The role of the Chairman is the more important in maximising the contribution of the board to the success of the company. That is evident from the above quotation. In the words of Sir John Harvey-Jones:

There are certain ineluctable responsibilities which lie upon him (the chairman), but above everything the entire position of the board. Only he can develop the board as a collective organisation, handle, select and motivate its members, and manage its work. The style and way in which the board works will have an enormous effect on the group as a whole, and the content of what it addresses itself to will decide to a large extent whether it is successful in influencing a large organisation. The actual way in which it works depends entirely on the chairman. (Harvey-Jones, 1989)

It should, however, be clearly understood that the chairman is chairman of the board not of the company. There is no legal status for a chairman of the company. His right to chair meetings depends on arriving within fifteen minutes of the due time to commence, since otherwise the directors may elect another from their number to take the chair. The contribution made by a chairman depends entirely on leadership (as Sir John Harvey-Jones emphasises) not on a broad, legally based authority. We shall consider leadership later in this book.

An earlier writer, Sir Walter Puckey, saw the duties of the chairman as follows:

1. He must earn respect
2. He must respect the views of others
3. He must control

4. He must co-ordinate
5. He must distinguish between opinion and fact
6. He must control the 'scope' of the discussion
7. He must lead, not follow
8. He must record progress.

It is obvious that, to perform these tasks adequately, a Chairman must have considerable managerial quality, and here lies the secret and often the root of chairmanship troubles, which some people try to avoid by combining the posts of Managing Director and Chairman. Frequently these men are first generation pioneers of the business, and they are unwilling (as yet) to accept a separate outside Chairman. They are not usually interested in an outsider who possesses only a prominent name but no real business experience, and they are slightly afraid of the outsider who possesses the management qualities of a real Chairman. (Puckey, 1963)

John Holbrook and Terry Pritchard (1965) emphasise the role of the chairman as 'a check on the Managing Director'. They see the chairman not as an initiator of policy but as responsive to, and (if convinced) supportive of, ideas proposed by the managing director. This ensures that proposals brought to the board have been discussed and agreed by two separate and powerful individuals. In the words of Sir Adrian Cadbury:

Both the chairman and the chief executive have responsibility to see that the company is working to a strategy which is understood inside the company and externally. Establishing a strategy is an issue over which they collaborate; it is not a separate responsibility of one or other of them. Strategy is a classic board responsibility and it is, therefore, in the chairman's field. (Cadbury, 1990)

The role of the managing director is primarily to deliver the business results required by the board from the company. In the context of the board he is another director, chosen to be the primary link between the board and the operating structure of the company. In the context of the company he is chief executive. Holbrook and Pritchard see the managing director as a catalyst for change:

The managing director is essentially the main stimulant to the Board in its task of policy-making. While legally the Board members are collectively responsible for company policy, in practice during a period of change it is the managing director who must bear the brunt of the responsibility. He may not necessarily originate ideas, but should be prepared and able to encourage the development of new ideas among his staff. One of the principal qualifications of the managing director is imagination; that is ability to recognize new and valuable ideas. The Board's essential role is to provide the check necessary and to examine the economic justification and feasibility of the ideas submitted. Subsequently, where a plan has been determined, the Board has to check on its operation. (Holbrook and Pritchard, 1965)

In his role as deliverer of business results, the managing director has full delegated authority from the board to manage the company's operations.

This requires considerable skills in motivation and managing people and in particular in delegation. Mills points out:

The chief executive who is slow to 'give away' some of his apparent authority is usually poor at appointing men who are good enough to assume some of his authority. He ends up by insisting that he has to do everything himself, in an ever-tightening circle in which he is both the centre and the circumference. The chief executive who begins without the slightest intention of spreading controlled authority will drive away good people, and thus weaken the initiative on which the quality of his own performance depends. The chief executive's best friend outside the boardroom can be the non-executive who can detect the effect the chief executive is having on his team, and can provide a diplomatic suggestion or two. You can distinguish the chief executive who will succeed from the one who may drive you into trouble by determining whether he would rather have a heart-to-heart chat with a good independent non-executive, or go to the dentist. (Mills, 1989)

The growth in the use of the term 'chief executive' has been paralleled by Robert Heller with 'the growing conviction that the supreme executive role was primarily strategic'. He continues:

This strategic emphasis, at least in theory, removed the necessity to have a separate chairman who controlled neither strategy nor tactics. His role was to preside over a board whose own function was to see that, both strategically and tactically, the executive management did its stuff. Today's theory, however, also holds the board responsible for strategic direction which supposedly makes the chief strategist the obvious, if not the only, logical choice to take the chair. (Heller, 1985)

Sir Adrian Cadbury sees the chairman as chief custodian of the longer term:

The chairman has a particular part to play in stimulating the board to reflect creatively on the company's strategy. He has the advantage over the chief executive that he has handed over the current year's results to the latter and so is free to concentrate his thinking on the years ahead. This is not meant to imply that the chief executive should be responsible for short term results and the chairman for longer term objectives. The development of the company is a continuous process and cannot be broken up in to annual increments. The chairman and the chief executive have, therefore, to work together to make certain that the actions taken in the company today are in line with their plans for the company tomorrow. (Cadbury, 1990)

The present phenomenon of combining the roles of chairman and managing director (more commonly chief executive) is questioned by many, not least by the Institute of Directors and most recently by the UK insurance industry. Geoffrey Mills suggests:

In cold logic, the only environment where the combination of the roles of chairman and chief executive can make productive sense is the small, privately-owned company with up to about 100 employees, when the chairman probably also types the envelopes during a crisis. Certainly once over about 100 employees – the boundary depending entirely on the nature and complexity of the business concerned – a separate chairman will invariably improve the objectivity of the board, and improve its control of management performance. (Mills, 1989b)

Sir Adrian Cadbury weighs the arguments for and against combining the roles of chairman and chief executive, and concludes:

There has to be someone on the board who is in a position to tell the chairman/ chief executive when the time has come for him to go, and to make sure in the meantime, that responsibility is being handed on to potential successors. If there is no such person on the board, then the posts should be split. (Cadbury, 1990)

The evidence points to the practice of combining the roles of chairman and managing director/chief executive as being widespread among larger as well as smaller companies. While for many companies there is no proof that the practice is damaging, the danger of one-man dictatorship is an ever-present threat, and the results can be catastrophic, as the shareholders of Guinness will be aware. The former Chairman and CEO of General Motors, Roger Smith, is personally credited by some observers with the Saturn Project, a $5 billion project to counter the Japanese. Unfortunately, few believe that it can succeed. At a time when organisation theory is pressing for the diffusion of management authority, it seems perverse and unproductive to seek an over-concentration of personal powers in so many of the Western world's big companies.

Executive directors

Executive directors are not only members of the board but have specific management functions and are members of the managing director's top team. This will often operate as an executive committee and will include selected managers who are not on the board as well as managers who are also board members. As we saw earlier, the evolution of the board brought about the inclusion of key functional specialists and later divisional general managers. In the United Kingdom this process has brought about a preponderance of executive directors on most boards, even though in some cases they are no longer speaking for their functions or divisions but are part of a carefully chosen board team. ICI is a good example of a company where directors are no longer the mouthpiece of their function or division, but that is an exception to the general pattern. Given the usual preponderance of executive directors on British boards (the reverse is true in the United States), the 'golden handcuffs' provided in terms of service contracts and pension rights, and the fact that the executive directors report to the managing director in the hierarchy of the company, there is growing concern that executive directors may not be free to indulge in what Jack Welch of GE calls 'spirited repartee', let alone challenge the position of the managing director. This makes the role of the board in monitoring, let alone dismissing, the managing director (see above) virtually unworkable in the absence of intense outside pressure. A survey by David Norburn (1989) of the characteristics of the British board in 1984, shows the typical executive director at that time to be quite inadequate for the work of a board.

Non-executive directors

The Institute of Directors' *Guidelines for Directors* states:

The present UK legal framework for appointing boards of companies permits the creation of boards composed wholly of full-time executives. This can be a source of weakness if such boards become inbred, lacking both the wider perspectives and the internal stimuli to perform that an external presence might provide. (Institute of Directors, 1985)

To enhance the company's sense of general responsibility, and to widen its strategic horizons, every board of a public company should, in the Institute's view, contain a proportion of suitable non-executive directors, with a minimum of two. The same considerations apply to any private company, large or small, which wishes to maintain an active control over its future and not merely react passively to events. The use of suitable non-executive directors will help a board to pay proper attention to the long-term strategic function of direction. These directors should have no contractual relationship with the company and should not be under the control or influence of any other director or group of directors. The use of such directors is not new, and its extension could be regarded as a return to traditional practice. A non-executive majority is still the norm in the case of many financial institutions. For many years the Institute has encouraged and helped companies to appoint non-executive directors. It is a practice now well established in the United States and has its parallels in the supervisory board of Dutch public companies. But it is extremely important to be clear what the proper contribution of such directors to a company should be.

The overriding consideration is that they participate to the full in the board's joint deliberations. Their legal duty, to act bona fide in the interests of the company as a whole, is identical with that of their executive colleagues. But within this framework their independence has three further contributions to make. The first is to widen the horizons within which the board determines strategy, both by applying the fruits of a wider general experience and by bringing into board discussions any special skill, knowledge and experience which is relevant to strategy and which the board might otherwise lack. The second is to take responsibility for monitoring management performance and the extent to which the management of the company is achieving the results planned when strategy was determined. The third is to ensure that the board has adequate systems to safeguard the interests of the company, where these may conflict with the personal interest of individual directors; to exercise a duty to the company in such areas as board appointments and remuneration; and to ensure the preservation of adequate financial information, whether or not a formal audit committee exists.

As the Institute of Directors points out, non-executive directors are not a novelty but have their roots in the custodial directors of the nineteenth century. Today, however, they are custodians not only for shareholders, but also for the other stakeholders in the company, not least the employees. Their custodial role extends beyond the present well into the future, and helps to protect the values and vision on which the company is being built.

If non-executive directors are to make a positive contribution to the board's performance, great care must be taken in their selection and they must be clear about the role they will be expected to play. Building a board is the job of the chairman, and he will be seeking a balance of knowledge and experience, and of temperaments and personalities, to help him in the work of the board. Meredith Belbin (1981) of Henley Management College has done intensive research into team structuring and has shown that teams consisting entirely of intelligent, innovative, articulate, 'big picture' people could not work together. The ideal model comprises a capable but not overdominant chairman, an ideas man, a highly ambitious driving personality to inject energy and enthusiasm into the team, a bright evaluator to act as a foil to the innovator, and a worker. This model does not necessarily translate directly into an ideal board, but the principles of complementarity and of checks and balances are worthy of imitation. This approach to team building is more important than 'tokenism' – the appointment of one woman, one black, etc., as a gesture. Where such people are valuable team members in respect of their individual contributions there is no tokenism only a net gain for the board. It is significant that few boards have yet seen the value of appointing foreign nationals – Sony is one of the pioneers in this dimension of team building.

Help needs to be given to new non-executive (and executive) directors, and this is a key part of the chairman's role. Sir Francis Toombs says:

I think a board gets the non-executive directors it wants really. If it provides plenty of information for non-executive directors, it gets good ones, but the problem is very often – and it's usually the chairman who does this – there is a lot of work involved in getting the papers into a form the non-executive directors can assimilate. (Ezra and Oates, 1989)

Sir Graham Wilkins sees the prime responsibility of non-executive directors 'to fire the chairman when he's not doing his job', as happened to his predecessor at Thorn EMI, Peter Laister.

Involving the non-executive directors in company functions, major presentations, social events, private board lunches for important guests, factory visits, exhibitions and other activities where they are involved as part of the top team is of great importance. Even more important is the practice of holding board 'away days' at which the board meets at a private location to discuss strategy, to analyse a potential take-over bid or to evaluate its own performance. There is no doubt that time invested in this manner greatly improves the potential of non-executive directors to perform effectively.

The type of non-executive director now being sought is changing. In the words of Dr Anna Mann, the headhunter:

The important factor now is not who the person is, but what he can contribute. Companies are seeking younger men who are currently holding positions as chief executive of perhaps substantial organisations and where they have specific experience in areas that are relevant to the company concerned. They are seeking people with track records, people who can demonstrate performance achievement, people with energy, pace and drive. It doesn't matter where these people come from or what their social or educational backgrounds are, so long as they demonstrate that they can do something for the business. (Ezra and Oates, 1989)

In addition to the pioneering work on promoting the concept of professional non-executive directors which has been done by the Institute of Directors and most recently manifest in the publication of Ken Lindon-Travers' (1990) book, the Bank of England and other financial and employer institutions have established an organisation named PRONED (1989) which seeks to promote the wider and more effective use of non-executive directors in the United Kingdom.

The company secretary

In the timeless words of Alfred Palmer (1953), 'The Secretary is a servant of the company and its agent for the performance of his secretarial duties.' In the early days of joint stock companies the secretary had no fiduciary role at all. In *Newlands* v. *The National Employment Accident Association* (1885) Lord Esher stated:

A secretary is more a servant; his position is that he is to do what he is told, and no person can assume that he has any authority to represent anything at all: nor can anyone assume that statements made by him are necessarily to be accepted as trustworthy without further enquiry, any more than in the case of a merchant it can be assumed that one who is only a clerk has authority to make representations to induce persons to enter into contracts.

The dismissive attitude of Lord Esher has been rectified over time and by the very real contribution made by company secretaries. The establishment of the precursor to the Institute of Chartered Secretaries and Administrators in 1891 gave a professional foundation to the role of company secretary which has been strengthened over the years. Lord Denning's assessment of the company secretary in a 1971 judgment contrasts tellingly with that of Lord Esher:

A company secretary is a much more important person nowadays than he was in 1885 (at the time of the Esher judgment). He is an officer of the company with extensive duties and responsibilities. This appears not only in the modern Companies Acts but also in the role which he plays in the day-to-day business of companies.

Other than the director or directors, the company secretary is the only statutory officer named in the Companies Acts. He may, or may not, be a director as well as company secretary but the roles are distinct. No company can be without a company secretary and the statutory duties which he will normally be required to discharge are specified in the Companies Acts, together with penalties for non-compliance. The company secretary is appointed by the board and is responsible to the board. Geoffrey Mills sees the company secretary as more than just an officer of the company:

Some argue that his daily functions are so detailed and specific that in practical terms they exclude him from an active role in the broader strategic deliberations which characterise the agenda. Others, that as he sits there all the time, and is privy, if not party, to every nuance, he might as well be a director. He is very much the Keeper of the Board's conscience, as well as being the Keeper of its records, and he is the prime internal source of legal information affecting Board decisions. Sometimes the question is solved by combining the roles of finance director and company secretary, though the functions of the two are quite different in character. Decision on this question, as indeed on the question of any appointment to the Board, should be made on the principle that a man's personal qualities and personality are much more important than his specific background. If still in doubt, he is better in than out. One of the most effective directors whom the writer has met, with the knack of always putting his finger on the critical factor in any complex case, happened to be a company secretary. This knack would have been of equal value to the Board if the man's daily role had been quite different. (Mills, 1981)

The Institute of Directors queries the practice of electing the company secretary to the board:

Some companies consider it undesirable that the offices of director and secretary should be combined. A secretary has certain statutory duties for which he is legally responsible in his own right. As a secretary outside the Board, he can give independent advice on matters for which he is responsible; if he is also a director he may become bound by collective decisions which conflict with his statutory duties.

In smaller companies, however, reasons of status or even expense may dictate the decision to appoint one person as secretary and director. The exercise of the dual role in no way, of course, reduces the secretary's obligations under the law. (Institute of Directors, 1985)

The 1980 Companies Act brought in provisions (s79) for the secretary of a public company to be qualified. Among suitable qualifications is that of the Institute of Chartered Secretaries and Administrators; others are UK-called or admitted barristers and solicitors and members of the main accounting bodies. Setting higher standards for company secretaries has led to a widening of the scope of their work. In addition to his statutory duties, a company secretary will often have many of the administrative tasks of the company, including property administration, personnel, contracts, legal matters, pensions, fleet management and the custody of key and sensitive documents. In one of his judgments Lord Justice Salmon stated, 'the secretary is the chief administrative officer of the company.' With the emergence of the concept of compliance in the Financial Services Act, many company secretaries in the field of financial services may now also act as compliance officer to help secure compliance with the detailed provisions of the Act. Such responsibilities are onerous as the dismissal and negligence charge against the compliance officer of National Westminster Bank over the manipulation of the Blue Arrow share launch in 1989 clearly demonstrated. The use of company secretaries in other fiduciary roles is expanding, reflecting Geoffrey Mills' perception of them as privy to every nuance of the board's deliberations. It is not uncommon for the company secretary to be involved in confidential negotiations, carrying the authority of the board implied in his office, and to be consulted on issues which relate to the board's conscience. In the words of Ewan Mitchell (1978): 'The company secretary has considerable status and very real powers to contract on the company's behalf. If you wish to restrict those powers you must do so by letting your suppliers know of those limits.'

Rather than seek restrictions it is suggested that the role of the company secretary should be further expanded. Ewan Mitchell sees him as the link between directors and between the directors and shareholders. The role of the company secretary in corresponding with shareholders and in helping the chairman to prepare and shape the annual report and accounts is emphasised by Sir Adrian Cadbury (1990) in his recent book, *The Company Chairman*. Given the perceived need to make boards more effective, the role of the company secretary in that process is of great potential importance. The process of identifying and selecting non-executive directors who will be able to make a significant contribution to the company will involve careful research and sound judgement. While the judgement will finally be exercised by the chairman and the board, the rest of the process can be substantially assisted by using the company secretary. He will have a detailed inside knowledge of how the board works and of its interface with the rest of the company. He will be the curator of the board's history and of the evolution of its 'chemistry' and ways of working. A wise chairman will involve the company secretary in the development of the board not just as record-keeper and 'conscience', but as a full member of the team.

What of the company secretary in the board's strategic role? Where there is no strategic planner employed by the company, which is frequently the case with medium-sized and smaller companies, the company secretary should be used to organise and conduct the planning process. This role fits with the training of a qualified company secretary and the Institute of Chartered Secretaries and Administrators is developing post-qualification training in strategic planning for its members in association with the Strategic Planning Society. The company secretary as strategic planner has the advantage of being in tune with the nuances of board thinking and is usually a trained analyst and researcher. Much of the detailed work of strategic planning can be overseen by him, even if he does not have the time to carry out the whole task single-handed.

Where the company has a strategic planner, the company secretary's role in the planning process is important both in organising and facilitating board strategy meetings and 'away days' and in working as part of the board team on strategy. Where there is a strategy or planning committee of the board, the company secretary should organise its meetings, record its deliberations and carry out tasks commissioned by that committee. The role of the company secretary in identifying and analysing mergers and acquisitions, where discretion is of the utmost importance, is described in an interesting article 'The administrator as corporate strategist' by R. J. Barron (1989). The company secretary's training enables him to understand the issues involved in mergers and acquisitions (strategy, market shares, accounts, valuation of companies, legal matters, taxation, etc.), enabling him to do the requisite research, brief the board and even be involved in negotiations. This is surely proof positive that the company secretary has achieved recognition of his pivotal position between the board and its external and internal environment.

3.4.   The board's responsibility for formulating and implementing strategy

The formulation and implementation of strategy are the means of achieving the objectives set for the company, and for ensuring its survival and prosperity. We have seen how the strategic task is defined and carried through; implementation is the realisation of the strategic task, and the whole process is sometimes referred to as strategic management. This subject will be dealt with in detail later in this book.

Professor Bernard Taylor of Henley Management College defines the board's responsibility for strategy as follows:

Strategic planning is one of the two key tasks of top management. The other job, of course, is making sure that the business is running smoothly. There are five main reasons for the board to get involved in planning:

1.   to improve the performance of the business, for the benefit of the shareholders, the managers, the employees and the stakeholders;
2.   to provide a philosophy and a set of principles which will guide the actions of the people involved in the enterprise;
3.   to set the strategy and direction of the business – usually for growth in products and markets, divestments and acquisitions;
4.   to monitor and control the company's operations, not just in the form of immediate financial results, but also in building for the future through improved productivity, quality, customer service, new products, the recruitment and training of staff, and
5.   to provide a set of policies which can be presented publicly in discussions with governments and other external bodies. (Taylor, 1988)

Although strategic planning is a key task of the board it cannot and should not be done in isolation from the realities of the business and of the outside world. The task is to ensure that the process is carried out imaginatively, thoroughly and effectively, and that ownership of the strategies and plans that result is spread throughout the company. In carrying out its task the board will need assistance from a wide range of sources within the business; the wider the range, the greater the resulting ownership.

Two key contributors to the process of developing strategy are the corporate planner and the company secretary. The former will have direct responsibility for the process and for the resultant plan, and will bring technical advice on planning issues as needed. The role of the company secretary is less immediately obvious but should be very powerful, as we have seen earlier.

In addition to its strategic role the board will need to be closely involved in 'issues management'. This is the process of analysing public issues which may affect the company, and of developing programmes to respond to them positively and in a way which furthers the company's business objectives. The Institute of Directors' (1984) *New Agenda for Business* is heavy with public issues and it is likely that the impact of external issues on most companies will increase as the business environment becomes more complex and intrusive. The link between strategic planning and issues management is well displayed in Figure 3.1 (Arrington and Sawaya, 1984). This shows how the two processes interrelate and shape each other. It is not without significance that a growing number of companies combine planning and public affairs; for example, Shell UK has a Director of Planning and Public Affairs. This is a recognition of the growing impact on corporate strategy of public issues such as the environment, and of the need to manage such public issues positively and proactively in order to deliver company strategies over the long term. Other public issues which might affect a typical company include political and charity payments, obtaining planning permissions and development grants, health and safety, third-party liabilities, relationships with national and local government, voluntary codes of conduct such as the OECD guidelines for international investment and the ILO tripartite declaration of principles on employment, and involvement with local society (co-operation in education, fund raising, etc.).

Another facet of issues management is the recent rise of the 'Corporate Communicator'. This role combines public relations, now considered too important to be left solely to outsiders, and internal communication of strategy and values. A recent survey by Smythe, Dorward, Lambert (1990) shows that a surprising 21 per cent of responding corporate communicators were board members, emphasising the growing need to improve the formulation and communication of board policy.

3.5.   How the board can discharge its responsibility for strategy formulation and implementation

The first item in *A New Agenda for Business*, published by the Institute of Directors (1984), is the upgrading of business leadership. The actions

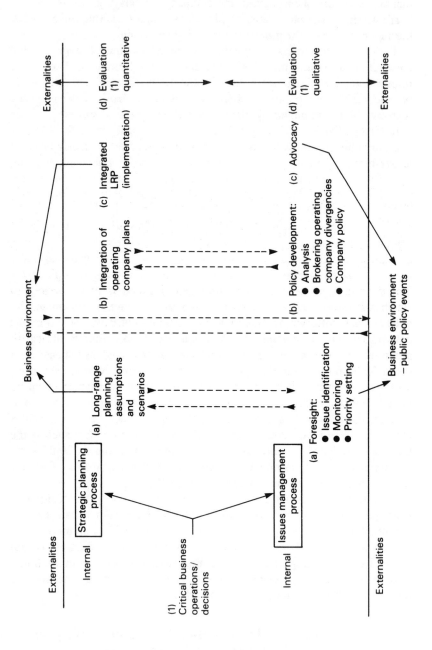

Figure 3.1   Issues management and strategic planning

earmarked as flowing from that key agenda item are professional development, strategic thinking, leadership training and business ethics.

Leadership is a growing issue in business because it is believed to be a key factor in differentiating successful companies from others in conditions of increasing complexity, competition and change. What does leadership mean in a business context? The whole of the book *Making it happen* by Sir John Harvey-Jones (1989), is a practical treatise on leadership applied to rescue ICI from an outmoded structure and declining profits, and to reposition the company to win back its threatened pre-eminence.

In his lecture to the Strategic Planning Society's 1984 National Conference, Sir Raymond Lygo drew a distinction between management and leadership:

Management is the art of organisation, the art of organising people and things to produce and achieve objectives. Leadership is the ability to inspire other men and women, to achieve things much greater than they would if they were left to their own devices in no matter how good a management structure. . . . Leadership has in it an element of service, service to one's fellow men, service to the company, service to each other. (Lygo, 1984)

The importance of the inspirational aspect of leadership in the services, to which Sir Raymond Lygo (a former admiral) referred, derives from the need to cope with battle, crisis and unpredictability. These conditions are now pressing home on business, and company boards have to deal with pressures and uncertainties which are more intense than those of earlier years. All businesses are having to cope with an accelerating pace of change; leadership can turn reacting to change into a proactive and creative seeking of change as a strategy for building future profitability.

A key element of leadership, counterbalancing the heroic aspects more readily associated with it, is judgement. Sir Geoffrey Vickers (1987), in his famous address 'The art of judgement', identified three types of judgement – reality judgements, action judgements and value judgements. The first reassesses the currently accepted view of external reality. The second is a judgement which underpins a decision to act. The third is a judgement of what is best of a number of alternatives. The action of Churchill in shipping tanks by sea to Egypt in 1940 when the United Kingdom was still threatened is cited as a combination of the three types of judgement: Churchill judged that invasion was not imminent (a reality judgement), that the tanks should be shipped by sea (an action judgement) and that they should go to Egypt rather than elsewhere (a value judgement). Good judgement is not only successful, it inspires confidence in those whose leaders have it. When Napoleon said 'give me generals who are lucky', he was simply recognising that good judgement is only validated by success and that luck is inevitably part of any action involving risk.

In order to provide focus and direction to the use of leadership for driving their business, many companies develop mission statements. We have referred to these earlier and also to mission statements for the work of the board. Mission statements arose from the emphasis placed on the import-ance of mission by Peter Drucker (1973): 'A business is not defined by its name, statutes or articles of incorporation. It is defined by the business mission. Only a clear definition of the mission and purpose of the organisation makes possible clear and realistic business objectives.' A mission statement should be inspirational and harness all concerned to goals which enhance and sustain long-term performance. Peter Schultz, Chief Executive of Porsche, talks of three men doing the same job on a building site. Asked what he was doing, the first said 'breaking rocks', the second replied 'earning a living', the third answered 'helping to build a cathedral'.

In an article in *Long Range Planning* Fred David (1988) reports on research done by questionnaire to *Business Week*'s top 1,000 companies. 181 responded of which 75 provided mission statements and 10 per cent had not written one. From analysis of the results of his research, Fred David identified the following common components of mission statements (though not all statements contain all nine elements):

1. Customers – who are the enterprise's customers?
2. Products or services – what are the firm's major products or services (best stated from a customer view point)?
3. Location – where does the firm compete?
4. Technology – what is the firm's basic technology?
5. Concern for survival – what is the firm's commitment to economic objectives?
6. Philosophy – what are the basic beliefs, values, aspirations and philos-ophical priorities of the firm?
7. Self concept – what are the firm's major strengths and competitive advantages?
8. Concern for public image – what are the firm's public responsibilities and what image is desired?
9. Concern for employees – what is the firm's attitude towards its employees?

Mission statements should not substitute for the specific objectives and strategies derived from them, but should be broad enough to accommodate significant change over time. In the words of George Steiner:

Mission statements are not designed to express concrete ends, but rather to provide motivation, general direction, an image, a tone and a philosophy to guide the enterprise. An excess of detail could prove counter productive since concrete specification could be the base for rallying opposition. Precision might stifle creativity in the formulation of an acceptable mission or purpose. Once an aim is cast in concrete it creates a rigidity in an organisation and resists change. Vagueness leaves room for other managers to fill in the details, perhaps even to modify general patterns. Vagueness permits more flexibility in adapting to changing environments and internal operations. It facilitates flexibility in implementation (David, 1988).

The idea of a mission statement to which others can add is perceptive. Like the old prints which the customer could colour to suit his or her taste but which remained unchanged underneath, the mission statement which can be filled out gives ownership and flexibility and yet remains identifiable and meaningful in its own right.

Sample mission statements from US corporations quoted by Fred David are shown in Figure 3.2. Work on mission statements for British companies has been done recently by Ashridge Strategic Management Centre and published by *The Economist* under the title *A Sense of Mission* (Campbell *et al*, 1990). An example of a mission statement for a small packaging and haulage business is shown in Appendix 3, together with that of the FI Group, a fast growing software house.

The board will exercise its role in the formulation and implementation of strategy in a number of ways. Some of those will be specific, others will be indirect and, in reality, the board should be reinforcing this process in every action it takes and every event in which it partakes. The specific areas of contribution to this role include the following:

1. The regular meetings of the board.
2. The company's planning cycle 'away days'.
3. Special meetings of the board (takeovers, crises, etc.).
4. Board luncheons for selected guests (customers, suppliers, etc.).
5. Annual reports and annual general meetings, extraordinary general meetings of shareholders.
6. Briefings for media, investment advisers, etc.
7. Strategy committee of the board.

1. *Regular meetings of the board*
Every board has its routine of meetings, from the minimal statutory meetings to approve the annual accounts and propose dividends to meetings of a frequency and length sufficient to carry out company business. Evidence shows that such meetings tend to develop a bureaucratic pattern and that the content snowballs with a growing accretion of routine issues. The picture of boards spending time on 'bicycle shed' matters, rather than the big issues which they should be facing, is an exaggeration which underlines what is often a true situation. It is easier to spend time on matters which are easy to comprehend and have obvious immediacy than on those which may only be dimly perceived and which may not become immediate during the time in office of the present directors. This is not to decry the need to devote time to what Sir John Harvey-Jones calls 'boiler plate' matters, but as he himself emphasises, such matters should be limited to a small part of the board agenda, leaving ample time to devote to significant issues which need fully to be ventilated.

How should board meetings belie Peter Drucker's comment 'Board meetings rarely go beyond . . . trivia' (Drucker, 1973)? This requires a

F. W. Woolworth Company
The mission of F. W. Woolworth Co. is to provide value to
consumers in North America, Germany and Australia
through distinctly individual but complementary retailing
businesses. These businesses are being managed, on a
decentralised basis, to generate levels of profit that reward
investors, sustain long-term growth, provide competitive
rewards for employees, and benefit the communities in
which they live and work.

Sunwest Bank
The purpose of Sunwest Bank is to provide financial and
related services in a manner that: Maintains a level of
earnings to support our growth and expansion, and
sustains the confidence of those that invest in us.
Anticipates and fulfills our customers' needs at a high level
of product quality and staff performance. Provides a
rewarding and challenging environment for our employees.
Responds and contributes to the social and economic well
being of the community and markets we serve.

Rockwell International
The leader in diverse markets, we are developing new
technologies and applying them to products and systems
in our four principal businesses — Aerospace, Electronics,
Automotive and General Industries. Our 103,000
employees, more than 17,000 of them engineers and
scientists, are dedicated to excellence in everything they
do, from implementing new technologies, to managing
complex systems, to making products of the highest
quality. This effort is serving the needs and meeting the
challenges of today's society. It also has given Rockwell
International a momentum for continued outstanding
financial performance.

Public Service Electric and Gas Company
Public Service Electric and Gas Company is an investor-
owned, business-managed public utility, franchised by the
State of New Jersey. Its primary purpose is to provide safe,
reliable and economic electric and gas service to its
customers at just and reasonable rates. In furtherance
thereof, it is the aim of the corporation to afford its
stockholders a return on their investment equivalent to
that of other investments of similar risks, and to com-
pensate its employees with remuneration and fringe
benefits competitive with other employment opportunities
in its geographical area and commensurate with their
contributions toward efficient corporate operations.

Figure 3.2   Four mission statements

decision by the chairman to manage the agenda actively, supported by his
fellow directors, and executed and sustained by the company secretary.
Such active management requires a clear identification of the various
routine tasks of the board and their timing (statutory tasks, cyclical tasks
(e.g. budgets), oversight of operations, share register, reports of board

committees, etc.). These should be shaped into a pattern which will allow the majority of time over the year for non-routine business. In reviewing board business, both routine and non-routine, thought should be given to Voltaire's famous comment: 'I am writing you a long letter as I haven't had time to write you a short one.' A great deal can be achieved by seeking concision in board papers and minutes. Some chairmen insist that board papers are of a limited length (e.g. two pages maximum). Sir John Harvey-Jones (1989) tells how he made a working committee more effective that way, supported by visual aids, and found that the effort took people directly to the nub of the problem. A firm policy in this area, sensibly administered by the company secretary, will not make the board less effective in its statutory and routine duties, but will ensure that only matters which really need to come to the board are allowed to do so, leaving more time for significant routine issues and for the board to deal with its strategic work.

The use of the time allocated to non-routine work is a key decision for the board. In much of the routine business of the board, the scene is set and the information provided by the executive, and non-executive directors are less well informed than their executive colleagues. In the board's strategic work it is important that balance is restored and that all directors are equally informed and involved as far as possible. The board may wish to allocate time in the non-routine area of the agenda to three key areas – monitoring, learning and strategy formulation. The monitoring role would comprise feedback on the strategic management of the company, beyond the routine reporting against plans and budgets, and based on systematic scanning of the company's environment. This would give early warning of longer-term changes and would 'close the loop' on earlier strategy formulation. The learning role would enable all directors to develop their competence jointly and severally, and would strengthen their effectiveness as a team. This might include specific exercises, or workshop sessions with outside experts or even inside specialists whose knowledge and experience might be strategically relevant to the company. Although the executive directors might have some advantage in such a situation, the balance of skills would still make the contribution of non-executive directors very important. The strategy formulation role is the output mode of the other strategic work areas. It may be difficult to plan the precise output, since many ideas will prove untenable or may be overtaken by events. Sir John Harvey-Jones used to set a dozen strategic tasks each year for his board to accomplish and these would cover the spectrum of the work areas described above (e.g. how to improve the allocation of information technology to the commercial aspects of ICI). Some direction or prioritisation of the process is necessary to yield usable results, yet the board needs to be open to the workings of serendipity and to major emergent issues (e.g. the rapid liberalisation of Eastern Europe in 1989/90).

2. *The company's planning cycle*

The question of organising the strategic planning function is addressed in Chapter 5, but the board's contribution to the effectiveness of the planning process is fundamental. Unless the board is committed to strategic planning as a key instrument of implementing the company mission, the ability of the planning process to support the board in achieving the company's objectives will be totally thwarted. Nothing is more futile than a corporate planning system which is not harnessed to real ambitions, and the leadership needed to animate the process must come from the board. Fuller discussion of the board's detailed contribution to the annual planning cycle will follow in Chapter 5.

3. *Special meetings of the board*

Some boards never have special meetings and leave the chairman full discretion to deal with issues which emerge between regular board meetings. This is evident in the limited time many non-executive directors put in annually. It may be significant that according to the survey carried out by PRONED (1989), 40 per cent of non-executive directors of companies with an annual turnover of less than £50 million spend ten days or less per annum on their company's business. Allowing for board meetings and committee meetings, that leaves little time for special meetings.

Special meetings take different forms and have various purposes. Some special meetings are called to meet crises, for example, the departure of the managing director or a threatened takeover bid. In the first case the chairman would have a private meeting with his directors and in the second would have his legal and financial advisers present. Where such crises are totally unexpected, the board is usually at a disadvantage. As Peter Drucker says, 'In every major business catastrophe . . . (since the Great Depression) . . . down to . . . recent debacles . . . the Board members were apparently the last people to be told that anything was awry . . . and it is futile to blame them. It is the institution (the Board) that malfunctions.' (Drucker, 1981) And to quote Dan Bavley from his article in *Long Range Planning* on 'What is the board of directors good for?':

It is in crisis situations that the value of the Board is tested. Yet most last-minute corporate rescues have been the work of a capable chief executive officer or the main outside financing body. It has been very rare for the Board to help save the corporation. Most companies don't have serious contingency plans for crisis situations. When they do, they refer to a limited set of possibilities. Less than half the companies (in a survey by Daniel C Brown) – 47 per cent – with less than $500 million in annual sales 'have a plan that would enable them to communicate quickly and effectively in a crisis'. (Bavley, June 1986)

Not only should the board be quick to meet in a crisis, but it should also have a contingency plan for communicating to employees, customers, suppliers, shareholders and the media in a positive fashion. Too often complacency before a crisis is compounded by embarrassed denials of crisis while the company struggles to pretend that nothing has changed.

Special meetings should also be used positively to help the board in its work. Where the board has a mission statement, or has formally agreed its terms of reference, a special meeting should be held, at least annually, to enable the board to evaluate its performance. This should not be part of a board meeting, where a board might report on progress made against specific tasks. The purpose of this special meeting is to evaluate, in an informal atmosphere, how well the members interact with each other, what skills may be missing, what changes need to be made. A board is a living organism and its chemistry is delicate and subject to change; like any organism, a board needs nurture and radical action to make it prosper.

None of the special meetings is more important than those devoted to strategy formulation. Most boards have found that this process is best carried out away from the pressures of the office, and it is now common practice for 'away day' sessions to be held in quiet locations in conditions of informality. Often busy boards will devote a weekend to strategy meetings, and these require punctilious organisation to be successful. Some boards hold strategy sessions as a 'think tank' with no agenda, but such arrangements can easily degrade into a kind of 'T group' with a loss of purpose and dignity. It is recommended that strategy meetings have a firm framework of timings, with a clear topic and action line for each session, even if not a detailed agenda for those who abhor a vacuum! Although the atmosphere of the meeting is informal, and, within limits of relevance and courtesy, participants are encouraged to contribute freely, the sessions must have a clear purpose and be taken at least to an interim conclusion.

One of the strategy meetings which is of particular importance is that which is held before the annual planning cycle. Such meetings are discussed in detail in Chapter 5.

4. *Board luncheons for selected guests*
An enterprising chairman will seek occasions on which he may entertain selected customers, suppliers, bankers and other parties with a close relationship, actual or potential, with the company. Some meetings with key contacts will by their nature need to be private or in a small group. Many others, however, will benefit from being staged with a wider audience. Involvement of the board in such events is of value not only to receive well, and hopefully impress, a number of guests, but also as a team exercise for the board. Such exercises, even for some companies in the form of grandiose annual dinners in livery halls, are also a way to develop the performance of the board and, in particular, of non-executive directors.

5. *Annual reports and company meetings*
The annual report and accounts is a statutory document which is expensive for any company to produce even if it is not printed in multiple colours as a

media spectacular. It should be seen not as a chore but as a major opportunity for the company to gain well targeted benefits. Many companies recognise this and it is interesting that there are annual awards for the best presented annual reports (as advertising media) and for the presentation of accounting data (for the Stock Exchange and accounting bodies). I have sought to create an award for a third category – for the annual report as a communicator of strategic direction – but my efforts have so far been to no avail! This third dimension is beginning, however, to take shape, and it will begin to be important for companies to show not just their past performance but to demonstrate that they are building a better future. The details of strategy are, of course, confidential, but the publication in the annual report of mission statements, the commitment to obvious future goals and reporting of progress towards those goals, and demonstrating the existence of an active strategic process (e.g. the use of a strategy committee) will do more to build confidence in the company and its board than any other single document. The annual report is addressed to shareholders and their confidence and support is crucial for the company's long-term success.

Company meetings are important because they are the usual interface between the shareholders and their board. Business at such meetings is formal, but questions are now becoming more frequent and interesting, and many companies offer a buffet meal after the AGM at which shareholders can talk informally to the directors. Many of the questions traditionally asked are pedestrian, querying small details in the accounts or the managing director's salary. The level of interest may be heightened by imaginative displays of new products, new factories or the impact of new acquisitions and alliances. The presence at the buffet after the AGM of representatives of new associates lends credibility to the company's strategic direction.

6. *Briefings for media and investors*
Often briefings for the media and institutional investors or investment advisers are given by the chairman and/or the managing director. Depending on the number of visitors involved, it can often be advantageous to do these briefings as a board. This not only helps to strengthen the board's competence in presenting issues to outsiders but gives the audience a stronger impression of the resources available to the company in its directors and of their ability to perform as a team. If the board is used to working on strategy, the penetrating questions which such an audience might hopefully ask would be handled with confidence and would strengthen the credibility of the company's future prospects.

7. *Strategy Committee*
Boards are usually empowered by the Articles of Association of their company to delegate their functions either to committees of the board or to management. The establishment of a sealing committee to handle powers of attorney and other transactions requiring the company seal is now quite

usual, and larger companies usually also have an audit committee and a remuneration committee. Audit committees have been required since 1978 in companies listed on the New York Stock Exchange and are increasingly established by UK companies as a consequence, often at the suggestion of their auditors.

We have seen the burden of work which falls on an active board, and the passing of detailed work to selected committees of the board is a practical alternative to longer and for more frequent board meetings. If it is helpful to delegate administrative detail to committees, it may be useful for many boards to create a strategy committee.

Some boards (e.g. ICI) prefer to handle strategy entirely in plenary sessions of the board, and this has much to recommend it where time permits and where all directors are fully briefed on the company's operations in sufficient detail to be able to contribute equally. In most cases the non-executive directors will not have in-depth knowledge of the company's history, operations, competitors and markets to match that of the executive directors, and it is, of course, unrealistic to expect that they should.

The audit committee usually comprises non-executive directors and the company secretary, and takes expert evidence from the statutory auditors and the company internal auditor on the accounting and other systems and controls in the company. Its members thereby not only exercise independent checks on the executive, but also learn much more about the detailed workings of the company. In *de Paula's Auditing* (1986) it is suggested that the audit committee should extend the scope of its operations to audit the performance of management. I believe that a separate body is needed to deal with matters outside the ambit of the statutory audit and that this should concentrate on strategy, which would in any case subsume management performance. The establishment of a strategy committee, comprising non-executive directors and the company secretary, would allow the board to take expert evidence from the corporate planner and from managers involved in strategic planning, to ensure that the detailed workings of the planning system were satisfactory. The advantages of using non-executive directors are first, that they will have experience of strategic planning systems in other companies and will be able to relate to best practice, and second, that the non-executive directors are outside the company hierarchy.

It may be advantageous for the strategy committee to operate on specific tasks delegated by the board, many of which will involve research which will test the resources and systems of the company. The committee may wish to use the company secretary and/or the corporate planner to handle specific work in detail since the non-executive directors will be able to devote only a limited amount of time. Nevertheless, the operation of a strategy committee will be a useful way of deepening non-executive directors' knowledge of the company's operations, as well as bringing new eyes to bear on the strategic planning process and systems within the company and relating them to best outside practice.

It should be recognised that, according to Geoffrey Mills (1981), one in seven of the larger UK companies already has a planning committee. These committees may readily be adapted to the role detailed above where they are not currently engaged on the same task, with the same emphasis on non-executive director membership.

Parenting styles

While many boards will be developing strategy for businesses reporting directly to them, there is a growing number of boards in larger and more complex companies which are in a 'parenting' role towards their subsidiary companies, divisions and strategic business units. In order to add value to the process of strategic management (the formulation and implementation of strategy) corporate boards need to analyse carefully their role and their relationship with the operating businesses in their group. Parenting is discussed in Chapter 7.

The issues of centralisation versus decentralisation and of the parenting style to be adopted by the corporate centre are very complex and, even in a stable situation, would have no ideal answer. The choice of style and pattern can only be tailored to each individual company, and will be subject to tensions, changes and new development as personalities and internal priorities change and as the pressures of markets, competitors and other outside influences ebb and flow. In the words of Sir Christopher Hogg, 'An organisation is like a pendulum. It swings from too much centralisation to too much decentralisation; and comes to rest only when the mainspring is dead' (Goold and Campbell, 1988).

Strategic controls

A survey done by the Ashridge Strategic Management Centre (Goold and Campbell, 1989), on the use by the largest 250 British companies of explicit strategic objectives in their control process, showed that only 15 per cent actually had such explicit strategic objectives, while 21 per cent claimed to be developing or considering such objectives, 24 per cent might use them at a future date, and 41 per cent did not use them and showed no interest in using them.

It was recognised earlier that long-term strategic objectives can rarely be quantified precisely because of the need constantly to relate the objectives and their quantum to best practice and changes in the external environment. The intermediate goals of a company need, however, to be specific and, where possible, quantified, as do the milestones towards their achievement. For the purposes of strategic control, therefore, it is necessary to have some such objectives, no more than ten in number in order to achieve focus, and stated in such terms as market share (per cent), key unit costs, key cycle times, order completion times, service response times, number of new product introductions, and so on. These objectives are then broken down into the action subsets needed to deliver them, which are allocated to specific individuals with clear datelines for delivery, and built into the key action programmes of the relevant parts of the company, with milestones for progress where delivery is extended over time.

Milestones are found to have the following added value when they are specific:

- Greater clarity and realism in planning.
- More stretching standards of performance.
- More motivation for business unit managers.
- More timely intervention by central managers.
- Clearer responsibilities that make decentralisation work better.
- Avoid back-door target setting.

While problems associated with explicit milestones include:

- Inflexibility in implementing strategy.
- Misdirected motivation towards the wrong goals.
- Increase the cost of the control process.
- Encourage bureaucracy in performance reviews.

On balance the research found that informal strategic controls were frequently chosen by default, although the difficulty of establishing explicit milestones in businesses with strong linkages, high uncertainty, rapid change and complex key success factors was recognised. Nevertheless, it was concluded that many companies not using explicit strategic controls would benefit from their introduction.

Corporate renewal

One of the greatest challenges facing any board is that of corporate renewal. Any organisation has an inbuilt tendency to conservatism and to bureaucratic sclerosis. The proud history of many a company is given as the justification for failing to take the risk of innovation and change, and a boardroom which was once thriving with purposeful activity becomes a museum of past glories.

The process of corporate renewal is not a simple drive for rejuvenation, since the characteristics of youth are not all positive, and the process of maturity implies positive learning which differentiates the experienced company from the neophyte. Corporate renewal is a process which encourages adaptability, creates change and promotes innovation, building on the accumulated learning of the company but challenging the received wisdom behind which complacency and prejudice seek to entrench themselves.

The board's responsibility for corporate renewal is seen by Patrick Haggerty of Texas Instruments to be as follows:

1. Assuring that the corporate structure, policies and practices are realistic, sufficiently elastic, and yet powerful enough to couple not just with the external national and international environment as it now exists but as it will be through future years and over the entire corporate span of interests;

2. Assuring that the corporations's products and services are truly innovative and really are contributing in a major way to constructive change in the world around it;

3. Assuring that an innovative, aggressive, properly educated and experienced staff of professional managers, scientists, engineers, and other specialists is available and being generated in sufficient depth and talent to meet the corporation's long-range goals. (Haggerty, 1980)

Given the leadership of the board and the resources referred to above, the pursuit of innovation will involve close monitoring of Peter Drucker's (1986) seven sources of innovative opportunity:

1. The unexpected (success, failure or outside event).
2. The incongruity – between reality as it is and as it ought to be.
3. Innovation based on process need.
4. Changes in industry or market structure that catch everyone unawares.
5. Demographic changes.
6. Changes in perception, mood or meaning (for example, the new emphasis on the environment).
7. New knowledge – scientific and non-scientific.

This monitoring requires not only a systematic scanning operation referred to earlier but needs a consistent and perceptive input from the board. How this input can be achieved is a matter for each company to organise to suit its own culture, industry and pattern of working. Texas Instruments has been moving towards having directors whose principal occupation would be corporate renewal:

This would ensure our having high-level, capable people who have the time to study, to think quietly about and to comprehend the impact of the rapidly changing internal and external environment and the relationship of both to our corporate self-renewal. These directors would have no operating responsibilities. Their duties would relate entirely to their functions as directors and advisors to the board. (Haggerty, 1980)

In addition Texas Instruments sought non-executive directors with skills complementary to those of the selected executive directors dedicated to corporate renewal. Dr Simon Wilder of STC recommends having a new business director on the board to challenge old ideas and champion new products. My own view is that the board's strategy committee, discussed earlier, should have responsibility for monitoring Peter Drucker's seven sources of innovative opportunity, taking care to be alert for signals from within the company (which might otherwise be suppressed by the system) as well as scanning outside horizons.

Smaller companies may feel that their strategic responsibilities are daunting. Often outside help may be needed to launch the process of formulating strategy, as the necessary skills may not be available internally and the work has to be done without impairing ongoing operations. Until the launching of the DTI Enterprise Initiative such help was often expensive, and too many smaller companies failed to develop a viable longer-term strategy and many of them did not survive. The DTI Business Planning Initiative started in January 1988 and by the end of June 1990 over 2,500 projects had been successfully completed. Demand for business planning projects now runs second only to marketing out of six specialisms on offer. Of firms interviewed in 1989 by independent consultants Segal Quince Wicksteed, two-thirds reported that the consultancy results achieved made them feel better able to improve their management strategy.

3.6.   How to make boards more effective

Earlier in this book the performance of boards, particularly in the Anglo-Saxon economies, was examined and found to be less than effective. Peter Drucker recently surveyed the operation of charity boards in the United States:

Many non-profits now have what is still an exception in business – a functioning board. They also have something even rarer: a CEO who is clearly accountable to the board and whose performance is reviewed annually by a board committee. And they have what is rarer still: a board whose performance is reviewed annually against preset performance objectives. . . . the key to making a board effective . . . is not to talk about its function but to organise its work. (Drucker, 1989)

Reference was made earlier to mission statements for defining the board's own tasks. This is an area which needs more development, not with a view to giving the board self-importance, but in order to set specific objectives and ways of working in the same manner as Drucker's charity boards. At present too few boards take stock formally of their effectiveness, and yet they expect value for money from all other organs of the company. Unless such assessments are made regularly there are few effective controls on the board, other than a hostile bid or the receiver's knock on the door.

Boards have to add value to company operations or they lose rationale and authority. Effective boards can add substantial value, as demonstrated by the revival of ICI in the early 1980s, whereas ineffective boards are exposed to predatory attack, either to acquire their company or to dismember it in the interests of increasing shareholder value. Even well-run companies like BAT and Vickers have been attacked in this way, but such companies have a better chance of resisting hostile bids or pressure to divest.

A study by John Aram and Scott Cowan (1986), into the information needed by boards to enable them to assist the management in increasing the economic value of their companies, came to some interesting conclusions.

Value creation is not just dependent on the quality of directors, the clarity with which the role of each is defined and the quality of the information provided to the board. All must interact and improve each other – 'approaching the ideal of a value-creating board requires development of a complex managerial system'. Commitment to this goal is needed, together with adequate time to prepare for meetings and a results-oriented agenda.

Value-creating boards exist in companies where management has spent the time and effort to develop effective planning and control processes, has obtained director involvement in these processes and has designed information systems to support management and directors' decision-making processes. Director involvement in goal and strategy formulation, management control and executive evaluation and compensation is critical in the achievement of an effective board because it provides a focus and structure to board decision-making. The research indicates that the director's role in executive evaluation and compensation is an area in which specific board practices and conditions can spell the difference between value-creating and other types of corporate boards. Time, place and agenda are again critical; however, as the basis for the financial reward system that drives the economic performance of the firm, the board's personnel and compensation functions assume heightened importance in the ability of the board to integrate management performance and shareholder interests over the long term. Specific challenges to the board or its compensation committee are 1) to ensure that the reward systems designed to balance short and long term performance actually function toward the desired balance and 2) to ensure that financial rewards are given to senior managers only on the basis of actual performance against predetermined objectives. Fulfilment of these standards requires an unusually high standard of board or committee decision-making ability. (Aram and Cowan, 1986)

Earlier we considered the record of performance of British and American boards, and drew attention to the risk that the better national performance of Germany and others in Europe would make the two-tier board system attractive as an EC norm. Examination of the strategic planning practices in most other European companies does not demonstrate that the United Kingdom is behind – rather the reverse seems to be the case. For example: Denmark was addicted to budget-style planning, according to an article in *Long Range Planning* by Ackelsberg and Harris (1989); and Belgium was short-term oriented and relatively unsophisticated in its planning, according to Caeldries and van Dierdonck (1988).

The last published comparative survey of British and Japanese strategic planning, by Kono and Stopford (1984), showed that Japanese planning processes are more centralised and authority flows from the centre (in contrast to the accepted idea of bottom-up consensus). The decision-making body in a Japanese company is the management committee; boards in Japan are more ceremonial and mainly comprise executive directors, who are usually not subject to deadlines for retirement. Since the last war, independent non-executive directors are few in Japanese companies. The power of small shareholders is negligible; that of institutional group ('Zaibatsu') shareholders significant, if they choose to exercise it.

It would seem, therefore, that the Japanese model runs counter to the central thesis of this book – that the board is responsible for the objectives and long-term strategic direction of the company. Reality in Japan is more subtle. While the key executive directors are usually free to steer their company by means of the executive committee, this is within a broad framework of consensus established with the key institutional and group shareholders and overseen by the board. While the executive directors appear to have total power, it is exercised by them as a group and is worked down through the company in task groups. This process makes Japanese companies very flexible in their operations and enables effective feed-back to the centre to take place. Before the last war the Japanese board was more like a supervisory board, and may in time become so again. In such a structure, the management committee would equate to the management board in the German model. The model British board would have the long-term strategic responsibility and the external sensitivity of a supervisory board, together with the responsibility for a closer oversight of strategic management than a supervisory board would normally exert. More importantly, its responsibility for ensuring corporate self-renewal would be proactive, rather than the reactive posture of the classical supervisory board.

In his book *Understanding Organisations*, Charles Handy (1985) says that non-executive directors are 'regarded more as a bearer of status rather than of stimulus'. This statement underlines the dilemma facing the board, at a time when management is increasingly decentralised and the role of the board has drifted towards symbolism rather than substance. We have seen how the board moved from direct representation of ownership, through the representation of functional management power and later to representation of divisional power, to a situation where the real exercise of power was outside most boards, and directors were left with the task of endorsing decisions effectively made outside the boardroom and placing themselves at risk for the consequences. Non-executive directors have often been kept uninformed of the implications of what the board is asked to do. In some cases they have fought against abusive chief executives, as Angus Murray successfully defeated Alan Bartlett at Newman Industries, but the few exceptions only highlight the dreadfulness of the general performance. This problem has been aggravated by the abdication of ownership by most shareholders, which has left the board with little strategic accountability and with pressure limited to sustaining the share price and increasing dividends. We shall look more closely at ownership later.

The process of isolating the board has been at work in larger companies for much of this century. It may be traced back to the development of functional management, which earlier had no board representation, and to the consequent creation of 'baronies' round each function. These baronies still exist in some public sector organisations (e.g. the London Passenger Transport Board before the Fennell Enquiry in 1987/8). Such baronies see no value in communicating with others, and seek to enhance their value by professional obscurantism. From the viewpoint of such groups, it was only sensible to tell the board merely what was good for it to know. A similar, but mutually hostile, group of baronies developed as companies divisionalised, and boards were seen as sources of finance for pet projects, battlefields for divisional advantage and a potential hinderance to divisional independence. It is significant that corporate planning began in most companies as a 'bottom-up' exercise, based on the budgeting process and collated at the centre by new and rapidly expanding departments. The information required existed, if it was available at all, away from the centre. The growing need for more information to run companies led to the creation of data-processing departments, who became another self-perpetuating barony. As such baronies were created and grew, the board became increasingly irrelevant in most public companies (even private companies had some of the same pressures), and operations were effectively autonomous in many cases. A flavour of the impotence to which boards have been reduced is found in an interview given by Lord Sharp to Kenneth Fleet of *The Times*. On arrival at Cable and Wireless, Lord Sharp found:

a very comfortable board. None of the board papers seemed to have any bottom-line implications. The company was engineering-led. Everything had to be the best. I also found the entrepreneurial activity was at a low premium, except for the wrong motives. How to employ surplus staff caused by the shrinkage of business was seen as a challenge . . . promotion was by Buggins' turn, based on the tradition of the civil service. Thus we had problems relating to compensation, high centralisation, lack of decision-making, lack of any real corporate strategy, restrictions on salaries and a lack of individual performance. All this generated a very comfortable environment, but not a very exciting one. (*The Times*, 16 June 1990)

It was the recession which followed the oil crisis in the 1970s which forced companies to decimate middle management and the staff functions which had grown over the previous thirty years. In order to deal with this situation boards had to have better information than many of them had seen for many years, and were thus able to win back the initiative from management.

Since that time, line management has won back authority, partly by dealing directly with trades-union problems, and partly by asserting its needs in respect of other functions where staff departments had grown too powerful. As a result, the idea that planning should be done by planners has been seen for the nonsense that it is. Line management has been forced to plan in order to overcome its crises, and the accelerating pace of change will make it impossible for that involvement to slacken. Planning departments have been decimated and the remaining planners allocated to support line management in its planning responsibility. Computer departments are now part of a management information network, including personal computers, external databases and communication systems. Information is seen as a resource too important to trust to isolated specialist groups.

How can the board benefit from this change? First, by differentiating clearly between its role and the role of executive management. Line management needs to be free to manage and develop the business within a framework which challenges it and does not uduly constrain its authority. The board must, however, provide the leadership to guide the company over the longer term and to empower management to deliver the results needed to steer the company in the direction determined by the board. To do this, the chairman of the board (there is no such thing in law as the chairman of the company) should be independent of executive management. Combining the chairmanship with the role of chief executive is tantamount to combining the judge and the defendent in the dock – guaranteed to confuse the 'jury' of the other directors! It should never be forgotten that a prime responsibility of the board is to control the chief executive and, if necessary, dismiss him. Where the chief executive is also chairman this task becomes unnecessarily complicated, particularly where there is a majority of executive directors. It is less difficult to dismiss a relatively new chairman/ chief executive, as with Peter Laister at Thorn EMI or where family influence is strong, as with the dismissal of Ernest Saunders at Guinness, but a well-established chairman/chief executive is likely to be too powerful to allow the board to carry out its role of over-seeing management as effectively as it should or be able to exact an excessive price for his departure in the manner of Sir Ralph Halpern of the Burton Group.

In the United Kingdom the board appoints the chairman and the managing director (now usually titled chief executive in larger companies). Other directors are appointed to the board without a specific role as director; executive directors will have management roles but the financial director, for example, is not a role appointment of the board in law. In the United States it is usual practice for some officials to be answerable to the board in the same way that the company secretary is in English law (though often not in practice). The practice of making the controller a board appointment in the United States (and sometimes finance officers and other key officials) ensures that key custodial posts are accountable to the board and not to the chief executive. Some of the tensions which present UK practice generates may be seen in the Guinness and Polly Peck scandals, and consideration should be given to legislation to provide for key custodial posts to be answerable to the board in the last analysis. This should also clarify the position of the company secretary, particularly where the chairman and chief executive are the same person, and give protection in the same manner as provided for compliance officers under the Financial Services Act.

Given an independent chairman and an effective chief executive, the board needs to organise its work carefully if it is to maximise its effectiveness. This organisation needs to clarify the role and tasks of the board, as we have seen, and to allow for performance to be reviewed regularly. All directors are equally liable at law and the chairman should ensure that non-executive directors are carefully chosen, inducted and regularly briefed, so that they are as aware of issues as their executive colleagues. While non-executive directors are unlikely to be able to devote sufficient time to learn the finest details of the company's business as executive directors need to do, every effort must be made to communicate all necessary information available to directors equally. The chairman must resist the 'us' and 'them' attitudes which still characterise too many boardrooms, typified by sitting on opposite sides of the board table and by the use of pre-board meetings to 'lighten the agenda'. Non-executive directors should be invited to sit on subsidiary boards where appropriate, and be used more actively on working parties and to represent the company. In this way they are better able to understand the workings of the company and to fulfil their role of controlling the management. If practice in respect of briefing non-executive directors does not significantly improve in the United Kingdom there is a strong case for legislation to ensure that non-executive directors have equal access to company information to match their equal legal liability to that of executive directors.

The strategic role of the board has been exhaustively examined in this book. For well-run companies this is the real task of the board and can only be achieved if the board works as a team. To do this requires the chairman to pick the team in a way that ensures that he has a mix of talents appropriate for defining and re-evaluating the long-term mission and objectives of the company. These talents will need to be equivalent to those of experienced world-class researchers who are then willing and able to work together in disciplined group programmes under an outstanding professor whom they respect. The performance of such men is greater than their individual contribution and they each bring to the task a whole network of contacts, insights and judgements which enrich and underpin the quality of the whole operation. In the same way the board has to be a window on the world, open to influence from stakeholders, shareholders and those who set the trends which will affect the company's future. A closed system is doomed unless it can be brought into the real world in time, as Lord Haslam is doing for British Coal, and it is part of the board's strategic task to ensure that the company is alert to all potential change, searching for and interpreting the weakest signals in a systematic search for possible threats and incipient opportunities.

In making itself effective, the board needs to give authority to management to run the company within established guidelines and towards agreed goals, and in return must be given the information and feed-back to enable it to function. With the rare exception of companies like John Lewis, there will be another party to the process – the shareholders. They it was who appointed the first directors and who renewed the mandates of individual directors according to the Articles of Association. They have no authority over the managers other than through the board, yet rarely do shareholders seek to exercise ownership, unless it is to sell the company or to wind it up! In the same way that the board is required to direct and control management, shareholders should logically direct and control the directors whom they have appointed.

This issue was explored recently in *The Economist*. It emerges that Anglo-Saxon attitudes to shareholding differ fundamentally from those in respect of other forms of ownership. A share is a betting slip for most shareholders, particularly the younger institutional money managers. Any dissatisfaction with, or unease about, the company can be settled by selling its shares. In Germany and Japan shareholders have been more proprietorial, and there is growing dissatisfaction in Anglo-Saxon countries with 'punter capitalism'. Some companies are going private (Virgin, Really Useful Group, etc.) and others are raising funds other than by public issue. Institutional shareholders may realise the need to recapture power over their investments and exercise control over the directors they appoint; the growing number of individual shareholders may help this process. If action is taken, publicly quoted companies will reassert their leading role in the UK economy; if not, the trend to proprietor capitalism through smaller and medium-sized companies will be strengthened. Proprietor capitalism through the Stock Exchange is perfectly workable, as the remarkable success of Berkshire Hathaway in the United States has proved, and there is no reason why this model should not be replicated in the United Kingdom. *The Economist* sees Hanson Trust as an example of a proprietor capitalist, although limited to basic industries and driven by acquisitions and unbundling of underemployed assets. The link between ownership and management drove the Industrial Revolution and created Britain's industrial lead in the nineteenth century. Ownership needs to become more assertive. In the words of *The Economist*:

It is possible – no more than that – that all big institutional investors in America and Britain will correct their faults and start behaving like real owners. Of the various options for reform, that is probably the best. It would restore a sense of strategic direction to many public companies, and it would help to ensure that they spent their money more wisely and more profitably. (*The Economist*, 5 May 1990)

A first portent of this change is the publication of the discussion paper 'The role and duties of directors' by the Association of British Insurers (1990). Ownership will need increasingly to embrace the managers and employees of companies, and their involvement as owners can only be positive, particularly in a climate of greater competition which will face us in the 1990s. The last word goes to *The Economist*: 'Those countries that combine proprietor capitalism and relentless competition will win the economic prizes in the 1990s and beyond.' (*op. cit.*)

4

STRATEGY AND STRUCTURE

4.1. The importance of structure in implementing strategy

Strategy and Structure (Chandler, 1966) is the title of a classic study of the development of decentralised corporate structures in the United States. Written in 1962, this was one of the earliest recognitions of the link between strategy and structure and of the contribution which organisation theory is able to make to effective management. Structure, and the people, systems, information and procedures which comprise it, is the tool available to management to deliver its strategies. If structure is ill-adapted to the task, the chances of delivering strategies is made more difficult – at the margin, totally impossible. Adapting structure to the specific needs of the business is, therefore, an essential precondition of success in achieving strategic goals, that is, effective strategic management.

Chandler showed how a number of major US companies had, from the 1920s onwards, developed independently the concept of divisionalisation or decentralisation as the best means of adapting their structure to the needs of rapid growth. Without the breakdown of the centralised and functional structure put in place when these companies had established themselves, it would have been impossible to have achieved their key strategy of rapid growth, and, for many of them, the secondary strategy of diversification. The importance of structure for the implementation of strategy may be gauged by the growth of consultancy in this area in the last forty years, spearheaded by firms such as McKinsey.

A key factor in the development of decentralised structures was the need to release executive management from the burden of operations in order to enable key executives to carry out their entrepreneurial responsibilities effectively. The study continued:

This situation arose when the operations of the enterprise became too complex and the problems of coordination, appraisal and policy formulation too intricate for a small number of top officers to handle both longterm, entrepreneurial, and shortterm, operational administration activities. To meet these new needs, the

Table 4.1. Comparison of traditional and emerging design factors in organisations

Traditional organisation design factors (1890s–1920s)	Emerging organisation design factors (1960s–1980s)
1. Uneducated, unskilled temporary workers	1. Educated, sophisticated career employees
2. Simple and physical tasks	2. Complex and intellectual tasks
3. Mechanical technology	3. Electronic and biological technologies
4. Mechanistic views, direct cause and effect	4. Organic views, multiple causes and effects
5. Stable markets and supplies	5. Fluid markets and supplies
6. Sharp distinction between workers and managers	6. Overlap between workers and managers

innovators built the multidivisional structure with a general office whose executives would concentrate on entrepreneurial activities and with autonomous, fairly self-contained operating divisions whose managers would handle operational ones. (Chandler, 1966)

John Naisbitt (1984) sees the process of decentralisation as one of his 'megatrends'. He believes that the drive to centralise industry, in order to improve control and reduce costs, is against the basic culture of diversity and democracy in the West. This led to the crisis of US industrial performance and the subsequent search for looser, more flexible, 'bottom up'-driven structures which are now emerging. He believes that the growth of local political initiatives will be paralleled in future business strategies and structures.

Rosabeth Moss Kanter (1989), who has chronicled much of the pattern and methodology of change in US business, sees an unworkable dichotomy between the traditional factors influencing organisation and the emergent patterns of today. Table 4.1 draws some key distinctions.

In the view of Kanter, the key way to deliver strategic change is through 'integrative action', 'the willingness to move beyond received wisdom, to combine ideas from unconnected sources, to embrace change as an opportunity to test limits'. Kanter contrasts 'integration' with 'segmentalism', which is evidenced by highly compartmentalised structures. The structures which Kanter sees as conducive to change are looser and open to effective and rapid communication. Matrix organisations can work effectively in creating change but teamwork is the key factor. Teamwork does not mean the destruction of the operating structure, but involves the formation of *ad hoc* teams to tackle specific agendas or the encouragement of integrative action by wider consultation. Teams come and go, and should never be permanent. They are means to finding holistic solutions to allocated tasks and to deliver more effective results than a formal structure would be likely to achieve.

4.2.   Various structural options

No two organisations are likely to have the same structure since the structure will have evolved from the original concept of the business, modified by history and experience and hopefully related to the present ambitions and policies of the company.

Most organisation structures will have begun as 'bureaucratic', to use Max Weber's term, and have been based on legal or traditional authority. Weber (1987) defines a bureaucratic administration as one which exercises control fundamentally on the basis of knowledge, both technical and experiential. Such knowledge is power and must be protected as a matter of priority. Burns (1987) contrasts 'mechanistic' (bureaucratic) and 'organismic' organisations in a manner similar to Kanter's 'traditional' and 'emerging' organisations referred to in 4.1. above, and it is likely that most present day businesses will be moving their structure from mechanistic to organismic to cope with the growing pressures of change which they face.

Charles Handy (1985) sees structures as a product of the culture of the business. He identifies in his book *Understanding Organisations* four main cultures and related structures:

1. *Power*
   Structure: web.
   Characteristics: centralised; strong financial control; results
                         orientated.
   Examples: Smaller companies; GEC.

2. *Role (bureaucratic)*
   Structure: temple (functions as pillars).
   Characteristics: functional; role driven; stable.
   Examples: most major companies.

3. *Task*
   Structure: net; matrix.
   Characteristics: task driven; teamwork; difficult to control.
   Examples: project or product management.

4. *Person*
   Structure: cluster.
   Characteristics: geared to individual objectives; difficult to
                         manage.
   Examples: co-operatives; partnerships.

These structures are rarely met in the pure forms identified by Handy. GEC is not a pure web structure, but has spawned other structures to enable it to grow and retains a strong finance link with each other organisation in order to bind it into the web. Companies with a temple

Table 4.2. Types of activity within a business

	Characteristics/location	Culture structure
1. Steady state	All routine parts (accounts, administration, production)	Role/temple
2. Innovation	R and D, marketing, planning, O and M, etc.	Task/matrix
3. Crisis	Marketing, parts of production, supply	Power/web
4. Policy	Policies, strategies, priorities, resource allocation	Power/web

structure often have net structures in product groups. The key evolution for such companies is often to turn the matrix sideways in order to empower the task or project dimension and relegate the functional line to a support role. The person culture is not often found in pure form since it is inimical to any overriding objectives. It is, however, a powerful influence on the working of partnerships and co-operatives, and can act as a restraint on the development of family-controlled businesses where personal objectives are not reconciled with the real needs of the business and power is not given to those willing and competent to structure and run the business to its full potential.

Handy sees the need to modify structures within an overall organisation so as to relate to different types of activity. He isolates four types of activity which are distinct and may be localised within a business (See Table 4.2).

It will be seen that structures cannot realistically be monolithic and that, in a business of reasonable complexity, they will need to be diverse and differentiated. Businesses are organisms and require diversity and flexibility in order to be able to develop and to cope with the traumas of change and conflict. Whenever a structure is at variance with the real needs of a business, there will evolve an unofficial pattern of working which seeks to overcome the obstacles presented by the official structure. With the accelerating pace of change there are increasing battles being fought between managers defending obsolete structures and non-existent jobs and those who have been given tasks to achieve without the support of a clear change in structure. Many reorganisations are effected at top level and not fully driven down the organisation, leaving large areas of the business subject to wasteful inefficiencies and costly delays.

Managements often appoint co-ordinators to seek to integrate the working of their differentiated organisation structures. The role of co-ordinator is key to the successful operation of the complex, multidimensional structures which characterise modern business. A co-ordinator requires not only the power of being recognised as an expert in his field of activity, but also the very special chemistry needed to defuse and resolve conflict and motivate people to work to company goals. He is, however, unlikely to be able to sustain his role unless management endows him with authority and demonstrates support. Lack of power and access to key information are the twin tombstones of many a gifted and motivated co-ordinator who sought to produce results from an untamed and resentful structure.

Another approach to structure is to see it as a series of systems. Stafford Beer (1979) developed his Viable System Model some ten years ago and it has been used quite extensively as a tool for building structures to cope with complex tasks. VSM uses the principles of cybernetics to separate and detail each system and subsystem, linking all internal and external nodes and ensuring total feedback. VSM is also used to assess the ability of an organisation to deliver the strategies it has chosen.

4.3. How to appraise structure and match it to the needs of strategy

We have seen that there are a number of distinct types of organisation structure which, in practice, are usually mixed in most companies to meet their perceived needs. Structures are, however, mostly the product of history and of circumstance, rather than of conscious analysis and action. Inappropriate structures can lead to significant problems. J. Child has an exhaustive list in his book *Organisation: A guide to problems and practice* of which the following are only a few:

1. Motivation and morale may be depressed because:
   (a) Decisions appear to be inconsistent and arbitrary in the absence of standardized rules.
   (b) People believe that they have little responsibility, opportunity for achievement and recognition of their worth because of insufficient delegation.
   (c) There is a lack of clarity as to what is expected of people and how their performance is assessed.
2. Decision-making may be delayed and lacking in quality because:
   (a) Necessary information is not transmitted on time to the appropriate people.
   (b) Decision-makers are overloaded due to insufficient delegation.
   (c) There are no adequate procedures for evaluating the results of similar decisions in the past.
3. There may be conflict and a lack of coordination because:
   (a) There are conflicting goals between projects or departments.
   (b) Mechanisms for liaison have not been laid down.
   (c) The people involved in operations are not involved in the planning.
4. Costs may be rising rapidly because:
   (a) The organisation has a long hierarchy with a high ratio of 'chiefs' to 'indians'.
   (b) There is an excess of procedures and paperwork. (Child, 1984)

These problems emphasise, if only from the negative perspective, the crucial role of structure in delivering results. If key strategies are to be delivered, great care has to be taken to ensure that the organisation is structured in a manner to support those strategies and not to fail them or even thwart them.

Appraisal of the ability of a company's structure to deliver its key strategies would cover the following main areas as a minimum:

1. Top level structure (and culture).
2. The distribution of power.
3. Head office's 'rules of the game'.
4. Differentiation.
5. Integration.
6. Systems, communication.

1. Top level structure

Any appraisal needs to relate the basic structure of the business to its key strategies. If the strategies are geared to innovation, diversification and key projects it does not make much sense to perpetuate a functional, bureaucratic structure. Equally, it may be unwise to dismantle immediately the functional structure and risk the loss of technical excellence and effective control which that structure gives. The change may need to be the creation or strengthening of a matrix structure, with a progressive move towards empowering the task dimension of the matrix.

The question of the number of levels in the structure will also need to be addressed. These have tended to become too numerous, and spans of control at each level too narrow, partly due to misunderstanding of Col. Urwick's doctrine on the subject. Tall structures and narrow spans of control push power to the top. Flat structures tend to have wider spans of control and disperse power. The trend towards more decentralised and matrix structures has usually brought a reduction in the number of hierarchical levels in organisations and wider spans of control. Rowbottom and Bills (Handy, 1985) see no need for more than five levels in most organisations, with a maximum of seven for the biggest. The Fulton Committee found departments in the Civil Service with nine levels and spans of control of two or three.

2. The distribution of power

Power is not a factor formally allocated on organisation charts, but it is the lifeblood which makes them function. Unless those who have to deliver key strategies, in whole or in part, are empowered to use the resources of the business to that end, the chances of success are greatly reduced. Power can more easily be passed down the hierarchy of a functional organisation than across matrices or into task groups. In complex organisations great care has to be taken to empower the 'driver', and equal care to place all others clearly in a support role. It is tempting to leave full power in the hands of those who are no longer the drivers, but such power is at best not used to deliver the key strategies, and at worst it may hinder their delivery.

Those in a support role need sufficient power to carry out their tasks effectively and to nurture and sustain their competence. They need the power to challenge the drivers where the latter are in danger of making a mistake, but not to hinder sound progress. Both the drivers and the support staff need power in proportion to the responsibilities placed on them, and the relevance of those responsibilities to the delivery of the key strategies.

The distribution of power is, therefore, a crucial part of equipping an organisation to deliver its strategies. It is also essential to establish and maintain a balance of power, both to enable checks and balances to work within the system and to pump the lifeblood of power as needed to all parts of the organisation.

3. Head office's 'rules of the game'

In bureaucratic organisations the policy and procedures manuals are usually thicker and more thumbed than elsewhere. Many companies have given up maintaining such manuals in the face of accelerating change and the pressures of more immediately rewarding work. These are two extremes of an important issue, emphasising policy rather than procedures.

Any appraisal will have to establish the policies needed to make the structure deliver the company's key strategies. Such policies will include those guiding the internal management of the business, trading, other external relationships, the standards to which the business will adhere, the allocation of resources and, most importantly, the system of priorities. Within these policies should be the ground rules governing the operation of the business, so that staff know the expectations of management and the limits to which they may manoeuvre in seeking to help deliver the strategies. The rules affecting sanctions and rewards should also be clear and geared to the.achievement of the company's goals.

4. Differentiation

Care will need to be taken to weigh up the diversity of the business in terms of markets, products, location, technologies, supply sources, and so on, and also to identify the different internal goals which may result. Lawrence and Lorsch (1967) term this 'differentiation'. Production may be seeking to automate while personnel is striving to increase recruitment. These factors will need to be identified and assessed and their implications reflected in the company's structure.

If a business is moving fast into diversity it risks losing effective control. It may be appropriate to break the organisation into multiple units or even to adopt a conglomerate structure. Any solution has, of course, to be relevant to the company's strategic goals.

5. Integration

Whatever structure is adopted as a result of the appraisal will need to be integrated appropriately. If a conglomerate structure is adopted it may only be felt appropriate to integrate the different businesses financially. Integration will also be effected, in part, by the 'rules of the game' referred to above. The other mechanisms of integration are involvement of top management in activities down the line, for example, on subsidiary boards, and the use of departments or individuals for co-ordination. Accessibility of the top management is important for integration, but care needs to be exercised to avoid weakening the authority of local management. The attendance of top management at local board meetings, in a non-executive role, enables integration to occur without any trespass on the executive role of local directors, provided that the non-executive directors play their role strictly and correctly.

The role of co-ordinators is becoming increasingly crucial as organisations become more complex and diverse. The need to empower co-ordinators has been referred to earlier; their personal attributes (as listed by Charles Handy) make sobering reading, as follows:

To be expert in more than one field of the organisation's work;
To be able to handle role ambiguity, incompatibility and conflict without letting the role pressure turn into strain;
To have good interpersonal skills;
To be highly committed to the organisation, since he will have little energy left for other activities. (Handy, 1985)

Finding enough such paragons will be a challenging task for every company.

6. Systems, communication

The organisation structure is a skeleton, which requires people to give it flesh, power to give it blood, and systems to provide its nervous system. The key systems identified traditionally are as follows:

1. Adaptive systems, relating the organisation to its environment and shaping its future,
2. Operating systems, dealing with business logistics and finance,
3. Maintenance systems, preserving the organisation and its employees,
4. Information systems, animating and integrating the other systems.

These systems are usually structured to meet the specific needs of companies, the key component of which is the management information system, enabling the top management to monitor progress against budgets, programmes and projects and to relate key data (e.g. stock levels, receivables) to preset standards. Such systems are rarely of value for 'hands on' management, but can be of great value against a longer-term perspective. To monitor the delivery of strategies a management information system would need to establish milestones, that is, dates by which specific results are to be achieved, and record progress systematically. Such a system does not substitute for formal review of strategy milestones, but provides an agreed basis for recording progress and, hopefully, early warning of any likely failure to achieve a future milestone.

Communication is the essential life spark to animate any organisation.

Communication is a two-way process – how often does the office 'know-all' seem to be permanently on 'transmit' and never on 'receive'! Listening is an essential ingredient of communication and care should be taken to check that key points have been properly heard and, if necessary, confirmed in writing. Many companies communicate key messages by 'cascade'; that is, by holding successive meetings to take the message down the line. Such procedures run the risk not only of distorting the message but of losing the original conviction behind it. These difficulties are sometimes dealt with by sending a video message from the managing director to all parts of the company. There remains the missing magic of his presence. In the same way as medieval monarchs travelled round their kingdoms in order to retain them, today's top management has no real substitute for its presence at minimum intervals in all parts of its business.

4.4. How to cope with mismatches caused by events

The pace of change is accelerating and the impact of events on companies is becoming increasingly significant and immediate. Managements need greater understanding than ever before of how organisations work and how they can trim the sails of their organisation to stay on their strategic course. Organisations are living organisms, and the key to successful adaptation to change and to external events is the ability to learn.

Organisational learning is a phenomenon recognised and documented by, among others, Argyris and Schon in 'Organisational learning: a theory of action perspective' (1987). Organisational learning is not necessarily the sum of the learning of employees; employees often know things which their organisation fails to recognise. Nor are organisational goals the sum of the goals of employees; the whole rationale of the organisation is to achieve tasks which individuals cannot do or are not primarily motivated to undertake. To achieve its task an organisation establishes a task system and allocates roles to those who will contribute to that system. A task system develops certain assumptions about its environment, performance norms and strategies to succeed which constitute its 'theory of action'. Such theories of action may not be explicit or formalised; they may be reduced to the concept of 'what works', which Argyris and Schon term 'theory in use' as opposed to the formally recognised 'espoused theory'. Within an organisation individuals constantly strive to improve their picture of the theory in use. This process contributes to the process of organisational learning, but these private images need to be supplemented by public maps, the attempts to codify jointly the general perception of how the organisation works in flow diagrams, procedures, and so forth.

The process of organisational learning requires, therefore, both the active development and refinement of private images and the checking and updating of public maps. If the latter task is imposed from the top it risks losing touch with reality. The process depends on the constant refinement and adaptation of private images and the consequent modification of public maps. People come and go, but organisations evolve and adapt until they break down. Learning is the process which enables organisations to renew themselves; a failure of the learning process leads to organisational entropy, which weakens task performance and leads to an undermining of organisational norms.

Managements can best counter the effect of mismatches between their actual organisation and the organisation needed to achieve their strategies by active encouragement of organisational learning. Individuals are agents for organisational learning, and this role should be stimulated by management by active review of existing public maps and clear statement of the resultant norms. Constructive criticism needs to be encouraged and acted upon, or else individuals will no longer learn as agents of the organisation and entropy will set in.

The mechanics of the learning process range from the development of corporate strategy, through the routine operations of the company both externally and internally, through the innovative and opportunistic chances which emerge, down to daily personal transactions between individuals. All blockages to the process need to be avoided and openness is essential for success. Failures need to be recognised and analysed openly and their implications understood by all. Tasks allocated to individuals should be known to their colleagues, and the rewards and sanctions attaching to such tasks should be clear and carried through.

The learning process is not only the best means of maintaining the alignment of structure and strategy, it is the heart of the organic process which perpetuates organisations and generates the strategies needed to sustain them and give them the chance to prosper in an uncertain and competitive environment.

4.5. Future trends in structure

Structures represent ways of organising people to achieve common goals. Earlier structures were concerned with concentrating power and later ones with achieving efficiency through specialisation. In the twentieth century people have progressively become better educated, more self-aware and less willing to tolerate a lack of fulfilment in their working lives. Communication has improved so that inadequate leadership can no longer be hidden, and the superior performance of competitors at home and overseas is a constant spur to those who are even half-willing to face reality. In his book *The New Realities*, Peter Drucker (1990) emphasises that organisations will increasingly be information-based and will have a preponderance of 'knowledge workers'. Job security is now a lost ideal for most employees and the likelihood of having to relearn skills several times in a working lifetime faces virtually all of us. Demographic changes will also reduce the number of young people entering employment, at least until the early years of the next century, so that retirement patterns will change, and the employment of older employees and action to assist married women with young familes to work flexible hours is now overdue.

From this it may be assumed that future structures, or work patterns, will have the following characteristics:

1. They will be less hierarchical.
2. Rigid job boundaries will go.
3. Power will move to match tasks.
4. Work will be less concentrated geographically.
5. Structures will be formed to meet tasks and then disbanded.
6. Full-time employees will be supplemented by external specialists.

1. *Hierarchies*
It may be expected that hierarchies will be more flexible, both due to the breakdown of large groups into 'strategic business units', that is, viable operating businesses in a federal structure, and to conscious efforts to reduce the number of levels in the structure. Hierarchies exist fundamentally to concentrate power at the top of an organisation. This is no longer possible to sustain when large measures of responsibility have had to be pushed down the organisation due to the complexity of modern business and must be matched by appropriate authority.

Elliott Jaques (1990) warns those who wish to dismantle hierarchies: 'The hierarchical kind of organisation . . . is the only kind of organisation that can employ large numbers of people and yet preserve unambiguous accountability for the work they do.' He is dismissive of groups: 'Whoever heard of promoting a group or firing one?' Finally he reminds us of the fundamental reason for hierarchy: 'It is the level of responsibility, in terms of time span, that tells you how many layers you need in an enterprise – not the number of subordinates or the magnitude of sales or profits.'

2. *Rigid job boundaries*
The need for clear job descriptions has been emphasised for years by organisation specialists such as Hay Group, and by personnel managers seeking to structure rewards in complex organisations. The value of job descriptions is not in question, but the work patterns of the future are likely to be more fluid and the job description risks having the news value of an old photograph. With the growing use of work teams and task forces the actual work done by staff may vary considerably over time. The constant will be the skills and experience they bring to such teamwork, although both skills and experience will also change significantly over time.

3. *Power matching tasks*
As work is increasingly broken down into tasks whose timely achievement is critical to overall success, it becomes essential to empower those charged

with key tasks with the authority to drive them through to a successful conclusion. Such power should, of course, be proportional to the task in hand and be surrendered when it is concluded. This means that power attaches to the role and not to the individual, a lesson that many overweening chief executives have learnt to their considerable distress.

4. Less geographic concentration

Concentration of operations in large sites has developed as a result of the economies of scale of highly automated manufacture or the use of large scale specialist facilities, such as airports. With the present trend to an increase in service businesses and the need to move manufacture nearer to individual markets, it may be expected that pressures for geographic dispersal will become greater. New manufacturing techniques and improved communications make such changes more practicable. Employees usually prefer to work in smaller units, and geographic dispersal not only allows units to be nearer their markets but also opens up the possibility of easier recruitment in many cases. The need for work to move to areas providing better pools of labour will be an issue of growing importance; the rapid growth of business in East Anglia, for example, is due in no small measure to the relatively good availability of skilled labour.

5. Flexible structures

There will be a growing need to reconcile more stable structures with the need to form task groups and to work as teams to meet specific needs. The idea of having no stable structure and operating by the formation of fluid coalitions or teams to meet emerging requirements has rarely worked well in practice, despite legends such as that of Apple Computer. It is likely that organisation structures will continue to have a framework which will probably be oriented towards the company mission and longer-term objectives. This will mean, in practice, that the basic structures will probably be built round core businesses, within which the structures will reflect the critical factors for success in each business; for example, for a pharmaceutical company the structure will emphasise the importance of research and development and of marketing. Within each of these areas and across all functions of the business, task groups will be formed with specific mandates and disbanded when those mandates are completed. While such task groups are operating they need to encompass the best talents of the functions involved and to have the power to drive through their mandate. Adequate resources need to be given to achieve success and the boundaries between different task groups and the demands made by them on the core structure will need to be effectively managed. Priorities will need to be negotiated in advance and carefully managed during the process. It should never be forgotten that teams come and go, but the core structure has to be able to sustain the company over the longer term.

6. External resources

In the 1950s and 1960s organisations grew without undue constraint, and developed a preference for inhouse competence in services which had traditionally been bought in. Companies like BP had their own travel department, and large legal, insurance, property management and other peripheral departments were common in larger companies. This monolithic approach broke down with the oil crises in 1973 and 1979 and the subsequent recession in the 1970s and early 1980s, and companies identified and scaled down to their core competences.

With the growing complexity of modern business and the need to ensure maximum flexibility, companies are beginning to question how to staff themselves for an uncertain and increasingly competitive future. The cost of employing staff (and the high costs of redundancy), together with the difficulty of attracting and retaining younger staff, call for concentration of effort on developing and retaining a primary core of managers and key specialists, and for seeking other solutions for secondary resources. This is likely to mean that there will be greater flexibility in manning manufacturing plant, with an emphasis on part-time and shift work, and greater use of subcontractors for work which is not design-sensitive. It will also mean that specialist work which is not part of the core competence will increasingly be contracted out to external specialists and consultants. The number of self-employed professionals and entrepreneurs is expected to expand to three million by the end of the century, according to Charles Handy (1988), compared with a total number in full-time paid employment of twelve million and some nine million part-time and temporary workers in a total working population of twenty-four million.

Future structures will be subject to other factors for change but their success will be subject to the same criteria as those of today. Are they an effective tool for delivering the strategies of the business and do they enable the business to renew itself to meet the challenges which it will face tomorrow?

5

STRATEGIC PLANNING:
HOW TO ORGANISE WITHIN
THE COMPANY

5.1. Reporting structure for planning purposes

We have considered the issue of organisation structure and its importance for the successful implementation of strategy. Structure has been seen to be the skeleton needed to shape and support the flesh, blood and nervous system of the company. The flesh we saw to be the people who work in the company and who are a major factor in its survival and success; the blood is the power which enables action to be effective; and the nervous system is the complex of systems and communications which direct and control the company.

The essence of strategic planning is that it relates to the company as a whole. It has, therefore, to be a process which touches and involves all parts of the business and in which all parts feel individually and jointly involved. The reporting structure for planning purposes is, therefore, the whole organisation structure.

It is, however, impractical to produce a corporate plan directly from the different parts of a sizeable company, each of which will have its own strategic ambitions and planning imperatives. It is necessary, therefore, to develop a hierarchy of plans, each of which is viable for its own unit, and the sum of which is consolidated into a corporate plan for the business as a whole. The hierarchy of plans is, of course, to be developed within a framework set by the corporate centre, in order to ensure consistency of direction, assumptions and action.

The hierarchy of plans which feeds into and forms the corporate plan is comprised of the strategic plans of each level of operation down to the lowest strategic business unit (SBU), that is, the smallest viable business activity. Such a hierarchy might comprise major subsidiary companies, divisions within such subsidiaries, and SBUs in those divisions, indicating three levels of consolidation up to corporate level. Within each strategic plan there may be another hierarchy – marketing plans, manpower plans, manufacturing plans, R and D plans, and so on. The corporate plan will also contain specific plans for functions under its control (e.g. corporate R and D, information technology) and the consolidated function plans where appropriate (e.g. manpower planning, total quality planning).

Having identified the hierarchy of plans, and thereby having established the nodes of the strategic planning system, it is necessary to organise the infrastructure needed to develop and finalise the individual plans. At one time, corporate planners were employed in large numbers in larger organisations, both at group and at subsidiary or divisional level. Plans produced by planners were found to have little effect in many businesses and the large corporate planning departments have been severely curtailed. Plans can only be meaningful if produced by the line managers who have to deliver the planned results. This has moved executive management into the driving seat of producing and executing strategic plans, with corporate planners acting as facilitators, or even as coaches, but clearly in a support role only.

5.2. Systems and information requirements

A company may be seen as a complex of systems. First, there are the systemic links of the company with its environment, which is itself a supra system. Secondly, the company itself has a number of interrelated and often competing systems (e.g. manufacturing system, sales and marketing system, research and development system, etc.). Thirdly, a company's internal and external systems may be integrated by a management system which meshes subsystems for planning, organising, controlling and communication. Typical of such systems is that propounded by Dr. Paul Miesing (1984) of the State University of New York. He sees the components of an effective planning system as follows:

1. Evaluation and rewards (identifying what management values including effective planning).
2. Resource allocation (to support activities providing returns in line with management needs).
3. Organisation structure (to achieve the results needed by the business).
4. Communication and information (to feed the system and to promulgate plans).
5. Culture and philosophy (clarifying management's values and ensuring strategies align with them).

To integrate such a system a number of linking mechanisms are identified, as follows:

- Bonuses and promotions (linked to performance against plan).
- Risk taking and innovation (to encourage creativity by giving autonomy).
- Meetings and reports (linked to motivation to communicate).
- Top management leadership (supporting the integrity of the planning system).

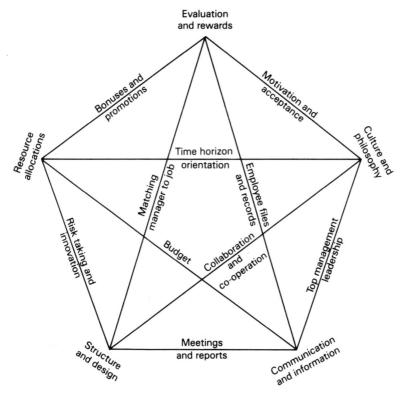

Figure 5.1 Integrating the components of a formal planning system

- Motivation and acceptance (having system supported by users).
- Time horizon orientation (offsetting tendency for short-term maximisation).
- Employee files and records (to maximise use of human resources).
- Collaboration and co-operation (to ensure support for the plan).
- Budgets (achieving alignment with plan).
- Matching managers to jobs (to ensure best performance in each role).

The resultant system may be shown diagramatically as in Figure 5.1.

This planning system will not meet the needs of all companies but does include the main elements needed for any tailor-made system. In designing such a system, Dr. Miesing suggests that attention should be given to the following questions:

1. Does the planning system meet the organisation's requirements?
2. Is there a proper trade-off between ease and elegance?
3. What will be the role of the planner or the planning staff?
4. Can commitment be attained at all levels of the organisation?
5. Can both long-run and short-run thinking be encouraged?

6. Is information timely and accurate?
7. Are planning procedures properly superimposed over the required task structures?
8. Is the current budget kept separate from long-run resource allocations?
9. Does the reward system provide proper incentives?
10. Will the system be subject to regular reviews and revisions?

Information requirements

Strategic planning systems depend enormously on information for their effectiveness. Information is not only required in great quantities but has to be as complete, as accurate and as up to date as possible. Information used in planning should be common to other relevant business functions, so that, for instance, corporate strategy is not built on data which differ from those used in the marketing function.

Businesses often generate vast amounts of data which are of no value for planning. Much of this information relates to past operations and some of it is purely mechanistic (e.g. clock cards). Seeking and manipulating information is expensive so that great care needs to be exercised, when developing a strategic planning system, in choosing the information needed to make it work. This choice relates to the value of information to develop and sustain hypotheses and to the potential for meaningful insights when disparate information is brought together. Kepner and Tregoe (1976) call information 'the raw material of management'. This implies that it is up to management to add value to information by manipulating it and by using it to a higher purpose. Appendix 4 lists some of the information typically useful for strategic planning.

Often key elements of the information needed to plan are unavailable. This may be because a company's systems do not record certain information internally; more frequently the missing data are external (e.g. market information, competition prices, industry trends, etc.). Commercial services such as the Henley Centre, *The Economist* and others can often provide useful data not readily available. In other cases it may be justifiable to spend money on sponsored market or competitor research. In considering such expenditure, the key questions are the benefit to be gained relative to the cost of buying the data from a reputable source, and the competitive edge which such data may give in an important market.

Weak or incomplete data can often be extended judgmentally. If data are available on one market and information on another not-dissimilar market is incomplete, the data from the one can be scaled across to the latter and the 'fit' tested against the limited data available and the judgment of people who know the market in general terms. This will provide a working hypothesis to be checked at the earliest reasonable opportunity. Where the quality of data is suspect, however, it is essential to qualify their value clearly in the records so that later use is conditioned by such qualification.

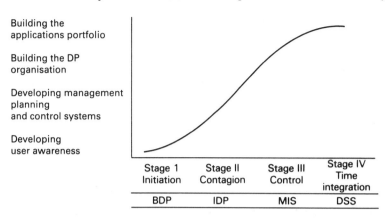

Figure 5.2 Four stages in the creation of an information system

Information systems

The development of computers has led to the concept and to some extent, realisation of information technology. This is the nexus between data processing and communications, enabling sophisticated integrated networks to be set up to handle and communicate data. The development of information systems is, however, not achieved overnight. It requires the right climate to enable work to be effective and top-level support to encourage its use. The process of creating such a system is seen as having four stages by Nolan and Gibson (1974), as shown in Figure 5.2.

Few companies have yet progressed beyond stage 3 (management information systems), and the attributes of the first three stages, as seen by Brightman and Harris (1985), are shown in Table 5.1. From this it will be seen that the attributes of the four stages move from simplicity to increasing complexity, from lack of modelling to increasingly sophisticated modelling and from low-level organisation to top-level organisation/ involvement.

The planning and implementation of information systems is a difficult process. A relevant case study (Adriaans and Hoogakker, 1989) is that of Netherlands Gas, which was keen to develop an integral system, not a hybrid, so that it would be 'future-proof and consistent'. The information-systems plan was based on two key premises:

- Information systems must support the strategic objectives of the company.
- Information must be treated as one of the assets of the business.

Table 5.1. Attributes of information system performance

Attribute	Basic data processing systems	Integrated processing systems	Management information systems
Applications	Payroll, inventory personnel record keeping	Production scheduling, sales analysis	Production control, sales forecasting, capital budgeting
Data base	Unique to each application, batch update	Common to task within a system, batch update	Interactive access by programmers
Decision capabilities	No decision models	Simple decision models	Management science models
Type of information	Summary reports	Summary reports, operational information	Scheduled and demand reports, management oriented information flows
Highest organisation level	Submanagerial levels, lower management	Lower management	Middle management

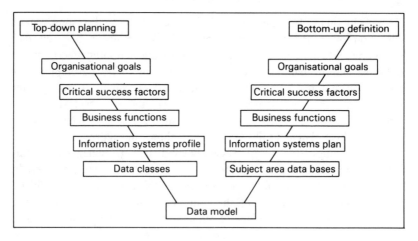

Figure 5.3 Steps in information systems planning

The structure of the study was based on Arthur Young's SISP methodology and is shown in Figure 5.3. The specific steps taken were as follows:

1. Establish the company's goals through interviews with senior management.
2. Establish critical success factors in order to set priorities.
3. Determine business processes and the relevant information needs by talking to operational management.

4. Study the existing systems and evaluate their effectiveness and organisational environment.
5. Construct a data model at corporate level, showing classes of data and their interrelationship.
6. Divide the data model into subject area data bases.
7. Design the information system architecture, detailing the relevant subsystems.
8. Determine future information and automation policy.
9. Draw up plan to modify existing systems or to redesign appropriate systems from scratch.

The process was co-ordinated by outside consultants and carried through by a team of four Netherlands Gas employees with systems experience and knowledge of different parts of the business. The team also included two consultants, one to co-ordinate the team and the other to contribute technical expertise on automation. Interim results were discussed and refined with a group of user representatives. The project had a time span of six months maximum in order to retain interest and support in the business. Specific decision points were built into the study plan to act as milestones. Regular reports were made during the study to the management board in order to elicit the decisions needed.

Following approval of the information systems plan it was necessary to carry out in-depth studies into specific processes; in the case of Netherlands Gas these were commercial, operations and new construction processes. These studies involved users more than the overall plan study and formed the basis for the relevant systems development.

A key factor in implementing the information system is the appointment of a data administrator, who is tasked with ensuring uniformity of data and its interchangeability within the system. The data administrator (and in the case of Netherlands Gas, the data base administrator also) is involved actively in the design of the information system as well as in its subsequent administration.

Knowledge-based systems

We have seen how the growth of information technology has put new power into the hands of management, both to plan and to operate its business more affectively. The evaluation of systems through the four stages (basic data processing, integrated data processing, management information systems, decision support systems) creates a progressively more powerful tool for management.

The concept of 'artificial intelligence', the creation of a non-human system which replicates the processes and output of the human mind, is now the golden fleece of information technology. Knowledge-based systems are a branch of artificial intelligence in the same manner as robotics and natural language systems. In the view of Robert Mockler and D. G. Dologite (1988), a knowledge-based computer system has the following distinguishing features from information or support systems:

1. They contain symbolic programming and reasoning capabilities.
2. They contain a knowledge-base about a specific decision domain or situation, which is in large measure distinct from the inferencing mechanism.
3. They contain an inference engine, or inferential reasoning capability, which is a large measure distinct from the knowledge base.
4. They can handle uncertain, unknown and conflicting data.
5. They allow a programmer or user to modify segments of programmes relatively easily.
6. They are non-procedural, as opposed to conventional programmes which are more procedural.
7. They have a facility to explain its advice or reasoning process.
8. They use heuristic ('if – then') rules extensively, but not exclusively.

In parallel with computer developments there has been work done to define approaches to developing generic strategies for typical industry situations, notably by Michael Porter and Richard Hamermesh. These enable a heuristic approach to be taken – if certain market and company conditions obtain, then a certain type of strategy might be worth consideration. Such a generic approach is no more than a first step in corporate planning but it indicates the direction of the subsequent work to be done.

Mockler and Dologite (*op. cit.*) detail the design of a knowledge-based system capable of recommending a generic strategy. This system has the characteristics referred to above and works by comparing the possible strategies in its 'then' list with the 'ifs' stored in the knowledge-base until it finds one where all the 'ifs' are true. This system operates at what knowledge-based systems experts term the 'colleague' level of sophistication. Less sophisticated is the 'assistant' level, more sophisticated the 'expert' level.

More recent systems can 'forward chain' rather than 'backward chain', that is, they can move from 'if' to 'then' using rules, rather than testing 'then' options against the groups of 'if' in the system. This is more germane to human thinking but requires much more computer power. Expert knowledge-based systems are seen as useful guides for a planner seeking strategic alternatives, and all levels of system are felt to be helpful to train staff for planning work. A promising expert system for marketing planning has been developed by Malcolm MacDonald at Cranfield.

Effective strategic planning does, however, require complex inferential reasoning skills to make assumptions about future market conditions and to identify key success factors in specific future environments. It would seem that, even in theory, knowledge-based systems are likely to have limits also in terms of cost: benefit ratio. Their future probably lies in systematically narrowing options, leaving the human planning staff to the final exercise of judgement.

5.3.   The planning horizon appropriate for the company

In 1932 Konosuke Matsushita announced a 250 year plan for his infant business, which has subsequently become one of the world's largest and most successful companies. This plan has never been revealed in detail but it is known that Matsushita's enormous success in the United States was clearly foreseen. Few businesses plan to such long horizons, but many are obliged to take a long-term view of their markets by the nature of their operations. It takes over 100 years to grow most hardwoods, and extractive industries, such as oil and mining businesses, have to view new projects over periods of up to half a century. This makes such operations highly speculative in many instances.

Dr. Leemhuis (1985) of Shell distinguishes three planning horizons. The first, up to five years in time, he terms 'cyclical'; from five to fifteen years is a horizon which will indicate trends; beyond fifteen years is 'exploratory'. Igor Ansoff (1979) postulates two stages in the planning horizon. The period over which a business can construct forecasts 'with an accuracy of, say, plus or minus 20 per cent' is the planning horizon of the company. This 'proximate period' is usually from three to ten years; beyond that lies the 'long term period' up to the time horizon, which may be very long indeed. Within Ansoff's 'proximate period', data are adequate for directly measuring return on investment.

In deciding on the planning horizon appropriate for a particular business it is important to differentiate between planning and futurology. Lord Tennyson forecast the aeroplane in his poem 'Locksley Hall' written in 1842; Jules Verne, H. G. Wells and others have been equally prescient but their vision goes beyond the range of strategic planning into the world of speculation.

Following the oil crises in 1973 and 1979 many companies shortened the time scale of their plans and three-year plans are now quite usual. The pay-back on projects has also been curtailed in many companies and it is not unusual for major projects to be established and monitored outside the formal planning system, where the pay-back period is at variance with the planning horizon. The natural planning horizon is the period, like Ansoff's 'proximate period' over which returns on investment and key ratios can meaningfully be established.

The need to establish a practical planning horizon for corporate plans does not preclude work on the long-term period which will guide longer-term strategy and help to shape future corporate plans. The growing pace of change and major discontinuities, such as Eastern Europe, are making a growing number of companies eager to have futures advice. Consultants such as SRI are reporting a rapid increase in demand for long-range planning advice, according to *Fortune* magazine (Fisher, 1990). Techniques such as scenario-building, developed by Shell, are being increasingly adopted as a means of exploring future possibilities and their likely impact on the business.

While it is no longer realistic (if it ever was) to build ten-year corporate plans in full detail and the horizon for structured plans is now no more than three to five years for most companies, it is important to maintain a long-term planning period which relates to the imperatives of the business (100 years to grow more trees) and which explores key issues beyond the structured planning horizon. Work done in this longer period may be done by visionaries, futurologists or by others who have the imagination and creativity to challenge accepted dogma. This work needs to be kept close to the business and the indulgence of 'blue sky' thinking avoided, and it needs to be accountable over time for having contributed to the strategic direction of the company.

It is a sobering indication of the poor state of strategic planning in small businesses that a recent survey (El-Namak, 1990) in the United States covering 357 small businesses found that only 18 per cent 'had a strategy level where there was a knowledge of next year's company and industry sales, anticipated company profits and profit implementation plans'. Lack of systematic planning was identified in numerous surveys, starting with Mayer and Goldstein in 1961, as a major reason for business failure. On the other hand, in 1977 Potts found that 'outsider based' strategic planning had achieved significant improvement in profitability, employment and productivity for small firms which were monitored over a five-year period.

5.4. The planning cycle

It is tempting to think that a strategic plan, once written, will be valid for a considerable period of time. Well-drawn strategies should be robust and not need to be changed to meet every movement in the company's share price! In the same way that 'the price of freedom is eternal vigilance', the effectiveness of a strategic plan can only be realised by a constant process of checking and review. This process is usually termed the 'planning cycle'.

In theory a planning cycle can run over any period of time; in practice most companies find that too long a cycle makes planning insensitive, too short a period makes it impossible to achieve stability and value for effort expended. Given that most companies need to account and report to shareholders on an annual cycle, and that the budgetary cycle needs to coincide with the trading year, it is now usual practice for the corporate planning cycle to mesh with these statutory and managerial imperatives. A few companies have moved beyond this stage to rolling three-year plans with emphasis in the intervening years on key issues and major projects, but this requires a mature planning process.

For a company whose trading year coincides with the calendar year, budgets need to be in place no later than December of the previous year. Budgets should be derived from the relevant year of the corporate plan and are usually based on the assumptions and outline figures in the plan, modified in the light of the latest circumstances and with the figures being developed in the full detail needed for ongoing control of the business.

It is obviously necessary, therefore, to complete the corporate plan before budgets are prepared and approved. This may mean that the plan has to be approved in June of the preceding year in order to approve budgets by December. Work on the corporate plan would, therefore, need to start immediately after finalising the budgets for the current year, thus creating the rolling annual planning/budgetary cycle known to many companies and shown in Figure 5.4.

The main stages of a typical planning cycle are shown in Figure 5.4. and include the following where both 'top down' and 'bottom up' planning are required:

1. *The economic/political environment assessment*

It is essential that all contributors to the corporate plan work on common background assumptions if plans are to be consistent and capable of consolidation. A document is needed which assesses the external influences on the plan and takes a reasoned and structured view of those factors which are likely to shape the plan. Such a document needs to be prepared with great care and to involve expert opinion from subsidiaries as well as that of corporate staff. It is not unusual for external experts to be consulted in preparing the assessment, mainly to ensure that internal wishful-thinking is tempered by objective advice. Much of the content of the document will be economic, but there will also be a significant political content (e.g. Government policy, anticipated legislation, etc.) and certain key themes may be featured (e.g. the environment, progress towards European unity, Eastern Europe, etc.).

The assessment needs to be both far-ranging to stimulate intelligent reaction and focused on issues and themes which impact on the business. It is not an academic treatise but a stimulus to creative and informed planning, focused on the business.

2. *Board involvement*

It is important that the board should be involved, and be seen to be involved, in the planning process and should launch the cycle. The degree of involvement may vary depending on the style of the company, but a resolution of the board to initiate the cycle is the minimum involvement. An increasing number of companies wish to involve the board more comprehensively in the process and it is a growing practice for the board to have a strategic review, often over two/three days at a location remote from the pressures of the office, at which stock is taken of the company's strategic stance and of the issues to be faced in developing the corporate plan.

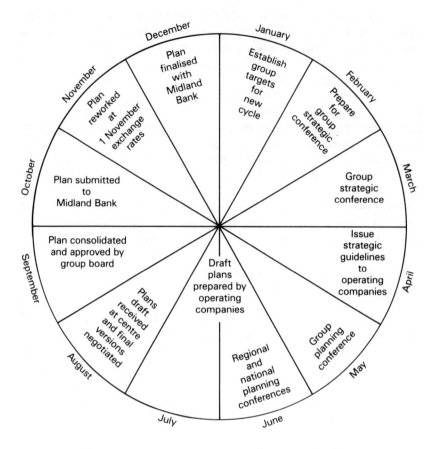

Figure 5.4   Annual planning cycle (Source: Thomas Cook Group)

Such strategic reviews may be highly structured or may be in the form of a think tank, or some combination of both extremes, depending on the style and preference of the chairman. Whether or not there is an agenda, it is essential to prepare a number of documents to brief directors before the strategic review. These documents should include the economic/political assessment (in draft) and an assessment of the current year's performance against plan and budget. Unless the meeting is totally 'free form' it is usually found helpful to list the issues facing the company and to remind directors of the objectives and strategies in the current corporate plan.

A key part of strategic reviews is to break down the formality which usually conditions board meetings and to encourage challenges to accepted thinking. This is facilitated by holding the review away from the office and by isolating the participants as far as possible from day-to-day interruptions. Some chairmen encourage informal dress for review meetings and avoid the use of tables which remind participants of their regular board meetings.

However the meeting is structured, it is essential that the chairman has a clear objective towards which the review is steered (with due discretion), and that the key points which emerge are not lost. A blackboard or flip-chart are useful tools in this regard, preferably the latter, since space is limitless and earlier data can readily be retrieved later in the review. It is often found useful to employ the company secretary as facilitator in order to capture points on the flip-chart as they emerge, and help bring forward loose ends as the meeting progresses. The main thread of the meeting is, of course, held by the chairman.

During the review it is important that the non-executive directors are encouraged to participate fully. A strategic review should bring up the unaskable questions and challenge the status quo; the non-executive directors should have the wider experience and mental flexibility to have insights which would not be so readily obtained from executive directors. In a board meeting the non-executive directors may need to query the orthodoxy of their executive colleagues; in a strategic review it may be the non-executive directors who are leading the discussion and the executive directors who are testing their ideas for practicability.

Following the strategic review, the board should record the issues which have emerged and the priorities attached to them by the board. These will be included in the chief executive's document which launches the cycle and will be recorded as a board paper to support the formal resolution to initiate the planning cycle.

3. The chief executive's 'setting of the scene'

The planning process is legitimised and given impetus by the authority of the board. The cycle needs, therefore, to be initiated with board authority and with a personal message from the chief executive. Similar arrangements will apply to subsidiary boards and their chief executives.

The message from the chief executive will refer to the timetable of the cycle in order to mandate the expenditure of time needed to complete the plan. It is not usually appropriate to detail the timetable in such a message; this can be sent separately, together with the appropriate planning documents.

The chief executive's message will be sent to subsidiary or divisional chief executives, together with the heads of corporate functions. Background information to the message will include the economic/political assessment and provisional results for the year about to terminate, compared with plan and budget.

The message will set the scene, usually be drawing lessons from past performance and by emphasising the group's key strategies. The main issues, threats and opportunities facing the group will be alluded to, mainly to stimulate appropriate reactions in the subsequent plans. The pattern of capital investment will be referred to, if this needs to be highlighted at this stage in the cycle due to capital scarcity.

The contents and tone of the message are the prerogative of the chief executive. Each has his own style, and the message will be interpreted in accordance with the company's culture. It is important that the message is positive, comprehensive and that the same message is received by all involved in the planning cycle.

Some chief executives write personal letters to each subsidiary and divisional chief executive, identifying the key issues of the subsidiary and the relevant strategies, and allocating capital in outline over the plan period. Such personal involvement can be helpful but the important issue from the standpoint of the corporate plan is that data and documents should be common and transparent to all. Unless the process is open and totally shared it cannot work.

4. *Planning conference*
The chief executive's message may be considered sufficient to launch the planning cycle at top level, and the planning arrangements within each division may be left to the discretion of its own chief executive. Planning is essentially about participation, however, and is less about filling in forms than about the discussion and trade-offs needed to arrive at plans to which as many people as possible are committed.

In order to encourage participation, and to take the strategic review process described above down through the different strategic operating levels of the company, it is common for companies to hold planning conferences at these levels. In the case of the Thomas Cook Group, there is a group planning conference which is used to launch the planning cycle, to which delegates are sent from all major subsidiaries worldwide. The conference is chaired by the chief executive and it discusses the issues identified in the board strategic review, both in plenary sessions and in working groups. The papers prepared for the conference and the recorded output of the conference are a key input into the planning work of subsidiaries. They also reduce the scope of the chief executive's message and ensure that the message reflects not the views of one man, or even of the board, but the results of several days' lively debate by delegates from around the group worldwide.

In the Thomas Cook Group major subsidiaries also hold their planning conferences and the travel business holds regional conferences to launch and integrate local planning. Again, the principle of participation is paramount so that involvement gives ownership of the outcome and commitment to achieving the planned results.

5. *Planning documents, timetable*
A planning cycle is a series of compromises between the time available to plan and the daily pressures of the business, between allowing time for planning and waiting for the best assessment of the current year's results, and between creativity and precision. In order to allow sufficient time to

complete the cycle, with its inevitable interactions, it is essential to start at least six months before the deadline for completion. In some larger companies even more time is needed; a major public corporation has recently adopted a fifteen-month planning cycle because of its size and complexity, and to cope with 'the Whitehall dimension'.

Timetables have, therefore, to be tightly drawn and strictly adhered to. Unless management lends its authority to the maintenance of timetables, operational pressures will destroy the planning timetable and no credible plan will be achieved. While experienced planners like to build some flexibility into their timetables, the total process is likely to leave little scope for cushioning delays. Timetables should not, however, be built to accommodate the slowest contributor, since undue slack is demotivating. Once the process starts, all participants should sense a steady pressure to move from stage to stage, and this pressure helps to maintain momentum and interest.

The documents needed for a corporate plan relate, of course, to the shape and contents of the plan when completed. While some companies still produce plans which have detailed financial information, they are now the exception and the typical corporate plan of today has a framework of numbers which are ideally derived from the strategies in the plan and not extrapolated from the current year's budget! The slogan 'words before numbers' should constantly be repeated to everybody involved in corporate planning, and evaluating numbers against stated strategies is a key critique of any corporate plan submitted for approval.

For the typical corporate plan the relevant planning documents will specify the contents of the plan (e.g. objectives, strategies, key assumptions, key issues, competitor and market analysis, constraints, key action schedules, etc.), and will specify requirements for numbers over the plan period for sales, margins, expenses, operating profit, capital employed, working capital, capital expenditure and headcount, cashflow and outline balance sheets. Certain key ratios will probably be required (e.g. return on sales, return on capital employed, market share, sales per employee, etc.). The contents of a typical corporate plan are listed in Appendix 5.

The planning documents will reinforce the need to explore thoroughly the issues which the group chief executive has highlighted, and will give guidance on how to evaluate strategies, what competitor and market information is needed to underpin strategies and how to test them for sensitivity to variance in key assumptions. Guidance may also be given on how to structure key action plans in order to ensure timely delivery of strategies.

By proper use of the planning documents all plans should have a common minimum content and a basic internal consistency. Participants should be encouraged to expand the content of plans in areas which are important to them and to produce plans which they are likely to use rather than documents which are merely for submission to the centre. The key test for a plan is whether it is to be found under the writer's pillow each night or whether it is consigned to the bottom drawer of a filing cabinet in the outer office!

Other steps in the planning cycle will be considered later in this chapter and in Chapter 7 *Strategic Management*.

5.5. 'Top down' framework

We have considered earlier the board's strategic review and the chief executive's scene setting for the plan, involving a planning conference or in the form of a structured message. In whatever form the detailed input from the top comes to the planning process, it is a key component of that process and it requires careful work to make it effective.

While the board's strategic review will take stock of progress made towards existing goals and will have revisited the established strategies and explored the viability of new ones, the key judgements to be made are whether the company is on course towards its long-term objectives and whether it will have a short-term performance sufficient to protect it from competitive and acquisitive pressures. If these pressures have intensified or threaten to do so, there will be an urge to 'make the assets sweat' and to re-evaluate the trade-off between the short and long terms.

The key judgements arising from the strategic review cannot be made definitively as a direct result of the board's review meeting, but need to be worked out in detail subsequently. In the case of companies where planning is totally 'top down' a corporate plan can be prepared at the centre and relevant parts spun off to subsidiaries to be developed strictly within stated guidelines. This means that the strategies, roles and resources of the subsidiaries are dictated by the centre – in John Argenti's words 'the dog wags the tails'. Planning on a 'top down' only basis is common in highly centralised businesses, and it is not unknown for 'top down' planning to be carried out in subsidiaries or divisions who do not involve their SBUs completely in the planning process.

Even where the corporate planning process requires a 'top down' and a 'bottom up' contribution, which is now the usual case, it is necessary to develop the 'top down' framework independently as a model against which to assess the 'bottom up' contributions. This exercise is usually carried out at the centre, based on the board strategic review and the chief executive's message to launch the cycle. The 'top down' framework will evaluate the level of profitability, its rate of growth which is required to meet short-, medium- and longer-term objectives, the strategies needed to deliver such profits, the resources in funding and manpower needed to achieve those strategies, organisational implications and any constraints which may affect achievement of the required results.

This 'top down' framework should be ready in time to be compared with the consolidated plans of the subsidiaries or divisions. It should be ambitious and seek to stretch the organisation's performance beyond its historical trend line. Change is forcing companies to set their sights even higher as adequate performance ends in failure or takeover. The 'top down' framework should be seen as a series of targets, reflecting the board's view of what the company's performance should be if it is to continue to prosper in more demanding and competitive circumstances. It is, however, more than a 'wish list' – it has to be structured rigorously and have both internal and external credibility. It must balance the short and longer terms and it must operate realistically within identifiable constraints. What it should not recognise, however, is suboptimisation of strategies, inefficiencies and wastage, and the perpetuation of failure.

5.6. Structuring 'bottom up' submissions

In Section 5.4 we looked at the documentation sent to subsidiaries and divisions to guide them in preparing their corporate plan. This documentation, together with the chief executive's message and other corporate input (e.g. the economic/political assessment), provides a basis for a subsidiary plan and a set of issues to which a response is required by the centre.

If the planning work in the subsidiaries was only based on this input, it would effectively be 'top down' planning and would miss a major dimension of insight and contribution. 'Bottom up' planning has evolved from the budgetary process of building from the bottom upwards. Such a process is necessary for budgeting because of the complex of detail lurking in the depth of most businesses. If managements need a 'bottom up' contribution for budgets to make them more realistic, why should the same not be true for planning? The 'bottom up' structure of budgets also brings commitment at every level – a principle which is essential for meaningful planning. A 'bottom up' contribution to the corporate planning process is, therefore, increasingly recognised to be essential in order both to bring insight and reality to plans and to provide the commitment needed to fulfil them.

The structure of 'bottom up' submissions will be decided by the formats required by the centre, and detailed in the centre's documentation, but also by the requirements of the SBU chief executive concerned. Many such chief executives write plans in the format which assists their work, and then reformat the plan for submission to the centre. Since the latter will be the plan considered by the local board or management committee, on which delegates from the centre may sit, it is usually more practical to build round the group standard format, either by expanding it or by having appendices or supplementary parts to it.

'Bottom up' submissions will usually be derived from a planning process analogous to that of the group. There may be a conference; there will certainly be a local chief executive's planning letter; and the data from the centre will be passed down to the units contributing to the plan. The local chief executive will know that the centre will be building a 'top down' framework which will be stretching. He has, therefore, to encourage the highest bids from all parts of his organisation on the first round, since to go back later will be time consuming and demotivating. If the bids from below require resources which he knows are beyond the immediate scope of the group, he may, when his bids are consolidated, reduce them to commit his subsidiary to a plan with which it can work. Alternatively, he may submit the consolidated bids subject to the resources being found in time to produce the higher results.

Because 'bottom up' planning is most effective when people are given their head local chief executives need to put their key staff into stiuations where they will accept stretching challenges and grow in stature. On the other hand they have to ensure that they have the resources and training to have a realistic chance of success. They have to anticipate the questions which the centre will pose when it analyses subsidiaries' plans, and be aware of best practice in their markets and among their competitors against which they will be judged. They must prepare for the pressure to gear up their plans to meet group targets and must have worked out their priorities and possible trade-offs. Above all they must know the boundaries of ownership of their plan; the point at which the total personal commitment essential for the success of any plan breaks down and the plan is 'theirs' not 'ours'.

5.7.   The 'planning gap'

Igor Ansoff (1979) identifies the difference between a company's objectives and its current forecast as its 'total gap'. This may be negative, that is, the forecast is higher than the objectives and objectives can be increased to close the gap. More usually the gap is positive and action is required to close 'the discrepancy between aspirations and anticipations'.

We have seen how purely 'top down' planning may appear to achieve satisfactory results, but lacks the ownership by those who have to deliver results, which is crucial for success. A combination of 'top down' and 'bottom up' planning is more demanding as a process but has the virtue of involving more people and of generating commitment. It also has the advantage of contrasting aspirations with realistic anticipations – revealing a 'planning gap'. It is obviously preferable to identify this discrepancy during the planning process rather than in the course of operations and the planning gap can concentrate minds to very useful effect.

The process of gap analysis examines the causes of the gap and can identify possible remedies. If the gap has been caused by a weakening of results expected from group strategies, it will be necessary to understand why this has occurred. Often, earlier plans are found to be too optimistic or delays will have occurred in implementing strategies which have set back profit streams. Competitive reaction may have been stronger than expected. There may be any number of reasons for the gap.

Once the causes are identified with reasonable confidence it is necessary to seek workable solutions. These may range from minor remedial action to restore deadlines, right up to major acquisitions to fill significant gaps. Gap analysis is ideal work for a team, since it is highly creative and requires a wide range of knowledge about the company, markets and competitors. John Argenti (1989) finds gap analysis very powerful, and sees the need to analyse past trends carefully in order to be able to interpret future gaps intelligently. Instead of contrasting one set of targets with one set of forecasts, John Argenti finds it creative to have 'minimum' and 'satisfactory' targets contrasted with 'optimistic' and 'pessimistic' forecasts. This process gives greater sensitivity to the process and forces issues of risk to the surface. Again, teams provide better results and can provide the dynamism to drive the process through multiple difficulties and disappointments.

5.8.   Analysis, iteration, refinement

The nub of the corporate planning process is reached when the 'top down' and 'bottom up' plans have shown a planning gap, and where the process of gap analysis begins to raise real issues.

We talked earlier of gap analysis being done by teams. Such an approach is not only fruitful in terms of ideas but, if staff from subsidiaries implicated in the planning gap are involved in the team, the process can protect ownership of their plan. Even where this is not possible (e.g. overseas subsidiaries), it is important to involve them in the process and negotiate any changes with appreciation of their difficulties.

Changes will come, not only through gap analysis, but from detailed analysis of the content of plans submitted by subsidiaries. These plans will have been written against a tight deadline and many subsidiaries may not have the planning resources available to the centre. Mistakes will be found and statements without supporting evidence will need to be checked. Often it will be found that the strategies on which the plan is built are not robust enough when tested by sensitivity analysis. This involves changing plan assumptions and reassessing plan results. In many industries a significant change in the price of oil will cause profits to wilt significantly; others are sensitive to exchange rates of currencies; others react to interest rates; few are insensitive to any key economic factor. Some change arising from adjustment to key assumptions has to be accepted; the whole purpose of making assumptions is to arrive at a workable set of results. It is, however, where such changes have a disproportionate effect that caution is required, particularly when the key assumption is volatile and the negative change may realistically be foreseen.

All changes are likely to require consequent adjustments to other parts of the plan and all of these have to be followed through meticulously. Planning is not a financial exercise and prime attention has to be given to the qualitative strength of a corporate plan, but lack of consistency in figuring the results of the qualitative process detract from the realism of the plan, since those responsible for the strategies do not see the full ramification of what they propose.

The analysis of plans and negotiation of changes is highly iterative, and time has to be given in the schedule to complete the process satisfactorily. It is likely that earlier changes will be more radical, as being more obviously needed, but there will need to be some refinement or fine-tuning towards the end of the evaluation process.

Changes may also need to be made in the allocation of resources, particularly if strategies are geared up to achieve higher profits or increased market share. Such changes in resources may affect the plans of other divisions, as we shall see later. Changes may also be needed in the key-action programme which underpins the delivery of the subsidiary's strategies, if this is found not to be sufficiently realistic.

5.9. Allocation of resources

The allocation of resources is one of the critical issues in the planning process. It is an unusual business whose ambitions do not outpace the resources needed to sustain them, and hard choices are forced on most managements at this stage of the cycle. The resources considered in this context are finance and people.

Finance

Assessment of the financial implications of the corporate plan will need to be made in a number of areas. Are pre-tax profits sufficient to sustain an acceptable level of return on capital employed; can the cash flow sustain the necessary levels of working capital and capital expenditure; are stocks and debtors turning over at acceptable rates; is the ratio of loans to equity sound? These and other figures will need to be analysed and tested against hypothetical changes in plan assumptions (e.g. pressure on margins from competition, increases in interest rates, slower payment by debtors, etc.).

From this assessment of the plan's robustness will come a picture of the level of capital expenditure which can realistically be sustained over the plan period without undue risk. The 'top down' framework will have gone through a similar process and the 'bottom up' consolidation will have been subjected to gap analysis to try to bring both into line. Before deciding on the financial resources to be written into the plan, it is essential to ensure that the refined plan which has emerged is sustainable.

Once the level of capital expenditure which can be prudently committed has been established, it may be necessary to adjust the corporate plan. All expenditure in the draft plans will have been subject to 'hurdle rates' (minimum rates of return) or other criteria (e.g. for company cars). It may be necessary to ration capital by increasing hurdle rates, keeping company cars longer before resale or setting priorities. Some capital investment may be needed for strategic reasons, even though it does not pass competitive assessment on financial criteria. These and other judgments will need to be made with the involvement of the subsidiaries concerned, and with the implications being understood and accepted by them.

Inclusion of capital allocations in the corporate plan is, of course, no specific authority to spend money. The capital expenditure written into the corporate plan will form the basis for capital budgets. Where those budgets include specific projects such expenditure will need to be approved by the board as a result of a formal detailed submission. In an article 'Capital budgeting: the state of the art' in *Long Range Planning*, Roger Mills (1988) refers to three phases of capital budgeting: first 'the creation phase'; then, 'the decision phase'; and thirdly, 'the implementation phase'. Phases one and two may be subsumed in the planning process, the third phase in the budgetary and control processes.

Mills' article presents a study done for the CIMA into the appraisal techniques used in the United States and the United Kingdom. Theory favours the discounted cash flow (DCF) technique, which forecasts the net incremental cash flow generated by a project (discounted to present value) from which the cost of the investment is deducted to produce a net present value. The DCF model can also accommodate factors for inflation, risk and uncertainty. In actual practice it was found that the largest companies continue to use 'payback period' as the basic measurement. Payback period is the time required for the sum of annual operating surpluses to equal the original outlay. Where a discounting technique was used, 'internal rate of return' was favoured. Internal rate of return is the discount rate needed to reduce projected cash flows to the same sum as that of the original outlay, that is, reducing net present value to zero. It would seem that the availability of financial planning models for personal computers is making the use of internal rates of return more common, mainly as a crosscheck on payback calculations.

People

Allocating financial resources is a key part of the planning process; but providing for human resources is probably the most critical part. 'Talent is the critical resource not money', in the words of Norsk Data's Chief Executive, Rolf Skar, quoted in *Shaping the Corporate Future* by Barham and Rassam (1989). Most corporate plans detail headcount by grade, and cost staff requirements accordingly. This is, of course, necessary, and movements in headcount will be closely monitored in appraising such plans. Few planners take the next step of developing job specifications for all new posts planned; these follow later if the staffing requirement is added to the establishment at budget time. Failure to think through the tasks required, and the person profile for those needed to do them, at the time of preparing the corporate plan is a major weakness in many corporate plans. Unless these key issues are faced in the planning process, time will be lost in filling the posts effectively and the human resources plan will almost certainly be out of tune with the true needs of the business.

Allocating staff is not only a costing exercise but is an investment, the true implications of which are not always reflected in corporate plans. In the same way that it has been estimated that each child costs its parents £70,000 to bring to maturity, each recruit has to be sought and interviewed, inducted and given an ongoing programme of job experience and training. These costs are not all lost, since many of them add value to the person involved. The value of staff is an asset shown on no balance sheet, and the added value of experience and training is also unrecorded in financial terms. The only way to realise that added value for the company is to plan the use of talents more effectively, so that people are constantly challenged and produce benefit for the business as they grow themselves.

Human-resource planning is one of the weakest links in the logical chain which is the planning process. Much more thought needs to be given, not just to the strategies which will produce the profit streams needed by the business, but to the identity, nature, skills and requisite talents of those who have to deliver those strategies.

5.10.   Key action programmes

We have dealt so far with the 'what', 'with which' and 'why' issues of planning; there remain the 'how', 'who' and 'when' issues to be settled. These are the drivers for delivery without which plans remain 'wish lists' and little will happen. The impetus for achieving the corporate plan is built into the key action programmes, which take each of the strategies in the plan, break them down into discrete parts, identify the numerous tasks needed to accomplish those parts and allocate specific responsibility and deadlines for such accomplishment.

Key action programmes require enormous care to prepare, and the analysis of the strategies into stages, the identification of those who have a role in achieving those stages, the dissection of the interplay involved in such achievement and the consequent listing and scheduling of tasks is enormously detailed and demanding. The process has been likened to disassembling a watch, with the concomitant fear of losing a key part! Often it seems like an endless series of Russian dolls or the onion which is never fully peeled! Even worse is the identification of cross-linkages and interactions between individual action plans, where failure to complete one action may interlock the completion of another which may not even be related to the same strategy.

The development of key action programmes requires, therefore, great attention to detail and co-ordination across the whole company or group. We referred earlier to the hierarchy of plans, and the linkages between these plans are not only the group strategies but also the key action programmes to deliver them. These need to cascade down to the lowest operational level in order to achieve tactical actions which contribute to the total programme.

Key action programmes will, therefore, be developed at top level in the corporate plan, covering the wide scope of activities needed to drive corporate strategies. These top-level actions will be broken down into the group functional plans (e.g. research and development, personnel, information technology, etc.), and picked up in the relevant subsidiary or divisional plans and driven down that hierarchy of plans (e.g. manufacture, marketing, etc). Action programmes driven from the corporate plan will mingle in lower-level plans with key actions needed to deliver functional and subsidiary/divisional strategies, and great care is needed to follow the linkages down the hierarchy of plans and to identify critical cross-linkages which will need to be managed.

Great care needs to be exercised in specifying the detail of key action plans. The actions to be undertaken must be detailed precisely yet comprehensively. The name of the person to undertake the action must be clearly stated; this person is fully responsible for delivering that action and will be accountable for the performance of those whose key actions support his commitment. The deadlines for completion must be firm but realistic and the measure of success must be clearly stated (e.g. to increase sales of product X in territory Y from £A per annum to £B per annum). Resources allocated to achieving the specific action should be clearly stated (e.g. funds allocation, man-hours, specific individuals, etc.).

The key action plan in the latest corporate or subsidiary plan should be preceded by a critique of the key action plan for the relevant period in the previous year's plan. This critique does not need to agonise in detail about the reasons for failure or to luxuriate in success; it is only necessary to identify the main tasks, the results obtained and give a short explanation of significant variances. Where actions are aborted, this should be stated; those carried forward should appear in the new key action plan.

The format of key action plans depends on individual taste. Some companies like to set them out sideways across an A4 sheet to give greater width and to give the added impact of a changed dimension. Others prefer to develop them vertically, giving ample space for detail with clear indexing in the left-hand margin and names and deadlines thrown into relief in the right-hand margin. Examples of typical formats are shown in Figures 5.2 and 5.5.

The importance of formatting lies in making the key action plan clear and compelling. This section of the plan requires action, and the presentation has to convey this and make it happen. Key action plans need to be reviewed formally at least quarterly, and some formats include boxes to allow results to date to be noted and comments made. This also has the advantage that the latest key action plan sheets can be sent to those concerned for their progress report, and facilitates the issue of updated sheets afterwards.

Because of the importance of the key action programme, it is essential that the discipline of regular review is maintained and that any emerging delays or difficulties are dealt with expeditiously. The board should be involved in the regular review and should see the top-level review in detail, annotated to reflect any emerging problems at lower levels. Performance against key actions should be a major factor in personal assessment at all levels, and encouragement should be given to give early warning of emerging difficulties so that corrective action does not have to await the regular review.

Key action programmes are one of the main tools for enabling management to turn plans into reality. They are a key bridge between planning and operations and a major instrument of strategic management, of which we shall speak in more detail in Chapter 7. Table 5.2 is an example of a vertically formatted key action programme, and Figure 5.5 shows a vertically formatted key action programme with updates.

5.11.   Contingency and continuity planning

We spoke earlier about the sensitivity of plans to variations in assumptions and how these could be tested by sensitivity analysis. Plans are even more at risk as a result of unforeseen events, or events whose occurrence has been discounted as highly improbable. The sort of events which are the contingencies against which managements may need to establish a continuity plan include fire, flooding, explosion, loss of power, loss of computer records, fraud (and hacking), terrorism, strikes, industrial espionage, kidnapping and assassination. It will be seen that some of these events are more expected than others, many are insurable (at a price) and few would be fatal to larger and well-established companies. And yet, the pressures of modern business are making some parts of a company critical for its survival. The lifeblood of modern business is information, and the ability to communicate it rapidly and with confidence is essential for a company's health. Computer breakdown or the loss of key information-transmission systems can be very damaging. Massive fraud destroyed British and Commonwealth and seriously damaged Ferranti. IBM has suffered from industrial espionage to a serious extent. The sort of events which are the subject of contingency planning cannot be discounted without careful investigation. The damage they can do is too serious and too immediate in its impact for insurance to be more than a partial answer to the problem.

Contingency planning, or as Ron Ginn (1989) prefers to call it, continuity planning, is a serious matter that requires careful assessment and continual review. The key first step is a systematic examination of the business and of the impact of the different types of contingency listed above on its performance. All such events are not equally likely to occur, nor, equally damaging; it is certainly unlikely that they would all occur at one time! For this reason, continuity plans are usually prepared as modules; this is also important in that different people will have responsibilities for each

Table 5.2. Key action programme

Action	Aim	Responsibility	Cost	Date	Target(s)
International relations					
Play full role at UPU Washington Congress, and as members of the new EC and CCPS.	To ensure BPO interests advanced, and damage limitation in other areas: • Terminal dues • Air conveyance rate • flexible regulations • priority/non-priority option • streamlining UPU • bar-coding and track/trace • international business reply	RMI2	HQ staff	December 89 (Congress), and throughout 90/91	–
CEPT agency (Unipost)	To support, and influence, work of CEPT agency.	RMI2	HQ staff	Throughout 90/91	Market research; transport study; Q of S monitoring; product planning.
Development of favourable attitude to postal service on part of EEC Commission.	Participate with commission in formulation of their policy in this area.	RMI2	HQ staff	Throughout 90/91	–
To give practical assistance to Third World countries (e.g. supply bar-code labels).	To achieve service/product improvements in some countries.	RMI2	20K	Throughout 90/91, depending on available opportunities.	–

Source: Post Office

Company/operation: Australia

Authorised by: ☐
Date:
Worksheet no: ☐

Operating plan

Key action no.	Key action and planned financial result	Responsibility	Date implementation planned	Date of implementation actual	Disposition or status of key action and achieved financial result
10-FY80	**Definition** To improve representation in New Zealand, Europe and Fiji by installing TC Australia inbound competence. Our association with Silver Fern in New Zealand will be terminating and the plan is to set up an inbound division under the control of TC Auckland. Additional representative effort will be researched in West Germany in conjunction with the Frankfurt office of TC. In Fiji, it we are to hold Japanese business, we must improve our operating effectiveness for movements entering that territory under our control				
	Objective To underwrite the planned level of performance by an extension of representation and operational efficiency				
10.1	**Strategy** Install an inbound division in New Zealand				
10.1.1	Select and train a manager and staff	General manager inbound	1.11.79	15.12.79	The managerial duties were combined with the present manager of wholesale. Staff were recruited and trained and it is operating very effectively
10.1.2	Promote new arrangements in overseas markets	General manager inbound	1.11.79		The new arrangements were very well promoted overseas and a major portion of the Japanese market is now being handled by the office in New Zealand
10.2	Research the viability of opening a sales office in West Germany in conjunction with TC Frankfurt	General manager inbound	1.1.80		Research was conducted into the viability of opening a sales office in West Germany in conjunction with TC Frankfurt. It was determined that at this time it was not a viable proposition and a consultancy firm, PROMO Tourism was retained to keep a watching brief on the market
10.3	Examine the effect of establishing operational representation in Fiji	General manager	1.1.80	1.7.80	The effects of establishing an operational representation in Fiji were studied and it was determined that with the introduction of direct flights from Japan, this could be a very viable office. It was opened on 1 July 1980

Financial effect
A large share of the traffic to Fiji and New Zealand has been captured by the two new offices established in FY80.
The financial results for New Zealand are found in their review of key action No. 8 FY80 and the results for Fiji
are expected to be near the breakeven point by the end of the financial year.

Figure 5.5   Key action performance review (Source: Thomas
Cook Group)

eventuality, and cannot burrow through an Armageddon plan to find their section when an emergency occurs! Continuity plans should be developed by teams expert in the hazards to be planned for and in the sensitive parts of the business to be protected. Often these teams will continue their responsibilities by maintaining and updating the plan and will be on call for action if disaster strikes.

The key to continuity planning is anticipation and preparation in careful detail of counteraction. Ron Ginn quotes fourteen areas of activity to be planned in the case of protecting a small data processing centre as follows:

1. Management.
2. Administration.
3. Transportation.
4. Replacement equipment.
5. Technical support.
6. Application support.
7. Communications.
8. Alternate site.
9. Data preparation.
10. Production control.
11. Internal user liaison.
12. Evaluation.
13. Salvage.
14. Personnel/PR/security.

All of these will have numerous subsets and will need to be planned in detail. It should be remembered that there will be a state of trauma when the plan is implemented, and that its operation will need to be quick and purposeful to be successful. Training is essential to make staff aware of the likely impact of a disaster, and to give them confidence in dealing with it.

Insurance planning is linked to continuity planning, and the one does not substitute for the other. Insurance cannot act fast enough to protect a company from the impact and disruption caused by disaster; it does, however, enable the cost of lost equipment and trading profits to be recovered, and help fund the cost of implementing the continuity plan. Effective continuity plans help to focus on the areas where insurance is needed and can be cost-effective in securing cover economically.

In the same way as companies hold fire drill sporadically, continuity plans need to be tested from time to time. Testing is usually done in three stages: first, the testing of individual components of the plan; secondly, by integrated testing of a number of components in their plan sequence; and thirdly, a full-scale disaster drill. Plans are also subject to auditing to ensure that they have adapted to change and that the plan objectives remain valid.

5.12. Planning audits

The term 'audit' is applied to the planning process mainly to refer to the strategic assessment process referred to in Chapter 2 of this book. John Grieve-Smith (1985) uses the term in this sense in order to emphasise the need for sensitivity and deeper penetration than mere 'strengths and weaknesses' assessment often provides.

The other use of the term 'audit' in respect of strategic planning is, I believe, a more proper use, in that it is an exercise involving independent assessment of the planning process used in a company. Such an assessment might well be made by outside consultants, but should at least involve non-executive directors.

A model for such an audit is provided by R. T. Lenz (1985) in his article 'Paralysis by analysis' in *Long Range Planning* as follows:

Developing a planning culture, carefully examining strategic assumptions and using strategy review sessions as occasions for creative thinking are means of preventing excessive rationality in planning. A more formal procedure is also required in some companies as a counter-weight to the drive for administrative efficiency. We recommend periodic audits of the strategic planning process. These may be conducted by a task force comprised of both participants in the planning process and those with no direct involvement. The latter could be a consultant, an outside board member or an executive from another firm or division. The team should develop audit criteria after initiating their evaluation. The following are some criteria for getting started. This list is by no means all inclusive:

1. Do those engaged in the planning process understand its basic purpose and structure?
2. Does the strategic planning process facilitate the identification and interpretation of strategic issues?
3. Is there a balance between quantitative and qualitative information that sets the stage for innovative thought and action?
4. Given the utility of information obtained, is the time required to gather and interpret it excessive?
5. Does the planning process provide a means for fully discussing dissenting viewpoints?
6. Are managers encouraged and rewarded for entrepreneurial initiatives?
7. Are intangibles such as managerial values, aspirations and acknowledged responsibilities to society explicitly incorporated into final strategic choices?
8. Does the process provide adequate time for strategy implementation and evaluation?

Such audits are seen by Lenz as vitally important and the practice of having such audits seems gradually to be gaining ground. Given the growing cost of planning processes, it makes sense to see that value continues to be obtained for the expense incurred. More importantly, it is essential to open the process to wide participation and unconventional thinking; too many planning processes degenerate into bureaucratic justification of the prejudices of executive management.

I can testify to the value of planning audits from personal experience of carrying out an audit of the planning process of a major public sector corporation. The value of the independent investigator is that he can ask questions which might be difficult for an insider to put, can obtain franker answers than might be forthcoming to an insider and can relate the outcome to outside standards and experience which add a new dimension of judgment. Equally important is the better chance of the outside consultant to make his findings acceptable to top management and have them followed through.

In the same way that most major companies now have audit committees which are directed by non-executive directors and can act as independent financial watchdogs for the shareholders, I believe that non-executive directors have a role to play as watchdogs over corporate strategy. The concept of a strategy committee of the board was developed in Chapter 3 of this book. This committee is concerned with ensuring the strategic health of the company in the same way that the audit committee oversees its financial health. Part of the strategy committee's work should be to receive reports following audits of the company's strategic planning process, to discuss them with the consultant who has prepared them and to make recommendations to the board as a result. The consultant is, of course, reporting to the board as a whole and executive management should see his findings before publication, in order both to correct errors of detail and to have a chance of preparing replies to issues raised. What must not be allowed to happen is any manipulation or suppression of the findings of the audit, and the involvement of the strategy committee in the process enables the audit to be examined and discussed in detail with an independent and externally experienced group before its recommendations are formally passed to the board.

6

STRATEGIC PLANNING TECHNIQUES AND THEIR PRACTICAL APPLICATION

6.1. The value and pitfalls of techniques

This chapter is intended to give directors and non-planners a flavour of some of the techniques used by planners and to demystify them. Techniques are only as good as the quality of information which they manipulate and as the perceptiveness of those that use them.

Few subjects cause more dissention among planners than planning techniques. John Fawn sees them in a positive light:

Planning techniques are potentially very attractive to senior executives at corporate headquarters for the following reasons:

1. They give control back to top management. As companies grew larger and became more diverse, power probably shifted to divisional chief executives. . . . techniques . . . bring it firmly back to corporate H.Q.
2. They enable rational decisions to be made. Top Management can justify their decisions particularly to businesses which are to be run down/divested.
3. Resource allocation (particularly capital) between totally diverse activities can be solved.

Topdown planning techniques cannot be used in isolation. Messages received from any particular technique are only indications. If the same message is received from several techniques that message starts to gain credibility (Fawn and Cox, 1987).

On the other hand, John Argenti says in *Practical Corporate Planning*:

I do not believe that directional policy matrices, computer models, assignment charts, or any of the dozens of other modern planning techniques, can inject the necessary level of belief and conviction into the average senior executive to be worth more than a passing mention in my book . . . . What most (other authorities) have done, it seems to me, is to devise planning TECHNIQUES; they have not developed what I hope this book describes – an entire complete planning SYSTEM. (Argenti, 1989)

John Chandler and Paul Cockle dismiss criticism of the use of models 'in the context of social sciences':

We can . . . assert that men think in terms of models (quoting K. W. Deutsch). Only by mental manipulation of experience can rational decisions be made about future courses of action. Those who do not think in this way are called insane. (Chandler and Cockle, 1982)

R. T. Lenz warns about excessive rationality:

Although to some it may seem ironic, corporate planners are often victims of excessive rationality in planning. In their efforts to attain organisational respectability as vital contributors to strategic decision-making, the trappings of the 'science of planning' sometimes create a snare. The snare is slowly fashioned out of the increasingly intricate network of models, data, analytical techniques and formal procedures. If the process goes too far, these factors establish an intellectual cocoon of abstraction whose relationship to the administrative experiences of line managers is, at best, tenuous. Increasing sophistication can breed increasing irrelevance and the development of a ponderous planning apparatus. (Lenz, 1985)

The value of techniques in the strategic planning process is as auxiliaries. Human beings think in terms of models and, as Ben Heirs demonstrates clearly, we use our experience, imagination and reason both to construct and interpret those models:

The need to make sense of events and to construct a model of reality, which yields accurate and useful predictions about the future, is a fundamental human requirement. The obvious danger is that, faced with the monumental complexities of today's world, we may try to cope with them by devising models which are simplistic and artificially rigid, or by shutting our eyes to reality and constructing a model of the world which shows it as we would like it to be rather than as it actually is. (Heirs, 1989)

Techniques can be helpful in assisting the process of thinking but they cannot be any substitute of that process.

As John Fawn (Fawn and Cox, 1987) points out, one value of techniques is to give credibility to a given model by multiple corroboration. One of the dangers in planning is to produce a model of one man's reality; techniques such as Delphi help to remove idiosyncrasies and form wider-based judgements. The various matrix techniques and morphological analysis enable factors to be plotted spatially against different criteria. This can help to provide insights and establish meaningful patterns.

The building of scenarios is helpful in forcing managers to look outside their business and to identify the exogenous factors which may impact on it in a significant way. Building models helps to form working hypotheses of the interrelationship between key factors within and outside the business. Both scenarios and models are likely to be considerably less than perfect but the challenge of building them helps to shape the internal model of the mind which in turn will refine the external models over time.

In all use of techniques it is important to be aware of Lenz's warnings. Planning is a process which seeks to identify and explore the issues facing a company. It is not a science and should not be prescriptive. Techniques should support the process but must not usurp it. In his article 'Paradoxes in planning', John Robinson sets this memorably in context:

We conclude that the job of the planner is not to state the objectives but to elicit them; is not to predict the future but to help understand it; is not to make the key decisions but to help managers do so; and is not to produce a plan so much as to conduct the planning process. (Robinson, 1986)

6.2. Scenarios

Traditional corporate planning systems have developed a single 'base case' and tested it for sensitivity to identify any weaknesses or factors imposing high risk on the outcome. The danger of the base case is that it is consciously or unconsciously an extrapolation of past trends or is too much influenced by internal wishes. To think unconventionally is not always politically expedient in a business proud of its proven formulae for success, and yet to 'think the unthinkable' is often crucial when a major discontinuity looms or a sudden change in predicted circumstances can wreck not just strategies but the companies which launched them.

In the late 1960s and early 1970s Pierre Wack of Shell developed a number of alternative scenarios for the future of the oil business. Scenarios were not new; Herman Kahn of the Rand Corporation had been writing scenarios in the 1950s, but Shell had taken scenarios to a higher level of sophistication. The insights obtained from Pierre Wack's work enabled Shell to foresee the likelihood of oil crises in 1973 and 1979 and, although these insights challenged received wisdom, they were accepted by the management.

As a result the technique of scenario planning has developed credibility and it provides a method of thinking the unthinkable that is politically acceptable. Scenarios are basically qualitative in content, rather than complex numerical models, although variations of the technique generate and derive varying amounts of quantitative data.

While Herman Kahn was developing all-encompassing scenarios, his colleague Olaf Helmer developed the Delphi technique, which exploited a judgemental approach to forecasting. This technique itself is explained in a later section but has been developed into a scenario technique known as 'cross-impact analysis' which is explained below.

One key decision to be made in scenario planning is the number of scenarios to be developed. Theoretically the number is unlimited, but the marginal value of extra scenarios declines rapidly. The minimum possible number is two and this has been championed by Peter Beck of Shell and has a strong following. Two scenarios imply that one is the 'base case' and the other the 'worst case'. The juxtaposition of these two scenarios provides,

Table 6.1. Economic backgrounds

UK Scenario	Average GDP growth rates, 1979–1980 to 2000 (% p.a.)	
	United Kingdom	World
(A) High growth based on services	2.6	4.5 (High)
(B) High growth based on manufacturing	2.6	3.3 (Medium)
(C) Medium growth	1.0	3.3 (Medium)
(D) Stable low growth	−0.4	3.3 (Medium)
(E) Unstable low growth	−0.4	2.1 (Low)

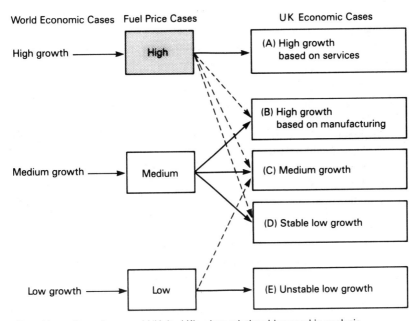

Note: Heavy lines show world/United Kingdom relationships used in analysis

Figure 6.1   Scenario cases – world and United Kingdom

in practice, nearly all the insights that management really needs for the least expenditure of time, effort and money. Three scenarios were popular at one time but this forces attention on the middle position which can be chosen as the base case almost by default. In an article in *Long Range Planning*, Stokke *et al* (1990) describe the scenario planning used by Norwegian Oil and Gas (Statoil) for R and D which develops four scenarios, reflecting four distinctive environments in which the company might have to operate in the long term. It would seem that four scenarios are near the practical limit for most purposes, although the CEGB developed five scenarios for the Sizewell enquiry (Hankinson, 1986), as shown in Figure 6.1 and Table 6.1.

It is interesting to note that scenario planning was developed primarily by companies with long planning horizons (oil companies, power utilities, etc.) since it is, in practice, virtually impossible to plan realistically for periods beyond five years without an imaginative and judgemental forecasting tool. The insights which protected Shell from the oil crises of the 1970s were obtained by scenario planning in the 1960s and given increasingly sharp focus as the critical moment approached. This does not invalidate short-term scenario planning, which is a highly effective form of sensitivity analysis at the least, but short-term plans tend to be rich in detail which may obscure deeper messages. Longer-term scenarios are not cluttered by familiar details and require considerable work to shape out of the unknown. This allows weak signals to be picked up early, and gives time for those signals to be monitored and validated as their meaning becomes more apparent.

Scenarios provide insights and assist the choice of strategies in the shorter term also. Dr. Stephen Millett (1988) of Battelle identifies six such insights:

1. Whether future demand for the company's existing products and services will expand, stay constant, or decline.
2. Whether market conditions are becoming more or less favourable to existing products and services.
3. Are there opportunities for new products and services which the company could provide?
4. Whether there are changes in technologies affecting the mode of producing products and services.
5. Whether there are changes in competition, including the possibility of substitute products and services.
6. What is the degree of uncertainty facing the company and how much flexibility is needed in choosing strategies?

There are numerous variants of scenario planning. William Huss and Edward Houton (1987) identify three major categories: (a) intuitive logics as described by Pierre Wack in his articles in *Harvard Business Review* and as systematised and practised by SRI International and Royal Dutch/Shell inter alia; (b) trend-impact analysis as practised by the Futures Group; and (c) cross-impact analysis as practised by the Center for Futures Research (INTERAX), Battelle (BASICS), etc.

SRI International defines scenarios as 'devices for ordering one's perceptions about alternative environments in which one's decisions might be played out. Its method has the following steps:

1. Analysing the decisions facing the company with long-range implications and the company's strategic concerns.
2. Identifying the key factors affecting those decisions.
3. Identifying the key environmental forces shaping the key decision factors.
4. Analysing those key environmental forces.
5. Defining scenario logics (themes, principles and assumptions which shape the scenario).

6. Elaborating the scenarios (combining logics with the environmental analyses).
7. Analysing the implications for the key factors affecting the company's decisions.
8. Analysing the implications for the company's decisions and strategies.

The SRI International approach relies strongly on intelligent and perceptive teamwork, but can produce flexible and internally consistent scenarios over extended periods.

Trend-impact analysis relies on an independent forecast of the chosen key dependent variable which is adjusted under the impact of events. The Futures Group uses the following steps:

1. Select topic and identify the key scenario drivers (e.g. GNP, regulatory environment).
2. Create a scenario space, picking the likeliest combinations of drivers (one of which might be median GNP/loose regulatory environment).
3. Identify important trends and collect time-series data.
4. Prepare a naive extrapolation (using standard time series).
5. Establish a list of impacting events (by Delphi or by literature search).
6. Establish probabilities of events occurring over time, including years to first impact, years to maximum impact, level of maximum impact, years to steady-state impact and level of steady-state impact.
7. Modify naive extrapolation to reflect impacts.
8. Write narratives.

The Futures Group approach is useful since it combines traditional forecasting techniques with qualitative factors. It forces the identification of specific impacting factors and an evaluation of their probability and importance. It does not, however, evaluate the impact of events on each other and is based on one key variable which is quantified based on historical data.

Cross-impact analysis was developed as a method of interrelating intuitive forecasts. From this concept two major scenario planning methodologies have been developed – INTERAX (Interactive Cross-Impact Simulation) and BASICS (Battelle Scenario Inputs to Corporate Strategies). INTER-AX's approach consists of the following steps:

1. Define the issue and time period of analysis.
2. Identify the key indicators (the primary variables to be forecast).
3. Project the key indicators (using econometric models, etc).
4. Identify impacting events (Delphi, interviews, etc.).
5. Develop event probability distributions over time period.
6. Estimate impacts of events on trends.
7. Complete cross-impact analysis (events on events, trend impacts of events on trends).
8. Run the model (using Monte Carlo random selection of events) to build a set of probable future paths.

INTERAX combines the strengths of trend-impact analysis with those of cross-impact analysis. It also allows a picture to develop over time, and corrections to be made in the light of events. There is a weakness in the random selection of events in the model and little identification of which scenarios are more likely than others.

BASICS does not use Monte Carlo simulation and does not require the independent forecast of key indicators in step 3 of INTERAX. BASICS has the following steps:

1. Define and structure the topic including unit of measure, time frame and geographic scope.
2. Identify and structure the areas of influence.
3. Define descriptors (refined from areas of influence), write essays for each and assign initial probabilities of occurrence to each descriptor outcome or state.
4. Complete the cross-impact matrix and run the model.
5. Select scenarios for further study including the writing of narratives.
6. Introduce low-probability but high-impact events and conduct other sensitivity analyses.
7. Make forecasts and study implications.

BASICS generates scenarios which are consistent and likely to occur. It is structured using influencing variables ('descriptor states') and uncertain events, giving a broader set of outcomes and giving extra flexibility. Its main weakness is that it generates 'state' scenarios, that is, the scenario at the end of the time frame. This means that work is needed to interpret the paths to the 'state' through the time frame of the forecast.

The different approaches may be compared more readily by reference to Figure 6.2.

Another interesting approach to scenario planning is that developed at Reed International by John Chandler and Paul Cockle (1982). Their system is described in detail in their book *Techniques of Scenario Planning* but in outline, it takes the plan offered by the managers who contributed to building it as a base case. This plan is then subjected to changes to see how they and their underlying strategies respond. The system is seen as a wheel, with the centre representing the company and the rim the external environment (see Figure 6.3). The operation of the system depends on the interaction of changes in scenarios upon a number of structured models (macroeconomic, market demand, market supply) and a series of financial models representing the company. This is a very flexible system whose strength depends on the quality of the models, the building of which is described in great detail in the book.

Scenario planning is a demanding exercise and difficult to justify for smaller companies. Its real benefits are derived over the longer term, providing insights which might be difficult to obtain without the discipline of the technique. Scenario planning also helps to set boundaries to

Generic scenario generation steps	SRI	The Futures Group	INTERAX	BASICS
The topic	1. Analysing the decisions and strategic concerns	1. Identify key scenario drivers 2. Create scenario space	1. Define the issue and time period of analysis	1. Define and structure the topic
Key decisions	2. Identifying the key decision factors		2. Identify the key indicators	
Trend extrapolation		3. Collect time series data 4. Prepare naive extrapolation	3. Project the key indicators	
Influencing factors	3. Identifying the key environmental factors	5. Establish list of impacting events	4. Identify the impacting event	2. Identify areas of influence
Analysis of factors	4. Analysing the environmental factors	6. Establish probs. of events occurring over time	5. Develop event prob. distribution	3. Define descriptors; write essays; assign initial probabilities
Cross-impact			6. Estimate cross-impacts 7. Complete cross-impact analysis	4a. Complete cross-impact matrix
Initial scenarios	5. Defining scenario logics	7. Modify extrapolation	8. Run the model	4b. Run the program 5. Select scenarios for further study
Sensitivity analysis				6. Introduce uncertain events; conduct sensitivity analysis
Detailed scenarios	6. Elaborating the scenarios	8. Write narratives		7a. Prepare forecasts
Implications	7. Analysing implications for key decision factors 8. Analysing implications for decisions and strategies			7b. Study implications

Figure 6.2   Comparison of the steps included in each scenario analysis technique (Source: Battelle)

uncertainty and risk and to assist in the evaluation of strategic options. Most importantly, it can be a powerful stimulus to strategic thinking and involve numerous people in that most demanding and yet rewarding of mental exercises.

6.3.   Analysis tools

Planners have long been interested in refining and using techniques to assist them in the development of strategies. A key stage in that process is the analysis of all available data in order to shape judgements. Tools to assist analysis include the following:

Experience curve

This tool was developed by the Boston Consulting Group and helps to quantify the well-established observation that as production increases, unit costs fall to a certain irreducible level. It is to be expected that when

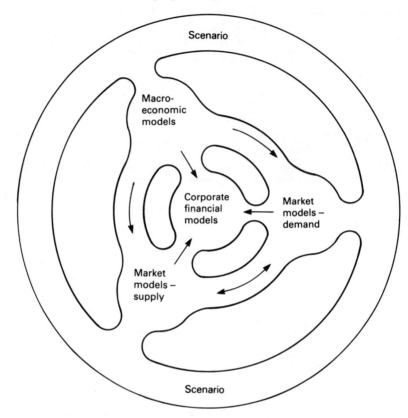

Figure 6.3   Transmission of influence through the planning
system

production doubles, unit costs will fall by a given percentage, characteristi-
cally 20 to 30 per cent. The working of the experience curve is recognised
by Michael Porter, who emphasises that it is valid for most business
activities, not just production. John Argenti (1989) points out the danger of
taking experience-curve theory as a justification for maximising market
share by acquisition, which has not always been successful in practice. In
his article 'The uses and abuses of experience curves' Jean-Paul Sallenave
(1985) demonstrates examples of experience curves derived from his
computer model. He concludes that they can provide insights and early
warnings, but should not be taken too literally due to limitations in the
quality of input data and the difficulty of making cross comparisons with
competitors whose technology and operating conditions may differ from
yours.

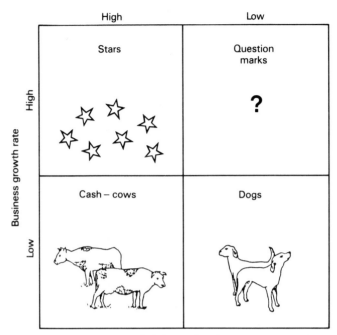

Figure 6.4 BCG matrix

Matrices

The classic tool of portfolio analysis (deciding in which businesses to invest) is Boston Consulting Group's directional policy matrix (DPM). This is a two-dimensional matrix setting relative market share against business growth rate and, as shown in Figure 6.4 (Grieve-Smith, 1985), is divided into four quadrants, as follows:

1. *Stars* are businesses which are growing rapidly and whose cashflow is at least in balance.
2. *Cows* are well-established businesses which generate surplus cash.
3. *Dogs* are likely to have low profits and should be disposed of, especially if needing further investment.
4. *Question marks* may become *Stars* if cash is invested to increase relative market share, or may become *Dogs* if growth should fall.

The individual businesses of a company can be located in the matrix and the shape of the portfolio estimated at some future time if certain strategies are followed. The DPM is a useful if simplistic tool for bringing out issues, but its assumption that maximising market share is always advantageous in terms of profitability is dangerous.

The DPM has been developed further by BCG and others. One

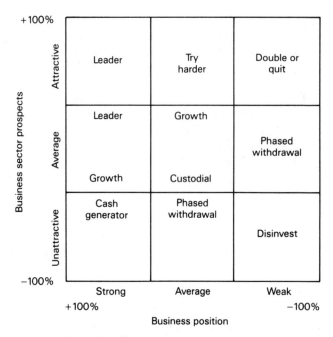

Figure 6.5   Company's competitive positions

development is the directional policy matrix of Robinson, Hitchins and Wade (1978), which merges a number of key factors into two factors: the business sector prospects and the business position of the company. The matrix is again two-dimensional but has nine boxes (see Figure 6.5). The principle is similar to the Boston DPM, but the build up of factors is more complex and the findings more nuanced. Given matrices for competitors the search for competitive advantage can be both structured and creative. It is also possible to project an ideal portfolio and determine how to move towards it.

A more comprehensive matrix is that of Hofer which plots competitive position against 'stage of product/market evolution'. A typical Hofer matrix is shown in Figure 6.6.

A more financially driven matrix is that of Patel and Younger. This plots the return of net assets against internal deployment of funds (i.e. the percentage of funds generated which are reinvested in the particular business). Businesses are categorised as 'embryonic', 'growing', 'mature' and 'ageing', and are plotted on the matrix as shown in Figures 6.7 and 6.8.

Matrices are a convenient way of displaying quantitative information spatially and of seeing situations in relative terms. They have an impact which raw figures lack and are as much a means of presentation as an aid to creative thought. (Examples in this section are taken from the article by Patrick McNamee (1984), 'Competitive analysis using matrix displays'.)

Competitive position

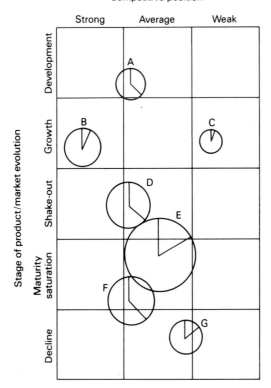

Figure 6.6   The Hofer matrix

Profit Improvement of Market Strategy (PIMS)

The Strategic Planning Institute was set up in 1975 and has developed an increasingly sophisticated data base of individual strategic business units covering a wide range of manufacturing, extractive and service businesses. The information recorded on each business includes its market environment, competitive position, state of competition and structure of its production process. The strategic moves made by the business over at least the last five years and its operating results are also logged. The database comprises more than 2,500 distinct businesses in the United States and Europe and is used to generate global strategies by identifying the global potential of the industry in which a particular business operates, the extent of that business and its competitors' globalisation, the appropriate level and type of globalisation for the business and its capacity for sustaining a global strategy. The steps involved are as follows:

1.   Work with participants in the programme to identify the business and countries to be studied.

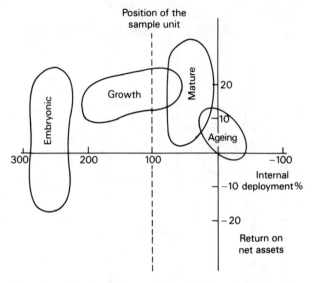

Figure 6.7 Patel and Younger's profitability and cash position matrix

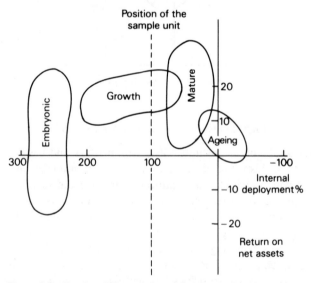

Figure 6.8 Patel and Younger's profitability and cash position matrix of a corporation by business unit

2. SPI staff spend time on site to help collect the data.
3. SPI staff help manage the data collection process to completion.
4. Conduct a data review session.
5. Analyse the global data against the PIMS global strategy framework.

6. Analyse the core data against the PIMS database of over 2,500 business units.
7. Develop and present strategy recommendations.

R. G. Wakerly (1984) of PIMS Associates claims that PIMS research has identified some thirty major universal factors which taken together, explain some 70 per cent of the profitability variations between businesses on the database. These factors relate to the 'shape' of businesses and not to their products. In particular, they relate to the structural characteristics of an industry (e.g. growth rate), the competitive position of the specific business (e.g. market share, quality rating), and capital and labour productivity (e.g. capital intensity). Wakerly quotes Bismarck: 'Fool you are to say you learn from your own experience. I prefer to profit by others' mistakes and avoid the price of my own.' The PIMS database constitutes a unique record of business experience on a wide scale. It has been found to give useful pointers to many companies and has no doubt saved many of them from expensive mistakes. Whether PIMS is a substitute for the learning curve of experience is more debatable.

Value chain

The value chain is a concept which has been popularised by Michael Porter though it has been used in various guises by consulting firms for some years. The value chain represents the selling price of a given product broken down into its various elements (cost of components, assembly costs, overheads and profit). This enables tactical make or buy decisions to be made, and provides a basis for evaluating vertical integration and acquisitions. The manufacturer of a final product might examine carefully the value chain of a supplier and conclude that he could run that business more profitably. He might equally look at the economics of distributing his product and find synergy in that direction. Value chain analysis can also be a timely warning of danger. Christopher Clarke (1989) quotes an example of a manufacturer of power semiconductors who was interested in forward integration by acquiring a leading manufacturer of variable-speed drives. Value chain analysis showed that the power semiconductor was only 4 per cent of the value chain of the variable-speed drive manufacturer. This meant that the benefit to the value chain of that manufacturer of even a 50 per cent fall in the cost of power semiconductors would not be significant.

Force-Field Analysis

Force-field analysis is a technique for evaluating forces affecting change which was developed by social scientist Kurt Lewin in the early 1950s. It involves a careful analysis of internal and external forces supporting and resisting a specific change targeted by an organisation. These are mapped

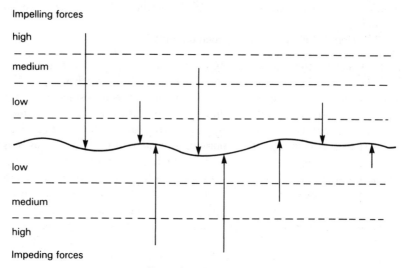

Figure 6.9   Force fields

against the present equilibrium point and the desired equilibrium point after the targeted change has been achieved. Examples of the types of forces involved are shown in Figures 6.9 (Ajimal, 1985) and 6.10 (Thomas, 1985), in which the length of the arrow indicates the relative impact of each force. An interesting case study in the use of force field analysis is written up by Dr Joe Thomas (1985) in *Long Range Planning*. It is admitted that the use of the technique for strategic planning has been limited so far, but force-field analysis can provide useful insights. It is a technique which is best practised by a group, both to remove individual bias and to widen ownership of the possible solution.

Delphi

Delphi is a method of forecasting based on structured interaction between chosen experts. It avoids direct confrontation between the experts which is a recognised weakness of panel discussions and is based on a series of face-to-face interviews or anonymous questionnaires. These seek reactions to hypothetical future events in a structured form which allows a statistical pattern of probability to be derived. The process is renewed, showing the range of answers and inviting respondents to revise their estimates. Interaction continues until a meaningful consensus develops.

The Delphi technique is valuable as an intuitive approach to forecasting and complements more mechanistic techniques, such as extrapolating past trends, using heuristic models based on a causal mechanism or morphological analysis (see below). Although the technique uses statistical methods to drive for a consensus, it does allow for comments which challenge and may

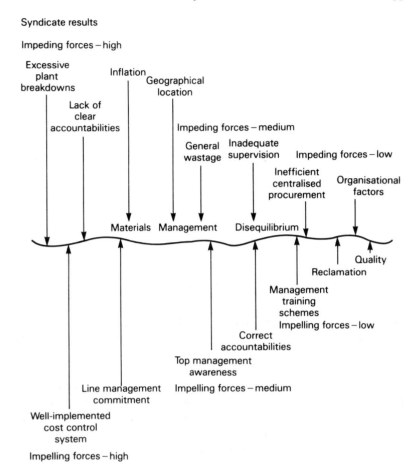

Figure 6.10   A force field analysis of a materials management
problem

change the basis of that consensus. Its main potential weakness is the ability
of experts to foresee discontinuities in their area of expertise which are
driven by factors outside the scope of their specialisation. Much of the skill
lies in the formulation of the questions put to the experts, and these should
allow for such outside eventualities wherever possible.

Morphology

Russ Shurig (1984) characterises morphology as 'a technique for lateral
thinking, for interdisciplinary problem solving, prophecy or forecasting,
fundamental research and creative speculation'! The Concise Oxford
Dictionary defines morphology as the study of the form of words (and, in
biology, of plants and animals). Morphology is essentially a method of

Information media preferences

	Voice (24,000 BC)	Image (12,000 BC)	Text (6,000 BC)	Data (3,000 BC)
Voice	(Voice is a medium for personal contact)	People prefer the use of speech rather than text, image or data when message is urgent, informal or personal		
Image	Message cannot easily be verbalised but can be displayed pictorially	(Image is a medium for visual display)	Message is complex, precise, external in origin or signed	Message is intricate or overview is needed or impact is important
Text	Message is complex or hard copy record is needed	Message is brief and/or verbal in nature	(Text is a medium for the preservation of thought)	Message is qualitative and/or non-numeric
Data	The use of data is preferable to the use of voice, image or text when the message is quantitative or precise			(Data is a medium for the preservation of measurement)

Figure 6.11   Comparison of information media to each other

classification (e.g. the periodic table of chemical elements) which is very comprehensive and painstaking. The technique is often used for innovation, since it is wide-sweeping and well-structured and is non-numeric in concept, even though numeric values may be attached to its results.

A simple example of morphological analysis is provided by Shurig in respect of information media, analysed against each other in their order of historical evolution, and analysed against the needs of the modern office (see Figures 6.11 and 6.12). An analysis of this type assists the differentiation of information and knowledge. Knowledge is meaningful information and is derived by the use of human reason. To equate information with knowledge is to equate machines with people. Knowledge is a specifically human faculty and only human beings can turn information into knowledge. 'Computers, telecommunications and databases are information tools whereas human brains, languages and morphology are knowledge tools', in the words of Russ Shurig (*op. cit.*)

Wargames

Like the concept of strategy, wargames are another contribution from the military to business practice. Wargames have been developed by most major powers as an aid to strategic and tactical decision making and as a valuable

Information technologies

	Voice	Image	Text	Data
Voice	Telephone Audio conferencing Audio processing Voice messaging	Audio graphics Video conferencing Picture phone	Dictation Voice annotation Display phone Text-to-speech	Voice recognition Voice ordering Voice I/O
Image		Micrographics Image processing Facsimile Photocopy Video	Fiche base Videotex Electronic blackboard Telecommuting Photocomposition	Graphics Computer aided drafting Aperture card base Optical character recognition
Text			Word processing Teletext Text messaging TWX/telex Electronic mail Text processing	Text base Computer conferencing Word processing and data processing
Data				Data base Computation Data processing Electronic banking

Figure 6.12   User needs and application areas or technologies by information media combinations

training tool for staff colleges. The analogy between the operational circumstances and objectives of military and business are strikingly similar in Figure 6.13, taken from Ginter and Rucks (1984).

Wargames are models based on military, political and scientific principles. Some factors in the model can be quantified accurately (e.g. artillery rates of fire), while other factors are more variable or indeterminate. Like scenarios and models used for corporate planning, wargames need to have a framework of assumptions, and judgement can be tested by varying these.

In practice most of the business models are built on a smaller scale and have less exogenous factors than military wargames. This is partly a function of cost but also due to difficulties in making such models user-friendly to decision-makers. Staff officers see wargames as central to their practical

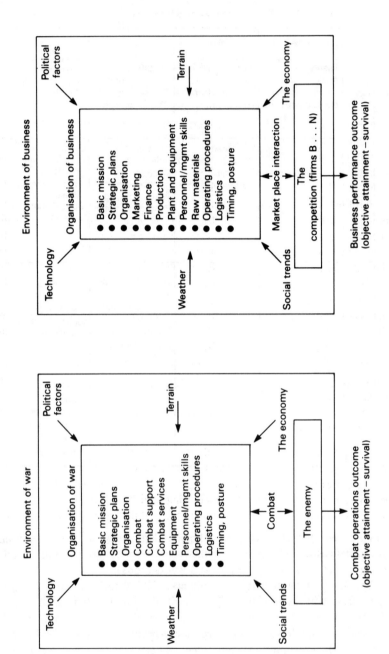

Figure 6.13   The military – business analogy

needs; decision-makers in business see them all too often as a theoretical self-indulgence of planners and a head-office overhead.

6.4. Modelling

Earlier in this section we referred to models which are attempts to formulate the relationship between different factors in order to predict a probable outcome. Models may be no more than equations which have been developed, tested and found to be useful. In these days of considerable computer power, models are more often developed to run on computers and may be of considerable complexity.

Models have often been developed initially to reflect the conventional accounting framework within which most businesses are managed. Such models enable the dynamics of the company's management and financial accounts to be captured, and are mainly monetary in nature. Many companies use such models for budget building and budgetary control, and the relationship between the different parameters in the model is usually established by convention or experience.

When models are developed for use in strategic planning it becomes necessary to distinguish between factors which the company can control and those outside its control. For the former, norms have to be established and built into the model; for the latter, assumptions have to be made and quantified for use in the model. In each case the relationship between parameters needs to be defined and expressed as a set of linear and non-linear differential equations.

Dr Kumar and Professor Vrat (1989) identify the following models classified by modelling strategy:

- Optimisation models (to identify the optimum among alternatives).
- Econometric models (to forecast performance in the light of exogenous variables).
- System dynamics models (which bring feed-back into consideration).
- Simulation models (used to imitate the realities of the system).

Models are also classified by Kumar and Vrat according to their characteristics:

- Deterministic models (with fixed values and no randomness).
- Probabilistic models (with multiple estimates with at least one operating characteristic given by a probability density function).
- Static models (which do not explicitly take the time variable into account).
- Dynamic models (which include time-varying interactions).

Classifications by methods of consolidation and the existence of recursive models, simultaneous models and logical models are also recognised. The main areas of application for models include forecasting and scenario generation, evaluation of alternatives ('what ifs'), budgeting, cash planning, investment and financial planning.

Kumar and Vrat (*op. cit.*) suggest that system-dynamics modelling offers considerable potential advantage for corporate planning, providing a 'flexible framework within which to view the interdependent operations of a system in a coherent and orderly manner'. Building such a model is an iterative process with seven identifiable steps:

1. Problem identification and definition.
2. System conceptualisation.
3. Model formulation.
4. Analysis of model behaviour.
5. Model evaluation.
6. Policy analysis.
7. Model use and policy implementation.

Schematic diagrams of systems dynamics modelling are shown in Figures 6.14 and 6.15.

The advantage of such a model for corporate planning lies in its 'causal view of reality', enabling it to break away from past patterns of behaviour by searching out meaningful patterns of interaction between individual components of the system which are often highly non-linear.

Models are also used for other planning applications, including manpower planning. Users are mainly large employers with well-defined hierarchies, long-service patterns and ongoing training needs. Such models are usually constructed to show manpower patterns at yearly intervals, based on past experience and projected ahead on structured assumptions. Manipulating such models can give a better insight into the dynamics of the manpower system and the results of possible policy changes. Models usually work on aggregate members, rather than on identified individuals. The latter approach is difficult to work effectively and may be subject to the Data Protection Act 1984. Data in the model can only be really useful, however, if it is based on computerised personal records and kept up to date.

6.5. Portfolio analysis

Earlier in this section we examined the application of matrices, based on the BCG growth rate market share (GRMS) matrix. Such matrices are used for gap analysis and, by mapping competitor data, for competitive analysis. They are also a key tool in portfolio analysis.

The theory behind portfolio analysis is that the company is an investor in a number of businesses, and attempts to optimise its return over the long run by a skilful choice of businesses which are diversified to spread risk and meet seasonality, and at different stages of development to ensure continuity. This theory was manifested in the earlier conglomerates, most of which have now disappeared or have been restructured. New conglomerates, such

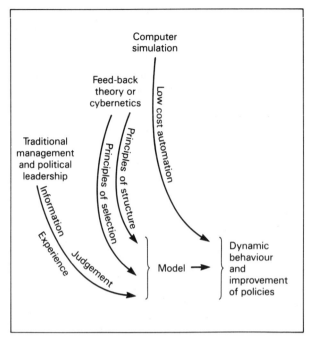

Figure 6.14 Background of systems dynamics method

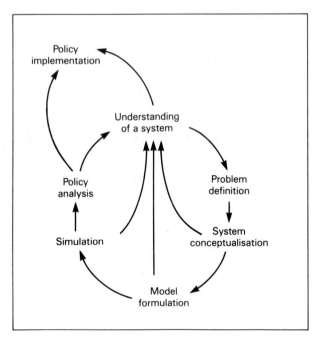

Figure 6.15 Overview of systems dynamics modelling approach

as Hanson, concentrate on mature businesses and avoid commitment to cash-hungry 'start ups' or high-technology businesses requiring heavy research and development expenditure.

The earlier concept has now evolved into portfolio management, which requires involvement in running the businesses rather than mere investment. To adapt portfolio analysis to make it contribute to a practical operation-planning system requires, in the view of Robert Walker, the resolution of the following problems:

1. The business units have to be defined fully.
2. The validity of available data is at best variable.
3. The growth rate market share (GRMS) matrix does not show in itself how the company intends to respond to the environment in terms of sales.
4. The response in terms of returns and profits is similarly not portrayed.
5. Only one competitor is considered for each business in the GRMS matrix.
6. A full profile of competitors is not provided.
7. The varied characteristics of fragmented as opposed to concentrated markets are not differentiated.
8. Differing market and competitive situations in the multinational environments are not considered.

This approach interlinks portfolio analysis with competitive analysis and adds an extra degree of realism. As John Grieve-Smith says:

The limitation of portfolio analysis is that it is primarily concerned with which individual businesses should comprise the corporation, rather than how they are run, or even their individual long-term strategies (save in the very restricted sense as to whether they are to expand, be run down or even liquidated). (Grieve-Smith, 1985)

Other limitations of portfolio analysis have been pointed out by Derkin-deren and Crum (1984). Because the technique is largely focused on cash flows, there is no easy way to reflect the effect of non-financial factors such as skill shortages, knowhow, management capability, and resilience. This last factor comprises the risk and endurance profile of the company and is crucial to the choice of sustainable and robust strategies. Portfolio analysis is therefore only one of a series of tools needed to analyse the strategy challenges of diversified companies, and is normally used to give pointers to areas where intensive work is likely to be fruitful. Linking portfolio analysis with competitive analysis to achieve a more involved portfolio-management approach is likely to provide better insights, but is no substitute for full analysis of key businesses, markets, competitors and products.

7

STRATEGIC MANAGEMENT: HOW TO MAKE IT HAPPEN

7.1. What is strategic management?

The term 'strategic management' has several times more definitions than practitioners! The working definition approved by the Strategic Planning Society states:

The essentials of Strategic Management centre on the creation of a clear concept of Purpose, Vision and Objectives at Corporate level, the dissemination of these in a meaningful way, the development of relevant strategies, goals, policies, etc., right through the organisation so that the resultant action builds towards achievement of Purpose, Vision and Objectives. Strategic Management in large organisations is most likely to be expressed in effective and relevant processes of planning and control and in appropriate organisational structure and culture where strategic criteria are continuously and evidently applied. Strategic Management also requires leadership. (Strategic Planning Society, 1990)

John Argenti sees strategic management having the following features:

- The organisation sets up a system for monitoring the company and the outside world. This does not consist of an occasional glance, it requires a system of scanning the items that have been singled out as strategic in nature.
- It therefore requires the posting of skilled 'look-outs' who have been properly briefed what to look for. The brief would include any early warning signs or signals that might herald a new strategic trend or event.
- The most important feature is that this scanning system must be firmly plugged in to a planning system (such as Argenti's). It is not much use knowing that some momentous event may happen next year if the company is not geared up to develop a strategic response to it.
- Therefore, the company must be organised in such a way as to allow it to act strategically once the strategy has been devised. This suggests that there must be a small management team at the top (including the chief executive) whose job explicitly involves making strategic decisions. The essence is that these top executives, whether they have day-to-day responsibilities for parts of the organisation or not, consider themselves the strategic planning team for the corporate whole. (Argenti, 1989)

Another way of looking at strategic management is shown in Figure 7.1 which appears in *Business Planning: An approach to strategic management* by Richardson and Richardson (1989). This shows strategic management at the hub of the business planning process, serviced by all facets of corporate planning and interacting with them. A more complex model of strategic management is provided by Yoo and Digman (1987), as shown in Figure 7.2.

Bernard Taylor identifies the following distinctive features of strategic management:

1. *The executive team are the planners.* They delegate operational control to the level below the board; they develop objectives and strategies for the corporation as a whole, and they require the chief executives of each business unit to present their strategies to the board for approval.
2. *The organisations are decentralised.* Their organisations are divided into autonomous units which are treated as separate businesses.
3. *The Chief Executive is a visible leader.* The top managers make a public commitment to a philosophy, a set of objectives, and a broad strategy and this is publicised inside and outside the organisation.
4. *Project teams accountable to top management.* Task forces and project teams are formed which cross functional and divisional boundaries and report directly to the Chief Executive.
5. *Internal marketing.* The company philosophy, objectives and strategies are communicated throughout the organisation via meetings and conferences, and by using modern marketing techniques.
6. *Problem-solving teams.* Teams are formed at section and departmental level to review their own performance continuously, and to make recommendations which will improve the company's productivity, quality, cost levels and customer service. This usually involves large investments in training.
7. *Profit-sharing and performance-related pay.* The top management encourages greater employee involvement in company affairs by promoting share ownership and incentive payments related to results. (Taylor, 1988)

As will be evident from these quotations, strategic management is firmly based on strategic planning and requires all its disciplines and techniques, and yet it is something much more than strategic planning. Strategic management is a commitment to using strategy to drive the business. This means that managers are the planners, and planning staff are there to support them. Strategic management is a commitment to action, and, therefore, to giving authority down the line to those who must deliver results. Strategic management requires strategies to inform all parts of the company and to involve all parts of the company in the strategic-planning process so that strategies are owned by those who must deliver them. Strategic management is, above all, about leadership – in the involvement of people in generating and delivering strategies, in foreseeing and coping with problems, in seeking innovation and change relentlessly and in constantly renewing the vitality and success of the company.

A recent book by Ralph Stacey challenges the planning approach to

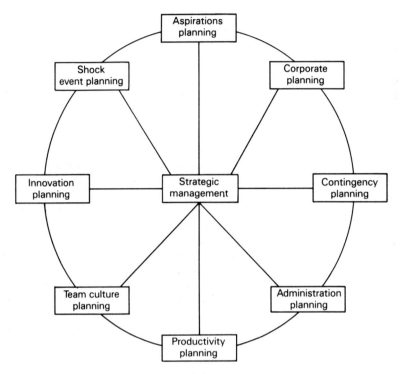

Figure 7.1   A total approach to planning strategic success

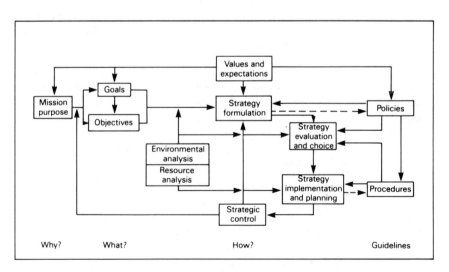

Figure 7.2   Integrated model of strategic management and
policy

strategic management and posits a game-playing approach, open to opportunism and reactive to challenge and change:

Strategic management in practice is a dynamic game and ability to play, ability to form multi-disciplined task forces is a major factor in success. Organisations which do not encourage experimentation, do not allow the emergence of task forces, do not develop managers capable of operating in this mode, are organisations which do not possess the flexibility required to play business games. And business games are realistic strategic management. (Stacey, 1990)

Stacey argues for the cultivation of short-interval control, based on rolling five-quarterly budgets, and the scrapping of long-term planning systems and procedures. He believes that the board has the role of 'strategic facilitation' – training and tasking people throughout the company to contribute to strategic management. A key part of that training must surely be the use of the strategic-planning system; the purpose of strategic planning is not so much to make plans as to take people through the process of strategic thinking. Without developing and using that skill, Stacey's dynamic strategic management will lack its basic fuel! More importantly, the board needs to set the strategic direction of the company, without which dynamic action down the line will be anarchic and unsustainable. With such strategic direction, many of Stacey's practical ideas enrich the fabric of strategic management.

7.2. The role of leadership in strategic management

Leadership in the context of the board has been discussed earlier in this book. Leadership in the context of strategic management is more akin to Burns's 'transforming leader' (Burns and Stalker, 1966) who transcends day-to-day management and focuses on the development of a new level of awareness among large numbers of people. Tom Peters in *A Passion for Excellence* sees leadership as the integrating factor in achieving excellence:

Leadership means vision, cheerleading, enthusiasm, love, trust, verve, passion, obsession, consistency, the use of symbols, paying attention as illustrated by the content of one's calendar, out-and-out charm (and the management thereof), creating heroes at all levels, coaching, effectively wandering around, and numerous other things. Leadership must be present at all levels of the organisation. It depends on a million little things done with obsession, consistency and care, but all of those million little things add up to nothing if the trust, vision and basic belief are not there. (Peters and Austin, 1985)

Leadership may take many different forms. Lord Weinstock of GEC sees his small HQ staff as a planning resource for the group. He does not require his operating companies to plan and controls them against budgets, capital proposals and a number of key ratios, including sales per pound of added value (productivity), profit to sales (margin) and sales to capital employed (turnover velocity). He uses his immense talents to push his operating companies to stretch their performance beyond the limits that they see to be possible. With an enormous grasp of detail he can comprehend the key issues facing all his businesses and spot the synergies between them. For him, strategy is largely an issue of maximising the returns on new technologies and shaping the future products of the group. Lord Weinstock almost seems to be able to run GEC single-handed and to have shaped the group in his own image much as Tiny Rowland has crafted Lonrho.

Leadership in conglomerate companies such as BTR and Hanson takes a different form. At the centre, the board is concerned to maximise shareholder return and, to do so, will acquire and dispose of businesses in the same manner as an investment manager buys or sells shares. Leadership takes the form of giving authority to the management of individual businesses to run them as they wish, subject to achieving negotiated targets. The rewards for achieving such targets are high; the penalties for failure are draconian. Businesses are subject to financial controls but their strategies are largely their own.

Some of the traits which are important for strategic management in all companies include the following:

1. Vision.
2. The ability to establish and nurture a corporate culture.
3. A commitment to total quality.
4. The ability to create and to give trust.
5. A commitment to change and innovation.
6. The ability to communicate and convince.
7. Total commitment to achieving results.

Let us examine these traits in more detail.

1. *Vision*

The Concise Oxford Dictionary defines vision as (inter alia) 'imaginative insight, statesmanlike foresight, political sagacity'. It is a faculty which is essential in business executives as much as in statesmen! Vision in one person is impressive; vision shared can be immensely powerful, as Mahatma Gandhi demonstrated earlier this century.

Strategic vision is defined by the Strategic Planning Society (1990) thus: 'A short succinct statement of what the organisation intends to be at some point in the future. This should embrace key areas of activity, geographical scope, size and shape, and distinctive competences. Vision acts as a filter for corporate options.'

Sir John Cuckney sees vision as a long-term unifying factor:

... apart from the corporate plan, the strategy and the mission statement you really do need to give some vision about the future of your company and a vision in which those working with you can share. You can usually tell an organisation that has a clear corporate plan but very little vision of the future. The lack of vision is reflected in the atmosphere among the staff and all the employees. (Ezra and Oates, 1989)

Anita Roddick (*ibid.*) criticises the retail industry for lack of vision: 'I have come across not one company which incorporates the pursuit of honest profits with social awareness, which provides a vision for themselves and their workers.' On the other hand Sir Adam Thomson (*ibid.*) had a clear vision for Caledonian Airways when it was launched: 'We had a grand design to develop a long-haul charter airline with the objective of gradually moving into scheduled services.'

The importance of shared vision cannot be overstated. By enthusing his staff to share his vision of punctuality and service, Jan Carlzon transformed SAS into a major force in business travel. Sir Colin Marshall achieved a similar renaissance at British Airways at much the same time, which is well described in *Managerial Leadership in the Post-Industrial Society* by Philip Sadler (1988). Vision was the unifying factor which enabled Boeing to transform itself from dependence on military business to world leadership in the civil airline market.

In the words of Lord King: 'Young men see visions; old men dream dreams. . . . It is the vision which generates the determination, and the dream which sustains the years of hard work.' (Ezra and Oates, 1989)

2. *Establishing and nurturing a corporate culture*
A corporate culture is the unifying force which makes a company distinctive. Its physical manifestations are the company logo, uniforms, and so on, but culture is more than image. It is a set of deeply held beliefs and values which come to be recognised by customers and others over time. The culture will include an attitude to customers, suppliers, local authorities, schools, and others, but it must have commitment to the longer term and to the use of strategic management to guide the company into the longer term.

3. *Total quality*
Commitment to total quality should be a key part of the corporate culture, referred to above. Quality is not an abstract concept; in practice it can be recognised where a product or service meets the requirements of the customer. The issue of total quality management is discussed in detail later in this section.

4. *Creating and giving trust*
Strategic management recognises that results can only be achieved by people who are committed to doing so. This commitment can only be achieved by involving employees in the strategic-planning process down the line and by harmonising their initiatives with the company's overall strategies. This requires openness about policies and strategies and a willingness to listen to people who are nearer the real problems and opportunities of

the business than the top management. Involving people in strategy, and empowering them to deliver mutually agreed targets, gives ownership to them of their strategies and creates mutual trust between employees and top management.

5. Commitment to change and innovation

Leadership requires a clear challenge in order to galvanise people into effective action. The biggest challenge facing most companies is change. Effective leadership does not just seek to accommodate change, it harnesses change as a motive force for improvement and innovation. Such commitment to change is a permanent spur to achieving improvement in results, internal renewal of the business and innovation in its products and services. It is laudable that at a time of recession, the board of Yale and Valor is protecting development expenditure and aiming its cost cutting at operational expenditure primarily.

6. Ability to communicate and convince

Leadership cannot operate in a vacuum. It requires a response in order to have an effect. This response comes through the ability to communicate effectively with all manner of people and to convince them that they should adopt the goals of the company. The effectiveness of Churchill's wartime speeches is now a legend; more recently the ability of Lee Iacocca to win support from the US Government, his suppliers and employees, and of many others was the basis of rescuing Chrysler from insolvency.

7. Total commitment to achieving results

Leadership needs to be obsessive, as we have seen. Cato the Elder ended his speeches in the Roman Senate for many years by calling for the destruction of Carthage (*delenda est Carthago*) until he achieved his objective. A modern obsessive leader is Warren Buffet of Berkshire Hathaway who runs the world's most successful investment trust. Far from seeing his company as an investor, Buffet behaves as an obsessive owner of part of the companies in which he invests. He seeks to exert influence on companies as an owner and is obsessive in accumulating capital and driving up his share price on behalf of his 'partners', the shareholders to whom he pays no dividends but whom he rewards with ever-growing wealth. If other investment managers behaved like obsessive owners, capitalism would be a lot healthier than it is today! If the employees in companies were to share ownership of their business and exercise that ownership to the full, the impact on the British economy would be revolutionary!

The role of leadership in strategic management is fundamental. The need is not so much for charisma and self-assertion; leadership has to be shared, propagated and sustained. A prime example of shared leadership, and not coincidentally of shared ownership, is the National Freight Corporation. When the opportunity came for Sir Peter Thompson and 10,300 employees and pensioners to buy the run-down and politically demoralised business, few outsiders believed that they could survive, let alone prosper. Yet within three years profits had quintupled and the unit share £100 invested had grown to £1240 in value. These profits had been achieved by empowering the workforce to use its professionalism to the full. Management takes great care to consult employees on key issues, to communicate the resultant strategies in detail and to bring as many employees as possible into share ownership. Ownership has now been widened further by the sale of a separate class of shares on the London Stock Exchange.

7.3.   Organising for strategic management

Organising for strategic management is not a once-for-all operation. Strategic management is both a firm and a flexible process; firm in its longer-term objectives, flexible in finding the best way to achieve them. This subtle combination of hardness and softness is characterised in the 'learning organisation', the detailed workings of which are demonstrated in the book of that name by Bob Garratt (1987). In principle a learning organisation is one which is continuously open to new ideas, continuously accumulates knowledge (not just information) and allows all its employees to grow themselves in the process. As will be seen later, a commitment to being a learning organisation involves constant effort and involvement but is, in modern times, the only way to achieve effective strategic management.

In the view of Tregoe and Zimmerman (1980) there are four key factors in organising for strategic management, as follows:

1. Getting the right people involved.
2. Having an effective process.
3. Knowing the end results to be achieved.
4. Getting the job done effectively.

1. Getting the right people involved
Tregoe sees the setting of strategy as the task of a relatively small group (typically eight to twelve). Exceptional people with special knowledge or 'high flyers' who can benefit from the experience are brought in to the process. A larger number of participants is believed to hinder rather than help the setting of strategy. A small, like-minded group is felt to help the chief executive to 'be comfortable enough to be candid'.

A key question is whether the board should be directly or indirectly involved in the setting of strategy. This has been discussed earlier and it should never be forgotten that the board is ultimately accountable to the shareholders for its stewardship. For the board to delegate responsibility for the strategic direction of the company would seem to be a risky act, if not a dereliction of duty. To leave the task solely to executive directors places the non-executive directors in the hands of their colleagues, since, at law, all directors are equally responsible for the conduct of the company's affairs and equally liable for the actions (or inactions) of the board. The involvement of the board should be the same for a strategically managed company as for one which is less strategically driven. As said earlier, the full involvement of the board in setting strategy is essential and the strategy committee of the board is a key instrument of strategic management.

Tregoe's approach of limiting the number of participants in the strategic process is inadequate. Equally the idea of 'comfort' for the chief executive is indulgent; strategic management is not a comfortable process, even though it needs wide support once the strategies have been hammered out into rough form. It is, however, true that a limited number of top managers have to give the company's strategy its final shape. Unless the widest involvement in crafting strategy is sought within the process, the ownership of the final strategy will be limited to those at the top who have no power to deliver it in detail. 'Bottom up' involvement must, therefore, be as complete as possible, even though the 'top down' framework will set the basic shape of the eventual strategy. Arie Nagel (1984) sees great benefit in the involvement of at least one outsider in the process in order to provide a critical perspective. The outsider might be a consultant; equally, the outside influence may be provided by the non-executive directors.

2. Having an effective process

A strategic management process is more comprehensive than a strategic planning process. It encompasses the strategic planning process which we have discussed earlier but involves more systematic feed-back and interaction. Feed-back is needed in order to adapt strategy to changes both in the external environment and within the company, and to adjust for performance against negotiated targets. An example of feed-back in the strategic management of technology at Goodyear is shown in Figure 7.3 (Lauglaug, 1987). This shows clearly that strategic management is a 'closed loop' system enabling results to feed back and modify the process of developing strategy. Few strategic-planning systems have the continuous feed-back and reassessment which is generic to strategic management.

The other generic feature is interaction. We have seen how line managers interact in developing 'bottom up' plans. This interaction is important in communicating plans and in transmitting strategic actions and project activity down through the business. Arie Nagel (1984) shows a model of interlocking working groups as a key instrument of strategic management, particularly in medium-sized firms or divisions of larger companies (see Figure 7.4). These structures are not permanent and will change as projects are completed or working groups are restructured. Groups should change at random intervals to enable success to be rewarded by promotion (or the reverse), and to ensure that they cannot become ossified. Strategic management is a structured process, but must not be allowed to become bureaucratic. Hence the importance of putting line managers in charge of the

Strategy   Implementation

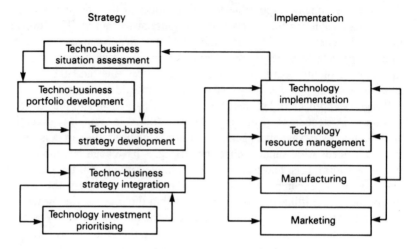

Figure 7.3   Strategic management of technology process

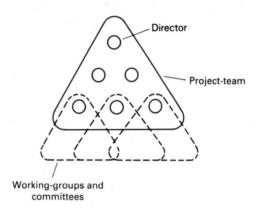

Figure 7.4   The linking pin idea applied to organising strategic
                management in medium-sized firms

process at all levels. Planning staff are involved as 'facilitators', to provide
support, information and guidance, but not to make decisions. Planning
staff need to make a conscious effort to keep the process open to participants
and to demystify any systems, procedures or techniques employed.

Procedures in strategic management should be kept simple but be
followed carefully. Simplicity helps the process to run purposefully, since
the objectives are not obscured or confused by systems issues. Procedures
need to be followed carefully since the process depends on quick and
effective interaction between a considerable number of people. In the same
way that discipline is needed to avoid chaos on the roads, 'the highway code'
of strategic management has to be carefully observed. A conceptual

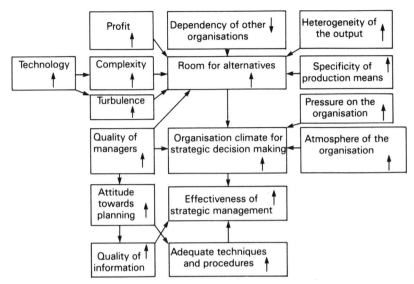

Figure 7.5 A conceptual framework for determining the
effectiveness of strategic management
(↑ = higher/better; ↓ = lower/worse)

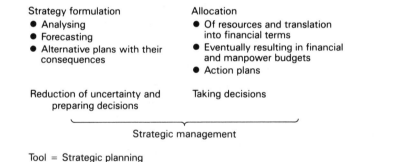

Figure 7.6 The elements of strategic management

framework for assessing the effectiveness of strategic management is shown
in Figures 7.5 and 7.6. (Nagel, 1984)

3. Knowing the end results to be achieved
Despite every effort to keep the strategic management process open and
simple, the numbers of people involved and the mass of detailed information
to be handled and absorbed make it inevitable that concern about the means
will tend to obscure the ends of the process. It is, therefore, critical to distil
the objectives sought into a clear statement and to keep this constantly in
front of all employees. It is also critical to break down the overall objectives

and establish key action plans to achieve the parts which will deliver the whole. This means that all involved must have a shared understanding of the objectives and of the strategies to achieve them, and be committed to them both. For an international company this requires that the remotest unit is fully involved in the process and fully aware of its place in the total pattern. Communications are crucial for achieving this and these have to be sustained as the process of strategic management moves through its phase of implementation. Feedback from the remoter units may be of great importance to sustaining the process and to making adjustments to the key strategies. Although these may need to change, the end results targeted must remain steady and clear to all involved. Budgets should reflect the goals set in the strategic management system and not be, as is so often the case, a separate, financially driven empire.

4.   *Getting the job done effectively*
Strategic management is a process for making current decisions, allocating resources and steering a company in the light of longer term needs. It is a management process not just a planning process. It is the basic working tool of line management and all other processes, procedures and systems are subordinated to it.

In organising for strategic management it is important that the role of the process as the main executive instrument of the company is recognised by all. This requires positive and sustained support from top management for using the process and their active involvement in both its planning and implementation cycles. Strategic management should subsume the budgeting process so that there is no confusion about the job to be done. Reward systems should be carefully attuned to the targets set by strategic management so that the importance of achieving results is emphasised both positively and, if need be, negatively.

'Getting the job done effectively' is monitored by key action plans, controlling projects by milestones and by strategic controls. Strategic controls are discussed in detail in Section 7.4.

An interesting example of the use of the strategic management process in a smaller company is the 1992 Working Party set up by Triplex Lloyd to shape and implement its European strategy. This working party was able not only to develop strategy, but also to involve employees at all levels and to unlock skills in languages and European experience which could be used to train others and to deliver the strategy. (Sharp, 1990)

7.4.   Establishing ownership of strategies and responsibility for achieving goals

Strategic management's purpose is to achieve results on a sustainable basis. To do so, it is essential to commit those who have to achieve results to perform effectively and to maintain that performance. Ownership of the planned goals and of the strategies to achieve them is the key to success.

The importance of ownership is increasingly becoming recognised. It is a major theme of *A Passion for Excellence* by Peters and Austin (1985), in which a wide range of examples is quoted. The Dana Corporation was revived by Rea McPherson on the principle 'turn the company back over to the people who do the work'. This was done by decentralising operations out to individual factories so that all functions were under the control of the factory manager. H. H. Robertson, the UK steel-cladding manufacturer, gives ownership by creating 'ginger groups' to tackle problems and opportunities which cut right across the formal organisation structure. At an extreme is the practice of Tupperware of holding sales rallies at which the top salespersons for the week are invited to sign their names on a blackboard in front of their peers.

Ownership may, of course, be achieved by handing the company to the staff. The John Lewis Partnership has prospered for many years on the basis of shared ownership. National Freight Corporation has been mentioned earlier and the recent spate of 'buy-outs' and 'buy-ins' has been motivated by the prospect of ownership, even if many such companies then convert ownership into capital gain by selling out to a major corporation subsequently.

Legal ownership of the company is not, therefore, the most compelling motivator. The history of workers' co-operatives is not entirely positive, and yet the need for individual recognition is important in all organisations whatever their legal status. Ownership in this sense is about recognition; even more it is about trust.

The impact of trust is well illustrated by a Japanese example from a US consultant quoted by Peters and Austin:

'In the US if ten people submit proposals and you only have funding for five, what you usually do is fund all ten at fifty percent of what was asked. So when a problem arrives, the fellow can lay it on the higher-ups: "They only gave us half of what we wanted". In Japan, they'd say no to five groups and yes to five groups. Then the five yes groups have got a problem: They got what they asked for. Now they've got to deliver.' (Peters and Austin, 1985)

The power of ownership is enormous. The old adage, 'a volunteer is worth two pressed men', is a significant understatement. Given trust and the resources to perform, I have found that employees down the line will commit themselves to targets more challenging than their supervisors would ever ask them to attempt and, since they have total ownership, will move heaven and earth to achieve them.

The essential concomitant of ownership, in order to achieve results, is power. The classical management dilemma of balancing responsibility with the requisite amount of authority needs to be solved if strategic management is to be effective. Participation in management does not mean that structure and power can be abandoned, as demonstrated by Erich Fromm in *Escape from Freedom*, where people who are given freedoms they cannot cope with slide into neurotic behaviour. Participation requires empowerment in order to be successful and such success can lead to remarkable results, as Rosabeth Moss Kanter (1989) shows in the story of Chestnut Ridge. This begins with a middle manager setting up a team to tackle production problems in the Chestnut Ridge factory of Chipco Inc., which led to a whole series of such teams and eventually the adoption by management of the use of teams for innovation. Initially, power had to be fought for, but it was won progressively until the teams became a permanent part of the structure. People-empowerment was critical for the success of David Clair's restructuring and rebuilding of Essochem Europe in the early 1980s.

In *Shaping the Corporate Future* Kevin Barham and Clive Rassam (1989) interviewed a number of managers from companies of different nationality. There emerges a disquieting question mark over the attitude of British managers to responsibility. Some Scandinavians felt that British managers were not used to taking responsibility; they expected to be given it. A senior French manager of Accor is quoted:

The British managers we have say they like our approach. It is very different at first for the British managers who join us, if they have come from a British company with different ways of managing. They usually come from our U.K. competitors and are not used to delegation and taking responsibility. It is a challenge for them. They have to forget one part of their habits. They must take decisions and take responsibility for them. When you explain to British managers that they must take responsibility, then they are very happy. Soon, they come to like our approach and then they bring new ideas. (Barham and Rassam, 1989)

Barham and Rassam are concerned that some UK head offices, fearful of change, are holding back managers down the line. A survey by Ashridge and Cranfield Management Colleges is quoted, which showed that many young managers in large organisations are keener to run their own businesses than to stay with their existing companies. Many of these managers are the rising stars needed to help their companies forge ahead into the future.

Mention has just been made of the influence of head offices on the operations of larger companies. It is by no means always as baleful as Barham and Rassam have suggested, but the danger of a negative influence has to be recognised and avoided. The role of the centre has been the subject of considerable study in recent years, not least by the Ashridge Strategic Management Centre. This role is named 'strategic control' and has three basic elements, as follows:

1. Agreeing objectives (ensuring that operating units have ownership and authority).
2. Monitoring results.
3. Incentives, sanctions, intervention.

Tensions	Strategic planning	Strategic control	Financial control
Organisation structure	Multiple perspectives	Separate responsibilities	Separate responsibilities
Planning process	Thorough review	Thorough review	Entrepreneurial response
Central leadership	Strong leadership	Business autonomy	Business autonomy
Objective setting	Strategic and financial	Strategic and financial	Financial
Nature of control	Flexible	Tight	Tight

Figure 7.7 Styles and tensions

Tensions	Ways of mitigating tensions
Organisation structure	• Businesses defined to encompass key points of competitive leverage (SBUs) • Businesses that need co-ordination structured into divisional groupings
Planning process	• Well-designed process
Central leadership	• Advice not instructions • Broad, unconstraining themes • Understanding the businesses
Objective setting	• Understanding the businesses • Slow rotation of managers • Short-term constraints, long-term objectives
Nature of control	• Broad goals • Manage upside/downside asymmetry • Growth expectation • Well-designed strategic planning process

Figure 7.8 Managing tensions

In developing this concept of strategic control, Michael Goold and Andrew Campbell (1988) identified three parenting styles, depending on the balance of planning influence and short-term profit needs (see Figures 7.7 and 7.8).

1. *Financial control*

This parenting style stresses short-term profitability objectives. Strategy is highly delegated and operating-company management is given clear personal responsibility for achieving profit targets. Control is not really strategic. Rewards and sanctions are totally linked to profit targets. Typical 'financial control' companies include BTR, GEC, Hanson and Tarmac.

2. *Strategic control*
This parenting style requires a strategic control process to monitor progress
towards financial and strategic goals. Monitoring is through shorter-term
programmes and through the use of milestones to measure progress towards
implementing strategies. Incentives, sanctions and central intervention are
all based on both financial and strategic criteria which are mutually agreed.
As much initiative as possible within the agreed strategic framework is left
to business-unit managers. Courtaulds, ICI and Vickers are typical 'strategic
control' companies.

3. *Strategic planning*
This parenting style also requires a strategic-control process but this is
complemented by a demanding strategic-planning process. Corporate management seeks involvement in the development of business unit strategies,
but is likely to set more flexible performance targets provided long-term
strategies remain on course. BP, BOC, Cadbury Schweppes, Lex, STC and
United Biscuits are typical 'strategic planning' companies.

It has to be open to question whether the corporate centre can realistically
add value to the planning process of its operating units. In a perceptive
article 'Strategic plans as contracts', Yvan Allaire and Mihaela Firsirotu
(1990) see strategic plans as contracts between 'agents' (the heads of SBU's)
and 'principals' (the corporate centre). They identify a basic weakness in
the contract in that the agent will have more detailed knowledge of his
business than the principal. This can lead to dangerous suboptimisation,
and has often been countered by the build-up of corporate planning staff to
bolster the contracting capability of the principal. The planning history of
GE is examined to show how 'culture-driven' planning (based on shared
values and goals), 'numbers-driven' planning and 'staff-driven' planning all
failed to produce adequate and sustainable results. When Jack Welch
became CEO in 1981, he heavily reduced the planning bureaucracy and
installed 'line-driven' planning. To restore balance, Welch has developed
a number of sector executives at the centre and is seeking to inculcate
generic values and policies in all SBU's. Line-driven planning is essential
for strategic management and better means of establishing effective
contracts with the centre will have to be found. Failure to understand what
was really happening in parts of Philips led the CEO, Cor van der Klugt,
to indicate satisfactory first-quarter earnings for 1990. In the event, the
outcome was a fall of $97 million and early retirement for Mr. van der
Klugt.
    The importance of strategic controls in increasingly being recognised by
companies of all sizes and complexity of structure. Work in this area done
by the Ashridge Strategic Management Centre has recently been consolidated in a new book, *Strategic Control* (Goold and Quinn, 1990).

7.5. Driving through strategies with sensitivity and flexibility

We saw earlier the importance of corporate culture as an unifying force within a company and with its external stakeholders. Roger Harrison (Handy, 1985) identifies four kinds of organisational culture – power, role, achievement and support. The power culture is authoritarian and hierarchical; the role or bureaucratic culture is also hierarchical but power is exercised through rules, systems and procedures. Most companies have discarded, or are discarding such cultures, as they are not effective in the modern world. An achievement culture seeks 'to make a difference in the world', and emphasises action, autonomy, innovation and the shaping of our environment. It is, however, very demanding and few can sustain it. A support culture works through relationships, creating trust and mutual support. A combination of achievement and support cultures can be very effective; for example, effective customer care can enhance profitability. The combination also allows a variety of personalities to find meaningful roles in the pursuit of the company's business and to work effectively together in teams. Such a corporate culture is essential if strategies are to be driven through to a successful conclusion in all parts of the company.

Success also depends on communicating the strategies effectively to all parts of the company. This is not a matter of talking, but requires careful preparation and interaction with a live audience. Many chief executives send video films to all parts of their company as their means of communication. Video communication avoids distortion of the message but cannot be effective in isolation. True communication requires interaction to carry conviction. JCB, for instance, uses workshops, briefing groups and notice boards to communicate news within the company. Interactive communication requires openness, which is a key quality needed to win support for company strategies. There are, of course, some few situations in which openness may be difficult. Strategies requiring takeover or disposal, for instance, need to be communicated with discretion until regulatory constraints have passed. Strategies which are competitively sensitive may also need care and good timing in their communication. These are limited exceptions to the need for openness and effective communication. An excellent example of effective communications linked to focused task groups is the process of launching Abbey National plc in 1989.

Reference was made in Section 7.2. to the concept of quality. The value of quality was first realised when the Japanese concept of 'quality circles' was tried in Anglo-Saxon companies and found to be a powerful motivation towards improving work practices. Out of this advance has grown the concept of 'total quality management' which John Oakland (1989) sees as 'a method for ridding people's lives of wasted effort by involving everyone in the processes of improvement; improving the effectiveness of work so that results are achieved in less time'. Quality is defined by the customer, who may be external but for many departments will be an internal customer.

A quality policy quoted by Oakland is succinct but comprehensive, as follows:

Total quality is meeting customers' requirements:
  both external and internal
  for all products and services
  all the time
This requires:
  total involvement of all employees
  total management commitment
  customer and supplier working together
  objectives, standards and systems which conform to the commitment to total quality
It is achieved by:
  conforming to requirements
  prevention not detection
  getting it right first time
  measuring quality, performance (including costs)
  Total quality is to be a permanent feature of the company's life. It will be implemented, monitored, nurtured and maintained by having an ongoing quality improvement programme. (Oakland, 1989)

Total quality management (TQM) involves a sustained process of seeking improvement in design, manufacture, distribution and all parts of the business with a view to maximising customer satisfaction. The customer is not just the user of the product; every internal department needs to identify its internal customers and negotiate with them the improvements they require in service and cost. TQM is normally launched by workshop sessions, which continue at intervals to provide training and new impetus to the process. Much of the detailed work is done by interdepartmental and intersectional teams which are formed and reformed as needed. The key to the effectiveness of TQM is to change the attitudes and habits of individuals, so that the search for improvement becomes a personal drive, and the use of teams is the mechanism for distributing the benefit of that individual drive.

John Oakland quotes Bill Conway, an American TQM guru, whose six tools for quality improvement are the following:

1. Human relations skills – the responsibility of management to create at every level, among all employees, the motivation and training to make the necessary improvements in the organisation.
2. Statistical surveys – the gathering of data about customers (internal as well as external), employees, technology, and equipment, to be used as a measure for future progress and to identify what needs to be done.
3. Simple statistical techniques – clear charts and diagrams that help identify problems, track work flow, gauge progress, and indicate solutions.
4. Statistical process control – the statistical charting of a process, whether

manufacturing or non-manufacturing, to help identify and reduce variation.

5. Imagineering – a key concept in problem solving, involves the visualisation of a process, procedure, or operation with all waste eliminated.

6. Industrial engineering – common techniques of pacing, work simplification, methods analysis, plant layout, and material handling to achieve improvements.

Many total quality programmes have been installed on a faddish basis and some have not survived the departure of their sponsoring chief executive. This is to be regretted, since there is a considerable synergy between total quality and 'bottom up' strategic planning. Total quality programmes provide a good deal of motivation and generate useful ideas for improvements and innovation; the 'bottom up' dimension of strategic planning provides a systematic cyclical mechanism for bringing the more strategic parts of this treasure to the surface to embellish the corporate plan. The discipline of planning helps to sustain total quality programmes while the latter reach people who would not normally contribute to the 'bottom up' planning cycle and whose contribution can only enrich the process.

Driving through strategies requires not only the optimum use of the company's own resources but a creative search for extra resources where these are needed. The usual way of bringing extra resources in support of strategies is to acquire them by recruitment, by mergers and by seeking fresh funds through loans or the issue of further equity. Where resources are needed in the longer term or where they form part of the core competence of the company, this makes strategic sense. Where resources are not needed permanently, or where the company cannot afford to acquire them without prejudice to its long-term health, it makes better sense to make more flexible arrangements.

Such flexible arrangements for staffing include, of course, the use of part-time employees and the use of consultants, and for temporary staff to handle special projects and short-term overloads. Most businesses now staff themselves to meet an average level of activity and will face increasing difficulty even to maintain such levels in the face of demographic change. As mentioned earlier, Charles Handy (1988) sees an employment pattern in 2000 where full-time employees will be some twelve million (four million less than today) and a similar number of self-employed and part-time contractors will meet the balance of demand. Demographically, there will be more older people and some 70 per cent of all jobs will require knowledge skills. Companies will need to improve their ability to use labour flexibly and to retain their core of employees constantly to increase productivity.

Flexible use of assets will probably see an increase in leasing rather than ownership, since that avoids tying up capital and being responsible for maintenance and repair. The ownership of property is another area where new thinking will be needed. Many older companies have acquired property over the years and some see property ownership as an earnest of their solidity (e.g. the joint-stock banks). Strategic management is concerned with achieving results, not with managing peripheral activities. Where property ownership is germane to the company mission, it will have specific strategies which merit close management; where the ownership of property does not contribute to the core activity, and may obstruct and/or obscure progress with the company's key strategies, its justification is difficult to find.

A key dimension of flexible resource allocation is alliance-building. This is not only an alternative to acquisition in many instances but is a strategy in its own right. Even IBM uses alliances in countries like South Korea where it is the only option for entry. Alliances take many forms, some of which are illustrated in Figure 7.9 (James, 1985). From this it can be seen that alliances are very flexible and can be adapted to meet a variety of needs. Alliances can also be extended as companies find it advantageous to do so; for example, the growing relationship between Rover and Honda. Alliances are invaluable for entry into difficult markets, for the acquisition and control of technology, for improving competitiveness (e.g. The SPAR buying consortium) and to enable businesses to co-operate across frontiers (e.g. the Airbus Industrie consortium). Alliances are frequently made for specific bids in the construction and contracting industries. Tactical alliances are also often made, such as, for example, the shops within shops in the high street. And alliances are a key strategy for smaller companies; for example, Autographics Software (Northern Ireland) uses British Thornton to develop its market in Great Britain.

Alliances depend on a balance of interest between the parties. Where this balance is eroded, or where the circumstances which favoured the relationship are lost, the alliance is likely to break up. Multiple alliances, such as those in the defence industry to produce aircraft, are notoriously difficult to control and decision-making is slow to achieve. Great sensitivity and much hard work are needed to make alliances succeed. Where they are used creatively they can produce remarkable results; the success of Glaxo is largely built on a network of alliances.

Attitudes to alliances among management advisers vary considerably. Michael Porter (1990 a, b) believes that most alliances hinder the ability of their members to compete effectively, leading to mediocrity rather than market leadership. Kenichi Ohmae (1989) disagrees: 'Alliances are not tools of convenience. They are important, even critical, instruments of serving customers in a global environment.' Gary Hamel *et al.* (1989) strongly favour collaboration: 'Competitive renewal depends on building new process capabilities and winning new product and technology battles. Collaboration can be a low-cost strategy for doing both.'

As companies increasingly need to operate on a global scale, the cost of doing so will inhibit all but the largest. This has led to networks of co-operation in the automotive, telecommunications, aero-engine and other

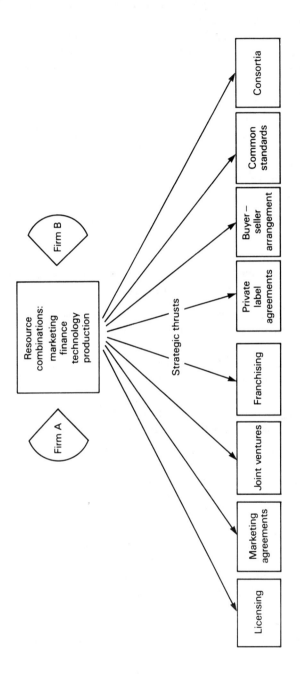

Figure 7.9 Basic alliance strategies

industries. Some of these became mergers or are cemented by cross-shareholdings such as those which typify Japanese and German industry. To be really strategic it is likely that alliances will evolve into mergers. Carlo de Benedetti contrasts living with a girlfriend and with a wife. Living with the girlfriend is easier but is not a good relationship in which to produce children.

Driving through strategies requires the support and active contribution of many people both inside and outside the company. It also requires a creative allocation of resources, and the intelligent use of the resources of others where there is mutual interest. Sensitivity is required, not only in dealing with independent parties but also in harnessing the co-operation of the company's staff. Flexibility is a crucial quality in the face of new operating conditions and increasingly competitive markets. Strategies will have to become increasingly flexible; goals will need to be sustained despite all difficulties.

7.6. The learning company and the growth of successful managers

We looked earlier at the concept of the 'learning organisation'. This embraces both the idea that an organisation should be seeking to renew itself through change and acquiring new knowledge, and the concept of the 'learning curve' whereby improved effectiveness is achieved over time through acquired experience of existing activities. The basis of the learning organisation is a sustained search for ongoing improvement and the regeneration needed to carry the process forward. This regeneration is dependent on skilful selection of key staff, a personalised programme of career development and effective succession policies. This is not a luxury reserved for large organisations; smaller companies such as Williams Lea, the printing group, are pioneers in management development.

The context in which managers are operating is changing rapidly. The external environment is increasingly turbulent and unpredictable, and the pace of change is being forced by international competition. In the words of a Deutsche Bank executive: 'The Japanese aim to design and market new products in half the time, with half the staff, at a quarter of the cost required today.' The pressure of environmental issues will also grow and complicate the task of management. To be effective managers will need to see their business holistically and be effective integrated business thinkers. This requires the breakdown of restrictive internal structures and greater flexibility in working. Key staff will have to be encouraged to take responsibility early in their careers and be given the support and recognition needed to retain their services. Managers will be all-rounders, with a variety of skills which are constantly rehoned or replaced to enable their performance to remain effective.

The obstacles to success are typified as follows in Rosabeth Moss Kanter's Rules for Stifling Innovation:

1. Regard any new idea from below with suspicion – because it's new and because it's from below.
2. Insist that people who need your approval to act first go through several other levels of management to get their signatures.
3. Ask departments or individuals to challenge and criticise each other's proposals (that saves you the job of deciding; you just pick the survivor).
4. Express your criticisms freely, and withhold your praise. (That keeps people on their toes). Let them know they can be fired at any time.
5. Treat identification of problems as signs of failure, to discourage people from letting you know when something in their area isn't working.
6. Control everything carefully. Make sure people count everything that can be counted, frequently.
7. Make decisions to reorganise or change policies in secret, and spring them on people unexpectedly. (That also keeps people on their toes).
8. Make sure that requests for information are fully justified, and make sure that it is not given out to managers freely. (You don't want data to fall into the wrong hands).
9. Assign to lower-level managers, in the name of delegation and participation, responsibility for figuring out how to cut back, lay off, move people around, or otherwise implement threatening decisions you have made. And get them to do it quickly.
10. And above all, never forget that you, the higher-ups, already know everything important about this business. (Kanter, 1989)

Given such politically driven bureaucracy, how does a company create conditions in which managers can grow? One approach to this issue has been to establish projects outside the formal hierarchy and structure of the business. Dupont was a pioneer of this approach and the IBM PC computer was developed in such a manner. This approach has been developed into 'intrapreneurship' – the idea of establishing entrepreneurs within the framework of a large or medium-sized company, rather than running their own independent businesses. The workings of intrapreneurship are closely examined in an article by Wesley Morse (1986), 'The delusion of intrapreneurship'. It emerges that the key motivators of entrepreneurs are the expectation of wealth and the need for personal autonomy. Few corporate reward structures presently allow employees to become 'seriously wealthy', neither in terms of earnings nor, more significantly, in capital appreciation. Phyllip Hwang of Tele Video Systems became $610 million richer when his company went public. The need for personal autonomy clashes directly with most corporate cultures, with the few exceptions, such as 3M and Hewlett Packard, proving the rule. In most cases even successful projects lead to disillusionment and the loss of the team which fought to achieve their success (e.g. The Data General 'Eagle' project).

If intrapreneurship is not the ideal model for developing future managers for larger and medium-sized companies, how can such companies best grow their future management? I believe that three factors are essential for success in this endeavour:

1. The need for harmony between the ambitions of the company and its developing managers.
2. Full exploitation of the learning process.
3. Creation and sustainment of a culture of change.

1. *Harmonising ambitions*

The differing agendas of management and its aspiring younger staff create misunderstanding and difficulties in the longer run. To accept totally the agenda of intrapreneurs creates problems as we have seen, since many of their peers will envy them and reject them, even if they achieve something in the shorter term for the company. It is necessary for the company to make its agenda known to all, and to encourage all who can to contribute to that agenda. Staff should be given space in which to grow their talents, and the resources and encouragement to do so, but need to relate their endeavours to the company agenda, which they should be able to influence if their arguments are cogent and timely. It may be significant that United Technologies believes that the managers of many overseas subsidiaries are 'shadow executives' and that failure both to listen to them and to allow them freedom to perform may be a future source of weakness in key markets.

2. *Learning*

Colin Carnall (1986) identifies the following five attributes of learning:

*   Learning is produced by exploring dilemmas or contradictions (to find new insights which can be exploited).
*   Learning is based on personal experience and experimentation. (People will only learn if they understand the problems and are brought into the process of seeking solutions).
*   Learning can be encouraged in a climate which encourages risk-taking, doing things, trying out new ideas.
*   Learning requires the expression of deeply held beliefs and will involve conflict. Only then can ideas emerge and be properly assessed before being incorporated into new systems, products, strategies, etc.
*   Learning can be helped by recognising the value of people and ideas. This involves developing learning styles which encourage individuals rather than close off discussion and creativity.

Learning is largely a personal process but, by being shared, it is possible for it to affect fundamentally the culture, capacity and effectiveness of organisations.

3. *A culture of change*

A culture of change recognises the reality of external discontinuity and competitive pressure and seeks to harness change to achieve long-term benefit for the company. Change appeals to the more vigorous and creative managers of the company and gives them the opportunity to learn and to grow. A culture of change requires that managers continue to perform and do not live on yesterday's glory. A culture of change generates the new ventures which are the real equivalent of entrepreneurial challenge. A company which can create and sustain a culture of change will attract, grow and retain the best managers and equip itself to compete in larger and more competitive markets with continuing success.

I have invited the views of Philip Sadler, lately Chief Executive of Ashridge Management College on this critical issue. He has kindly contributed a paper reflecting his considerable experience and insights, which constitutes Appendix 6.

7.7. Internal renewal and the perpetuation of success

We have examined the role of learning and of growing successful managers in ensuring the ongoing prosperity of the company, which is the long-term objective of strategic management. These are key parts of the process of internal renewal which is organically imperative for the long-term survival of the business.

Internal renewal is a process which combats the obsolescence, waste and decline which threaten every organisation. The corporate renewal cycle is typified by Bruce Lloyd in the following steps:

1. exploit the first specialisation
2. identify the point where the first specialisation is beginning to become deficient
3. identify a second specialisation for which there is a demand and for which the specialist knowledge and experience developed in step 1) could be appropriate
4. transfer from the old specialisation to the new, without ending up as a diversified group that has no specific skills
5. exploit the second specialisation. (Lloyd, 1989)

This simplified picture does not consider the wider implications of the process. For example, should the first business be sold or continue to be exploited; should the first business be shaken up and repositioned, and so on. It does, however, encapsulate the principle of creative change which is at the heart of the renewal process. Bruce Lloyd is one of the most perceptive writers in the area of innovation, entrepreneurship and corporate renewal.

Internal renewal is both a developmental and, for some companies, a recovery process. In both cases it is based on innovation though the mechanics will differ significantly. When Rosabeth Moss Kanter calls for an

'American corporate renaissance', she starts from the premise that US industry is not adequately competitive. Nor is it necessarily the older firms which lag – Proctor and Gamble are pioneers in team-oriented manufacturing. Nevertheless, renewal left too late becomes recovery.

In his book *Corporate Recovery*, Dr Stuart Slatter (1987) deals with the crisis and recovery strategies needed to turn firms from decline towards sustainable recovery. He defines 'sustainable recovery' as the development of sustainable competitive advantage in terms of economic factors (e.g. cost advantages in materials, labour or knowhow, or due to economies of scale or product differentiation), organisational factors (e.g. quality and expertise of management and effective implementation of sound strategies) and political and legal factors (e.g. government preference for national suppliers). It is a matter of fine judgement whether a company can recover from decline or whether it should be placed in receivership. The introduction of the concept of administration as a step short of receivership reflects both positive US experience and the experience that insolvent businesses are not necessarily irrecoverable. Dr Slatter shows evidence that, even after three to six years of declining earnings, over 20 per cent of firms were able to effect recovery.

The causes of corporate decline include lack of control, inadequate management, competition, high cost structure, problems with large projects and acquisitions, and poor financial policy. Dr Slatter identifies an ineffective board as a significant cause of decline since planning, resource allocation and control decisions are poorly made. He points to the following reasons for ineffectiveness (and consequent decline):

1. Non-executive directors who do not participate.
2. Executive directors who participate only when discussion directly touches their area of responsibility or expertise.
3. An unbalanced board, e.g. all engineers, not sufficient non-executive directors.
4. Lack of communication among board members, especially where there is a lack of consensus about company objectives.

Dr Slatter refers to research showing that companies whose boards have a high degree of consensus about objectives outperform companies where consensus does not exist. This may seem self-evident but it reveals a deeper truth that such boards are likely to work harder at clarifying and revalidating their long-term objectives and are thereby stimulating the process of internal renewal. This is the ultimate stewardship of the board of directors since it is the key to long-term prosperity over many centuries, which only a relatively few companies like Stora Kopparbergs, St Gobain, Hudsons Bay Company and Dupont have been able to achieve.

Developmental internal renewal is the process by which corporations realise their potential for vigorous and useful longevity. The President of Texas Instruments, P. E. Haggerty, states:

'We are convinced that corporate self-renewal begins with innovation, and that both useful products and services and long-term profitability are the result of innovation and that, as a matter of fact, profitability at a level above the bare fee for the use of assets results only from the innovation advantage and disappears as soon as the innovation has become routine'. (Haggerty, 1980)

Innovation to Haggerty means technological, manufacturing and marketing innovation combined; failure in any one aspect damages competitive advantage. Corporate renewal is, however, more than a systematic culture of innovation. It requires the company to be alert to changes in the external environment, which may threaten it or provide opportunities for profitable development. It requires a culture which is open to ideas and constructive criticism from all parts of the organisation, and which seeks to stimulate the learning process and to encourage people to grow in knowledge, experience and confidence. The company matures and develops the trust of generations of customers, but the people who animate the company are perpetually renewed and rejuvenating its activities and the products and services offered. This is a parallel to John Gardner's model in his book *Self Renewal*:

Every individual, organisation or society must mature, but much depends on how this maturing takes place. A society whose maturing consists simply of acquiring more firmly established ways of doing things is headed for the graveyard – even if it learns to do these things with greater and greater skill. In the ever-renewing society what matures is a system or framework within which continuous innovation, renewal and rebirth can occur. (Gardner, 1983b)

8

THE STRATEGIC ROLE OF THE BOARD IN THE 1990s AND BEYOND

8.1. Issues for the 1990s and beyond

A strategic planner is not a futurist, although he must evaluate the visions of futurists and build those that are significant into his scenarios. A planner needs to analyse trends and spot discontinuities; above all he needs to identify the issues which are likely to shape the future environment in which his business must operate and prosper.

The megatrends identified by John Naisbitt are as follows:

1. Industrial Society moving to Information Society
2. Forced Technology moving to High Tech/High Touch (i.e. human response)
3. National Economy moving to World Economy
4. Short Term moving to Long Term
5. Centralisation moving to Decentralisation
6. Institutional Help moving to Self Help
7. Representative Democracy moving to Participatory Democracy
8. Hierarchies moving to Networking
9. North moving South (a symbol of migrations elsewhere in the world; in Italy, South moving North!)
10. Either/or moving to Multiple Options. (Naisbitt, 1984)

These trends remain valid; we might add some (e.g. Marxism moving to capitalism), but they show the direction of change clearly enough.

The megaissues likely to face us as we approach the year 2000 include:

- Environmental protection versus growth.
- Coping with the breakdown of Marxist economies.
- The development of a wider Europe, with trading blocs in America and the Far East.
- The war against crime and drugs.
- Demographic changes in key economies.
- The growth of leisure in key economies.
- Increasing longevity in most countries, particularly Japan.
- The growth of religious intolerance.

- Growing difficulties with water provision in many countries.
- Replacing and developing infrastructure and transport equipment.
- Competition and deregulation versus protectionism (greater or lesser role of government).
- Future sources of power.
- Health care and the control of disease.
- Education.
- Morality.

Attaching to and derived from these megaissues are the specific issues facing the individual business. Enormous business opportunities are perceived in the opening of Eastern Europe, but so were they perceived with the opening of China a decade ago. *Plus ça change, plus c'est la même chose!*

Although most issues will relate to individual businesses, there are some business issues which are likely to affect a large number of companies. These include:

1. Globalisation.
2. Effective control.
3. Reactivity.
4. Ownership.
5. Product life cycle.
6. Customisation.
7. Motivating staff.
8. Education.
9. The role of the board.

We shall look briefly at each of these issues; the role of the board will be considered in more detail later.

1. *Globalisation*

The concept of globalisation has developed out of the teachings of Michael Porter, Kenichi Ohmae and others, and is increasingly recognised by businesses of all sizes. While General Motors is an obvious world-scale company, there are global-niche players like Alfred Dunhill, which have significant world-market shares. With the breakdown of barriers to trade this process is accelerating. Kenichi Ohmae sees the future development of 'the triad', a system of three major trading blocs based on Europe, the Americas and the Far East. If the triad rebuilds protectionist walls, we shall all lose; at best there are likely to be zones of influence for Europe, United States and Japan which will complicate the pattern of globalisation. Managing global companies will become increasingly difficult, as shown in *Managing Across Borders* by Bartlett and Ghoshal (1990). Local subsidiaries need powerful local managers and the difficulty of cross-fertilising ideas between subsidiaries is considerable. Successful companies like Philips and Ericsson give world-product leadership to particular subsidiaries which encourages both competitiveness and co-operation. The concept of global products is, however, very suspect. Few products are truly global in nature and competitive pressures will make local tastes a continuing major factor in design and marketing.

2. Effective control

Under growing pressure from change and with the increasing complexity of modern operations, the difficulty of maintaining effective control of a company will increase considerably. The growing plethora of task groups, skunk works, project teams and other *ad hoc* reactions to pressures on the company will need to be kept within a frame work of systems and procedures to retain control. Information technology will assist the process but it will need effective managers in key parts of the company to balance the leaders who are driving change. Warren Bennis sees leaders as challenging the status quo, managers as accepting it and as preventing change and complexity from degenerating into chaos. The board will need to oversee this process carefully in order to retain effective control.

3. Reactivity

I believe that suppliers to Ford Motor Company have to answer the telephone after no more than three rings or their contracts are at risk. Customers are demanding even higher levels of service from their suppliers and competitor pressure also makes reactivity crucial. Companies are now geared up to match competitors' new products in weeks, when previously they needed several months. The design-to-production cycles of new vehicles are down from five years to eighteen months and shrinking. Paris fashions can be pirated by mass production 'sweat shops' within a few days.

The need to be competitively reactive is going to become increasingly important just at a time when patterns of demand will be distorted by accelerating change. Customer commitment and flexible structures, with well-trained and committed staffing, will be needed to cope with this challenge.

4. Ownership

Ownership is likely to be the key to company success in the 1990s and beyond. At present ownership is diffused – shareholders are not exercising their legal ownership effectively, boards are not exercising ownership of their board strategies (where they exist) and employees mainly feel disenfranchised. Little has been done in most companies to recognise and encourage the ownership of outside stakeholders (e.g. customers, suppliers and others).

The board has a major task in exercising leadership in order to involve these different stakeholders in the destiny of the company. Shareholders should be encouraged to attend company meetings and to react to mission statements and other pronouncements on company policy. *Fortune* warns on 30 July 1990 that institutional shareholders, especially pension funds, are likely to become more assertive of their ownership in the coming decade, and this trend may move to the United Kingdom as fund managers find it harder to dispose of their larger holdings in key companies without price penalties. To take the initiative, greater use should be made by the board of the Annual Report and Accounts to inform shareholders of the board's strategic thinking and to demonstrate that the right actions are in hand to exercise strategic control. The existence of a strategy committee of the board, overseeing the executive, is an example of such action.

Ownership by employees is achievable at three levels. The basic level is to involve them in the strategic process so that they contribute to the formulation of strategy and are committed to their part of it. This ownership can be enhanced by a meaningful system of rewards (and sanctions) which recognises their commitment and gives them a share in its success. The highest level of ownership involves staff becoming shareholders in the company, either as a reward for their contribution, or as part of a scheme to encourage them to buy shares.

5. *Product life cycle*

The concept of the product life cycle has been criticised by Michael Porter and others as an imperfect planning tool. Perfect or not, it is the basis of most investment calculations, and there is growing evidence that product life cycles are shortening. This shortening is usually due to the introduction of improved products which make the original product prematurely obsolete. The race to perfect ever smaller and improved semiconductors is a case in point.

It is foreseeable that accelerated obsolescence will become an increasingly used competitive strategy in the coming years. Japanese car makers can produce new models in half the time of their US and European rivals and will press home this competitive advantage. This is not the planned obsolescence practised by US car makers in the 1950s and 1960s, but is a customer-oriented drive to offer substantial real improvements with each new product. Today's standard car has the specification of a luxury car of even ten years ago and competition wil accelerate the process of improvement.

Given shorter product life cycles, manufacturers will need to increase the rate and volume of production to recover their investment. This will intensify competitive pressure and force the process of rationalisation and specialisation.

6. *Customisation*

Pressure to increase market share will have to come to terms with a growing desire by customers to have greater choice and to personalise the products they own. There is now a growing dissatisfaction with standardised housing;

the market for self-designed or architect-designed housing is growing significantly, to the point where a new magazine for the personal housing market has been launched in the United Kingdom recently.

The need to customise products has led to the development of more flexible manufacturing systems and to the use of sophisticated IT systems to co-ordinate and control the exercise of options within a product package. This process is most advanced in the aircraft and vehicle industries but will certainly spread to other businesses in the coming years. McGraw-Hill is already planning to offer customised text books to major universities.

Talking recently with exhibitors at the British Interior Design Exhibition I was surprised to learn how many people now felt able to afford to commission artists to do original work. If a new age of patronage is dawning, individual taste will become a very powerful influence on most markets in the 1990s and beyond.

7. Motivating staff

The need to motivate rather than dominate staff has been an emerging theme through this last half-century. As knowledge rather than fixed assets increasingly becomes the key stock in trade of most companies this need becomes paramount. At a time when Charles Handy predicts that half the persons working for companies will be independent contractors or part-timers the need to motivate spreads beyond the payroll.

Signs of competitive markets for staff started to be apparent before 'Big Bang' and have been more evident since. Key skills are now in an international market and respond to the highest bids worldwide. Rewards are no longer totally linked to hierarchy, nor unfortunately, are they always linked to demonstrable success.

Motivating staff will be more than a financial exercise in the coming years. People are taking charge of their lives and seek fulfilment in their jobs and outside. The practice of career breaks is growing, not just for female staff. Motivating staff requires that their ambitions be reconciled with those of the company, and boards will need to develop a culture which both recognises the dignity and interests of the individual and motivates him to stay in the company and contribute to its development.

8. Education

As change accelerates, learning organisations are likely to be more success-ful than those steeped in tradition. The learning process requires encour-agement of education and of frequent re-education as different needs emerge. Education retains an elitist label despite sincere efforts by many to popularise it since the war. Progress with the Management Charter Initiative has been slowed by the restrictive action of the educators. The decline of education in the schools has yet to be reversed, and education may only be given a new sense of direction if companies become more actively involved with local schools and provide clear goals for those for whose future services they will increasingly have to compete.

The opportunity for continuing education will be a key factor in retraining employees, as demographic changes make their services increasingly marketable. In the 1980s, companies cut back heavily on education and training and apprenticeships became extremely scarce. In the same period German businesses strengthened their apprentice schemes and underpinned their theoretical education content. British companies will need to abandon the divisive distinctions between education and training and make education more freely available to all who are able to use it to good purpose.

8.2.   How companies may change in the 1990s and beyond

A recent edition of *Fortune* on 7 May 1990 features a self-managed team from General Mills' cereal factory in Lodi, California. Similar teams are being developed in a growing number of companies – Corning Inc. boasts 3,000 teams. Such teams are not temporary task forces or simple work groups; they force management to give up control and take on a defined task, as if they were an independent business. Such teams have developed from experiments at Proctor and Gamble, Digital and TRW and are now seen as the major productivity breakthrough of the 1990s in service and finance as well as manufacturing industry, particularly where there are significant cross-functional barriers to demolish.

The May 1990 edition of *Business* reports on the growth of Race Electronics, a small Welsh company which has built its business dealing with the Japanese electronics groups established in the United Kingdom and winning total acceptance by complete satisfaction of their rules on zero defects, just-in time and competitive pricing. The proprietor, Alf Gooding, has reinvested heavily in the business, has created an open culture within it, and steers it strategically and systematically. On the back of his total acceptance by the Japanese, Gooding is winning business in Germany and Sweden. Although the pressures of meeting the most exacting standards are intense, Gooding has managed to build a loyal team in his business and to retain them over an extended period.

On the other hand companies can ask too much of employees. *Fortune* on 12 March 1990 reveals how restructuring and heightened competition have led to an overexploitation of young achievers, causing personal crises and fading performance. The reaction of selected CEOs interviewed about the problem was that it would get worse with global competition and that executives had better 'sort themselves out'. This dichotomy is obviously not sustainable and points to the urgent need for CEOs to listen to what is happening in their companies and communicate better with the operating levels. The open communications of companies such as Alf Gooding's Race Electronics have to be developed in bigger groups or the devolved style of management needed in the 1990s will not work effectively.

Informality may be a feature of more companies in the future. The Apple Computer culture now pervades much of the software industry, as it has the advertising industry for much longer. The breakdown of hierarchies and increased team working make formal dress and behaviour out of place, particularly where there is no outside contact. Where people are valued as individuals there is no need for a uniform, although even the dealing rooms in the City show considerable conformity behind an appearance of sartorial freedom!

It is probable that companies will themselves develop less formal groupings in the 1990s. Size is no longer seen as a virtue *per se*; influence can be exerted through networks of associated companies, alliances, consortia for specific tasks and through franchising. A management consultancy business is being built by the Centre for Consultancy which is a grouping of independent contractors working within a common business framework and formula on the 'all for one and one for all' principle. This may be a model for other confederations of the future.

Not only are companies likely to have less formal groupings but they are likely to change shape amoeba-like to meet new challenges. The pattern of buy-outs and buy-ins seen in the last few years will continue, as companies redefine their core activities. Those that do not have strong innovating drives to create new businesses for themselves will probably continue to seek to buy them, although the number of businesses which can be bought and dismembered to release shareholder value will now decline until complacency creates the conditions for the next wave of take-overs in some ten years' time!

Manufacturing companies have achieved substantial rationalisation, productivity gain and customer orientation in the last ten years. This process has hardly begun in the service industries and will be at least as painful. Having spent millions on computer systems to control their business, the High Street banks will now have to spend even larger sums to reorient their systems to serve customers. In a survey on Information Technology in *The Economist*, N. Venkatraman of MIT is quoted as identifying five stages of exploiting IT:

1. *Automating existing jobs*   Jobs within a company are automated, typically to boost productivity – e.g. by installing a computerised accounting system. Little changes but the number of people and the capital costs of doing business.

2. *Electronic infrastructure*   Islands of functional automation are linked together. Nothing has to change in order to create ways of sharing information between all of a firm's computers. But without change there is usually little economic incentive to overcome the inevitable technical incompatibilities and battles over who does what. That incentive typically comes bundled up in one of three other sorts of change:

3. *Business-process redesign*   Just as Ford found it could do away with invoices (by using bar codes for goods received), computers enable things to be done in new and more efficient ways.

4. *Business-network redesign*   Creating links with suppliers and customers not only

creates new opportunities for changing business processes, it also changes the balance of competition.

5. *Business-scope redesign*   As part of the process of self-improvement, information technology enables some companies to move into new businesses. Merrill Lynch's cash-management account, for example, put the firm into competition with banks by each day sweeping the cash balances of brokerage accounts into interest-bearing securities. (*The Economist*, 16 June 1990)

Few businesses have penetrated beyond stages 1 and 2 of this process and some earlier attempts to inject an IT culture into major businesses appears to have failed at General Motors and, on a smaller scale, at Rover Group. The 'not invented here' syndrome is still very powerful even in the face of the radical challenges of the 1990s.

Major culture change is needed to break down functional boundaries which still abound in many businesses. These barriers are a major cause of delays in developing and marketing new products, and work on compressing development and manufacturing cycles by techniques such as 'simultaneous engineering' can have dramatic effect. British Aerospace has, for example, worked with United Research to reduce the manufacturing cycle of Hawk aircraft by some 50 per cent.

One possible model for companies seeking to encourage innovation without losing either strategic direction or control is provided by 3M (Minnisota Mining and Manufacturing). This company operates at three levels: corporate, sector and division. The corporate centre sets the strategic direction and has limited facilities, notably a major research facility. The four sectors (commercial/computer; industrial/electronic; information/ imaging; life services) are organised by market areas and have their own research and development facilities fed from the centre and feeding their divisions. There are some forty divisions, which are set broad targets and operate freely within a limited number of policies. One of these is that R and D expenditure must be exactly 6.5 per cent of sales (no more, no less), so that extra funds put behind a bright idea have to be taken from another project. Employees in the divisions are free to propose anything and have the right to spend up to 15 per cent of their time on 'blue sky' projects of their choice. If a project is adopted it receives a budget and has resources put behind it. The staff involved with the project grows as it develops until it becomes a major SBU. The 3M model shows that innovation can be actively encouraged at the periphery of the group without losing control. Projects are shaped by a strong culture derived and sustained from the centre and steered in a clear strategic direction. This does not mean that new businesses have to be directly related to 3M's core coatings and bonding capability (out of the technology for making advertising signs has come a billboard-leasing business), but they must be able to beat the new products hurdle rate of 25 per cent return on investment, contribute to the division's return on capital target of 27 per cent and the group's 20/25 per cent return on equity, and be able to sustain a high added value.

With such a proven culture of aggressive innovation; nurtured and owned by creative staff and perpetually reshaping and renewing the company, where is the need for the aggressive takeovers which have characterised the 1980s and, having mostly failed, have led to panicky unbundling and a new search for that elusive holy grail – shareholder value?

8.3. The changing role of the board

In view of what has been reviewed and discussed in this book and, given an increasingly confusing pattern of discontinuity and change, what is the future role of the board likely to be? I believe that there are four key elements, based on the present role and suitably adjusted, which are likely to comprise that role, as follows:

1. Achieving growth in shareholder value over the long term.
2. Representing the company to outside stakeholders.
3. Allocating resources to operating units.
4. Overseeing operations; rewarding and sanctions.

1. *Growth in shareholder value over the long term*
This is the basic strategic role of the board, identifying opportunities, coping with threats and establishing the strategic direction of the company. The issue of shareholder value is new and has been used as the pretext for many of the aggressive assaults which boards have suffered in recent years. To disarm such opportunistic moves, boards need to demonstrate that their profits performance is not just incrementally good but is competitive with that of outside businesses. As *The Economist* of 5 May 1990 says of Lord Hanson, 'the real skill . . . is to make the assets sweat'.

A recent survey carried out for Investors in Industry (1990) shows the growing importance of shareholder value as a long-term measure. Concern was expressed by finance directors about short-term judgements made by the City, and this echoes the results of a similar survey in the United States completed in 1987. The need to avoid undervaluation of shares is recognised, together with the concomitant obligation to take action to promote recognition of their true value.

2. *Representing the company to outside stakeholders*
Operating units will seek to develop the immediate loyalty of their employees and will have important stakeholder relationships (e.g. with customers and suppliers). A wider range of stakeholders will see the company as a whole and will judge it by its performance and external presentations. As the 3I report quoted above shows, companies have not presented themselves well to the City and many have suffered as a result. Many companies have been inept at dealing with environmental, health and other issues of public concern, and have suffered in prestige, if not in profit, as a result. With the

growing importance of outside representation it is the board that must provide leadership in carrying out this task effectively and in the long-term interests of the company.

3. *Allocating resources to operating units*
In order to maximise shareholder value over the long-term, companies will need to exercise ultimate control over the resources used by their operating units. Styles will differ; a company like GEC is unlikely to develop large numbers of managers at the centre for deployment within the group in the way that ICI or Shell have been doing. Some companies will run a tight treasury; Hanson does not allow its companies to have overdrafts and many pull significant cash balances back to the centre. Hanson does not allow its companies to seek acquisitions but only to concentrate on maximising return on assets.

It is probable that companies will need to give more discretion to managing directors of operating units in order to encourage innovation and a sense of ownership of their businesses. Innovation is not seen as important by many companies in the financial control mode (e.g. Hanson), but lack of innovation means that such groups can only maintain their earnings by constant change in their portfolio of investments.

Even where operating units are given more discretion and are allowed to build up their balance sheets, invest longer term and make acquisitions, the basic responsibility of the main company board for resources will remain. Resources allocated to an operating unit are part of a contract, the consideration for which is a planned and mutually agreed series of profit streams.

4. *Overseeing operations; rewarding and sanctions*
The board will almost certainly remain accountable to shareholders for the results of its operating units, even though it will be increasingly difficult to exercise detailed control should it wish to do so. Results are achieved by employees whom, in larger companies, boards can only influence indirectly; results are judged by shareholders who are usually reticent about their wishes until they sell their shares. Boards will have to work harder at understanding and influencing shareholders, so that results can be more clearly targeted over time; they will also need to create a culture in the company which encourages such results to be achieved. This will increasingly involve some measure of ownership, as discussed earlier, involving both rewards and sanctions.

Sanctions are as important as rewards. As companies gear up to maximise shareholder value over the long term they will be even less able to tolerate inadequate performance than in the past. Where employees are committed to freely negotiated tasks and have the prospect of real rewards, the evidence suggests that they will do much to bring inadequate colleagues into line. Where this fails there needs to be an open, clear and rigorous system of sanctions, tempered with humanity if severance is inevitable. The board must oversee the working of both the reward and sanctions policies.

How will these changes affect the shape and constitution of the board? It may be useful to consider some possible models for the future.

In his book *The Age of Unreason*, Charles Handy develops the model of 'the federal organisation' to cope with the need to devolve operations from the centre while leaving certain key issues affecting the overall organisation to be handled at the centre. He refers to the NEDO report in 1988 which criticised many of the large UK electronic businesses for breaking their structure into a number of individual businesses and leaving them to determine their own strategies. The results were seen as too short term and parochially driven. Handy likens this to allowing US states to make individual decisions about defence, and emphasises that the cores of federal structures are not just central bankers.

The centre has to be more than a banker. Only the centre can think beyond the next annual report or indeed, to quote one family business, can look beyond the grave. Only the centre can think in terms of global strategies which may link one or more of the autonomous parts. To leave these big decisions to the discretion of the parts can be a way to mortgage the future. The centre, however, is not in full control in a federal organsation. It is easy, in logic, to think of the centre taking the long-term decisions and leaving the implementation to the parts. That logic, however, reeks of the old engineering language of management, of decentralisation, and of delegated tasks and controls. It is not the new language of political theory, of people and communities. The federal concept requires the centre to act on behalf of the parts, if the resulting decisions are going to be self-enforcing – and they have to be because the centre does not have the manpower to control the details. (Handy, 1990)

The implications of such a model (which already exists) for the role and operations of the board are considerable. The board becomes 'an assembly of chiefs' which takes key decisions together on behalf of the federation, which are then implemented separately. Such a board cannot be run like a monarchy (who can even name the Swiss President?) but requires persuasion and the search for consensus. Leadership is expressed in ideas not through personality. Many Japanese corporations come close to this pattern and it is perhaps significant that Japanese boards are not noted for the presence of independent non-executive directors.

Another model of the future board might be the board with no executive directors. This is the upper tier of the two-tier board system long established in Europe, and would simplistically be a reversion to the early boards peopled by owners and their representatives. A few companies in the United Kingdom such as the Laird Group use this model, which requires an executive chairman in order to be effective. While such a board would be able to use a wide range of talents among its (non-executive) directors, it might have difficulty in remaining closely in touch with operational reality and thereby put its legitimacy at risk.

The Handy model has the merit of empowering the individual businesses within the company, with the centre providing new resources of people and money needed to sustain their development. It does not, however, open the board to new influences and ideas from the wider environment in which the company operates. As the pressure of change increases the number of factors affecting the company but outside its control, relative to those which it may hope to control, the need for an effective early-warning system becomes more imperative. A key part of that system is the presence on the board of a reasonable number of effective non-executive directors.

US boards have, on average, a preponderance of non-executive directors, whereas the typical British board will have one-third non-executive members. Given a separation of the roles of chairman and chief executive, PRONED sees no need to change that proportion, only a need to be more selective in the choice of non-executive directors and more committed to their effective use. If boards are to carry out effectively their strategic role, and to involve the non-executive directors in the strategic process, both through the strategy committee and in board deliberations, it will be necessary to give more time to briefing non-executive directors and to contract for more of their time than most companies presently request.

Greater involvement of non-executive directors on a board, where they will probably still be a minority, will require great skill and diplomacy from the chairman. The board will have a clear role and executive directors will need to relate to that role rather than act as delegates for specific parts of the business, in the manner pioneered by ICI with such success. Executive directors will continue to have deeper knowledge of the present business than their non-executive colleagues, but this is their specific contribution to the role of the board in the same way that the non-executive directors will bring outside experience, contacts and insight. On a well-structured board the mix of talents will be carefully balanced and targeted at fulfilling the role of the board. No one director will be allowed to dominate the board's deliberations, since they are addressed to the board's strategic role, for the success of which all are equally accountable to the shareholders and other stakeholders.

To borrow an image from Peter Drucker, the board in the 1990s and beyond should be like an orchestra. Each member is an expert performer as a soloist, but is willing to play under the direction of a conductor in order to achieve a performance which is greater than the sum of their separate contributions. The score is the role of the board and the skill is to interpret that role to satisfy a wide and critical audience of shareholders, stakeholders, analysts and professional specialists, all of whom expect quality in every note and, at the same time, a performance sustained through the length and modulations of a major symphony.

APPENDIX 1: A POSSIBLE
MONITORING SYSTEM

Monitoring should not be a mechanistic process, since its main wellheads are imagination, insight and creativity, but it needs to be structured and systematic.
The key characteristics of the monitoring process include the following:

- As wide a scan of outside horizons as possible.
- The ability to process large amounts of information into knowledge and then through to insight.
- A clear set of reference points identifying the 'norm' from which deviation can be monitored.
- A constant re-evaluation of the 'norm' (zero-base thinking).
- Alertness to opportunities for competitive advantage.
- Orientation towards understanding customers in depth, with imaginative segmentation and creative search for crosslinks.
- Alertness to direct and indirect threats.
- Awareness of changes in attitudes of 'stakeholders' (shareholders, suppliers, community, etc.) to the business.
- Alertness to discontinuities in key factors affecting the business.
- Sensitivity to changes of pace in significant patterns of evolution.
- Openness to conflicting interpretations of data.
- A willingness to challenge comfortable assumptions.

The structuring of such a process may involve the following:

- A total commitment and involvement by top management (including the creation of a board strategy committee).
- Involvement of a wide range of outsiders (non-executive directors, advisers, even mavericks).
- Use of consumer, adviser and other groups, where appropriate.
- Regular use of market, attitudinal and other research to evaluate hypotheses and validate trends.
- Close links with politicians, opinion formers, experts and lobbyists.
- The development of a well-structured database, linked to public and other databases, and widely accessible within the company.
- Making internal structures flexible and non-hierarchical to encourage creative thinking and wider involvement in the monitoring process.

The operation of such a process may include the following:

- The development of a linked series of scenarios (? three) in detail, built on data derived from the monitoring process, subject to rules to provide internal consistency, updated in real time and related to control scenarios fixed from a base date.
- The development of on-line facilities to model the effect of changes in key parameters of the plan, or of important assumptions to the scenarios to test the likely effect of such changes on the company.
- Such facilities would also be of value in assessing trade-offs and multilateral changes.
- The development of models to assess the impact of scenario changes and of changes in company strategy in major competitors, and the likely outcome of competitor reactions.
- Use of models to gauge the effect of different paces of change in key parameters.
- Use of models to assess the risk implications of outside changes and/or of changes in company strategy.
- Regular assessments of the company's market posture with a view to repositioning it to secure competitive advantage and/or enhanced return on assets employed over time.
- Regular assessment of human resources relative to the above.
- Exercises in lateral and 'upside down' thinking to challenge the strategy and structure of the company.

It should be recognised that the cost of a monitoring system may outweigh the resultant benefits unless it is rigorously controlled and regularly evaluated. Closest attention should be focused on issues which directly affect the firm's survival, and on those which are pivotal in achieving competitive advantage. Alertness to opportunities for restructuring or repositioning will be important, and any rigidities in the firm's structure or operations must be avoided. It seems a long time since Man walked in fear in the primeval forest, and his instincts have been blunted by generations of civilisation. New threats and an accelerating pace of change will make it essential to rehone those instincts to survive into the uncertain future of the twenty-first century.

APPENDIX 2: STRENGTHS, WEAKNESSES, OPPORTUNITIES, THREATS

A franchised petrol station

Strengths
1. Petrol company brand.
2. Franchise formula (layout, products, etc.).
3. Personal service.
4. Open twenty-four hours.
5. Space to expand.
6. Prime site.

Weaknesses
1. Limited ownership.
2. Declining traffic flow.
3. Limited storage tanks.
4. No rain cover for clients.
5. High reliance on slow-paying account customers.

Opportunities
1. Additional products (laundry, dry cleaning, groceries, etc.).
2. Commission products (insurance, car club membership).
3. Café, children's play area.
4. Rapid car wash.
5. Buy site on other side of road.

Threats
1. Planning permission for a rival station next door.
2. Forced buyout by franchisor.
3. Building of new by-pass.
4. Armed robbery at night (has happened once).
5. Son may leave business and move to another town.

Even this limited list begins to show a picture of a business which has some critical issues to face. The strengths and opportunities are qualified by significant weaknesses and threats. Can these be mitigated to enable the opportunities to be grasped? Are the opportunities worth grasping if traffic is declining and if personal service is threatened by the owner's son departing? It is out of these tensions that strategy has to be developed.

APPENDIX 3: EXAMPLES OF MISSION STATEMENTS

EPS Logistics Management

EPS Logistics Management has a mission to establish itself as a leader within the field of third-party logistics by providing a comprehensive range of services nationally to demanding and respected customers.

Success in achieving this will be measured not so much in financial comparison with the major haulage-based operators, but rather by the degree to which manufacturing industry regards EPS as an automatic contender for this business within the defined service field.

Financial performance is, however, a vital measure of success and the company's financial mission is twofold. First, at the end of the three-year plan, to have arrived at a position where we can consistently provide a return on assets which is substantially above the minimum return expected of group companies. Second, to produce a level of growth which will confirm the company's position as a major contributor to group growth over the next ten years.

FI Group plc

Mission statement: charter

FI GROUP is a group of companies which have sprung from seeing an opportunity in a problem: one woman's inability to work in an office has turned into hundreds of people's opportunity to work in a non-office environment. Because of its unusual origin, FI GROUP has a clear sense of its mission, its strategy and its values.

Mission FI Group's mission is to stay a leader in the rapidly growing and highly profitable, knowledge intensive software industry. It aims to achieve this by developing, through modern telecommunications, the unutilised intellectual energy of individuals and groups unable to work in a conventional environment.

Strategy FI Group's strategy is to maximise the value of its unusual asset base by establishing a competitive advantage over conventionally organised firms, and imitators of its approach, through cost and quality competitiveness. This occurs by the development of a methodology which ensures quality and by establishing a company ethos which binds people who work largely independently and often alone.

Values People are vital to any knowledge intensive industry. The skills and loyalty of our workforce are our main asset. Equally important is the knowledge which comes from the exchange of ideas with our clients and their personnel. It follows that human and ethical values play a pivotal role in the way in which an organisation like FI Group conducts itself. This is even more true in a structure as open and free as FI Group. To maintain a high level of creativity, productivity and coherence in such an environment requires a set of high ethical values and professional standards that any member of the organisation can identify with and see realised, and reinforced, in the organisation's behaviour. FI Group has defined for itself such a charter of values.

Professional excellences Our long term aim is to improve our professional abilities so as to maintain a quality product for our clients. It is also our aim to develop fully our professional potential as people and to develop our organisation in a way which reflects our own individuality and special approach.

Growth We aim to grow our organisation to its full potential, nationally and internationally. We aim to grow at least as rapidly as the software industry as a whole in order to maintain our own position as an attractive employer and a competitive supplier.

Economic and psychological reward We also aim to realise and enjoy fully the economic and psychological rewards of our efforts resulting from the development of the unique competitive advantage of our structure and capabilities. We aim to achieve profits, reward our work-force, maintain the Employee Trust and provide an attractive return to our shareholders.

Integrated diversity We have a commitment to consistent procedures worldwide as a means of lowering cost, but aim to conduct ourselves as a national of each country in which we operate.

Universal ethics We respect local customs and laws, but see ourselves as members of a world society with respect for human dignity and ethical conduct beyond the profit motive and local circumstances.

Goodwill An extension of our ethical view is a belief in the goodwill of others: colleagues, clients and vendors. We also believe that goodwill results in positive, long-term relationships.

Enthusiasm Finally we believe that enthusiasm for our people and our product, and the ability to engender that enthusiasm in others, is the most essential quality of leadership within the organisation. Enthusiasm promotes creativity, cooperation and profit.

APPENDIX 4: INFORMATION NEEDED FOR A TYPICAL STRATEGIC PLAN

External

1. Background information and statistics on key issues facing the company.
2. Political issues likely to affect the company with background detail.
3. Economic data on markets in which the company trades (GDP growth forecasts, balance and terms of trade, inflation, interest rates, exchange rate forecasts).
4. Specific market data (market size, market share of company and competitors, potential new competitors, expected changes in market size, market segmentation and relevant market shares).
5. Background data on potential opportunities and threats.
6. Data on key customers, competitors, suppliers and potential acquisitions/alliances.
7. Price sensitivities of key products in key markets.
8. Product life-cycle assessments.
9. Evaluation of brands – brand strategy.
10. Technical issues relevant to the business.
11. Shareholder profile – large holdings? – implications for company independence.

Internal

1. Cost data on key products with volume sensitivities.
2. Analysis of fixed and marginal costs.
3. Prospective step functions in fixed costs as volume changes.
4. Payroll data with sensitivities, e.g. effect of overtime increase or new recruitment.
5. Employee skills profile (to match against future needs).
6. Employee age profile (to ensure correct pattern maintained).
7. Schedule of key plant and equipment (to match against expected demand/obsolescence).
8. Schedule of purchasing (key items) – to enable savings, substitutions, etc. to be planned.
9. Analysis of key properties – own, rent, or sale and leaseback?

10. Review of insurances – with assessment.
11. Research and development – assessment of key projects.
12. Funding – how to fund the new plan.

Performance against present plan

1. Key deviations – why? – implications for new plan.

APPENDIX 5: CONTENTS OF A TYPICAL STRATEGIC PLAN

Company or division

1. Mission statement.
2. Long term objectives/objectives for plan period.
3. Executive summary.
4. Performance against previous plan.
5. Key issues to be addressed/critical success factors.
6. Internal factors affecting the new plan (strengths, weaknesses, changes, etc.).
7. External background to the new plan (political, economic, markets, competition, opportunities, threats, etc.).
8. Key assumptions underlying the new plan/key variables.
9. Review of established strategies (changes, retiming, etc.).
10. New strategies.
11. Resource requirements to support strategies – headcount – skills pattern – capital expenditure.
12. Key action programme to support strategies (broken down to detailed specific tasks, with deadlines and individual accountabilities).
13. Financial projections for plan period (with data for last three years and estimate for current year):
    - Profit and loss accounts.
    - Cash-flow forecasts or source and allocation of funds.
    - Proforma balance sheets.
14. Sensitivity analysis by key variables (showing impact on financial projections).
15. Worst and best case scenarios (showing impact on business and estimating probability).
16. Appendices:
    - Marketing plan
    - Manufacturing plan
    - Research and development plan
    - Manpower development plan
    - Plans of other key functions or strategic business units.

APPENDIX 6: DEVELOPING
TOMORROW'S DIRECTORS

The increasing speed of change in the environment constitutes a challenge to every leader in the business world today. In particular it is causing many of them to rethink their management development policies. But are they asking the right questions? Do they really perceive what are the critical issues that lie ahead? It is all too easy, for example, to be mesmerised by the obvious marketing challenges that face UK companies in the single European market after 1992, and overlook other more fundamental changes that are already occurring and which are gathering pace. There are other, equally significant shifts taking place in the business environment and in the practice of management which will have far-reaching consequences for the development of the next generation of senior and top managers.

The task for those engaged in management education is to understand how the critical factors that are changing the business environment are leading to altered decision-making processes and new forms of organisational structure in companies, and then map out the implications for the way we develop our senior managers and chief executives.

A new socio-economic framework for business is rapidly taking shape. It has variously been described as the information society, the cybernetic society and the post-industrial society. What are its chief characteristics?

The engines of economic prosperity will be the science-based or knowledge-intensive industries such as electronics, biotechnology and aerospace. Knowledge will increasingly become the scarce resource rather than labour or capital, and this will put enormous pressure upon companies to husband their resources of knowledge and their most talented employees, and to maintain them in the face of predatory activity from competitors. Manufacturing will become increasingly automated and will be linked to advanced data-processing systems. This increase in automation will act as a spur to greater quality, reduced lead times for the introduction of new products and more autonomy for individual production units. The new manufacturing systems, linked to an integral company database, will further break down the traditional functional barriers.

Employment will be dominated by service-industry jobs, and this will be true even within manufacturing companies. Already in Western Europe service-sector employment accounts for around 60 per cent of all jobs, and this figure is set to continue to rise. Work attitudes in the service sector, where the emphasis is on the use of professional knowledge-based skills and where individual responsibility for service delivery is both necessary and an important source of motivation, will have important implications for overall management practice. In these circumstances the job of the senior manager of the future will be different. He or she will be dealing with smaller numbers of people, more educated, more articulate and less inclined to accept managerial authority for its own sake. His or her role will be more that of an orchestral conductor rather than that of a commander – that is, bringing out talents, setting objectives and co-ordinating them for a wider organisational purpose.

The use of a common information technology will have profound effects upon business. Activities such as computing and telecommunications, which up to now have been seen as discrete, will overlap. The strategic issue for many companies will be how they use information technology to achieve competitive advantage by creating better products faster and by building more adaptive organisations. But these structural changes, generated by information technology, will demand new concepts of management, less rigid management practices and a wholly new approach to developing managers. Neither a systems-based, mechanistic view of management will be the answer nor will a purely people-oriented philosophy be the right way ahead, but rather a fusion of the two.

At the macroeconomic level, one implication of the wider use of information technology may be that it will enable companies to manage a complex mix of products and markets more easily than they have in the past. We may well see the return of the conglomerate. Thus, the lessons for Europe post-1992 are clear: advanced information-processing technology, a more open financial system and a single market will combine in a heady mixture to propel the growth of cross-national corporations. For the smaller to medium-sized companies, business life will become much tougher; they will have to adopt new strategies quickly in response to severe changes in their environment, and in order to do that they will first need to have managers who are adept at thinking through organisational and corporate change. Management development in the future will therefore have to put much more emphasis on providing senior managers with new tools for strategic thinking and decision-making.

These technical and social changes will combine with predicted demographic changes in Europe to produce new patterns of work and new career structures. Already we can see some of the effects of these forces at work: shorter working weeks, longer holidays, more self-employment and people working from home. By the turn of the century, those in their fifties will make up the largest segment of the working population. In Britain, roughly half of those in work will be women, many of whom will have interrupted their careers to bring up their children. Thus, these demographic and social factors will give an added push to the notion of continuous education throughout people's working lives.

Finally, attitudes towards business itself are already changing as a result of these shifts in life-styles and expectations, and this is a process which is going to become more pronounced. Managers in the future will be required to have far greater regard for public health and pollution hazards, concern for local communities and an awareness of the public's sensitivity to questions of business ethics. The interface between business and society is going to become much more complex, and for some companies much more difficult. Many of today's top executives still regard this as a soft issue, and one that does not really affect them. Yet increasingly, companies are paying the price for disregarding public opinion – in lost market share, lost reputation, boycotts and difficulty in recruiting.

Towards a new business culture

Changes in the external environment of business are increasingly going to be mirrored by changes inside business organisations. No aspect of company life will escape the impact of these changes. Research on 'Management for the future', carried out by the Ashridge Management Research Group (Barham and Rassam, 1989) provides a number of important messages.

The Ashridge research project looked at some of Europe's leading companies such as ACCOR, BMW, Burton Group, J C Bamford, Electrolux, ICI, Jaguar, Norsk Data and Shell UK, interviewing senior managers including chief executives. The attitudes of these companies suggest that organisations in the future will be flatter and more fluid in structure, with much more emphasis on managing lateral relationships than hierarchical ones. They will be decentralised, fragmented, with smaller units able to react swiftly to shifting market demands. The integrative mechanisms of companies will be quite different from what they have been in the past; instead of a strong authoritarian headquarters setting company-wide procedures, there will be a strong corporate culture, an inspired and flexible strategy and a co-ordinated database. These new company structures will be made possible by the advance of automated manufacturing systems and information technology. New technologies will not only provide managers with the tools to compete more effectively in the market place but also the opportunity to create more diverse and federated organisations.

The new organisation structures that will arise will produce a number of tensions for management, and one tension in particular. On the one hand there will be tremendous pressure on organisations to cultivate their knowledge base, to manage their most talented people for the greatest benefit of the organisation, while on the other hand the traditional legitimacy of managerial authority will come to be questioned. Indeed, the central problem with the knowledge-intensive oragnisation is that its rise has not been accompanied by new conceptual frameworks or practical guidelines for those senior managers who have to live within them. Already those companies which are at the leading edge of what might be termed knowledge-intensiveness are experiencing serious problems of management.

A critical factor here is that we have no proper system for accounting for knowledge; we do not know what it is worth and we do not know how to calculate a rate of return on it. Managing and husbanding knowledge will become a preoccupation of companies and it will inevitably affect corporate cultures. Reward systems and career structures will have to change. So, too, will the exercise of managerial authority and corporate decision-making. Meanwhile, the spectre of 1992, with the possibility of a truly open European labour market, will add another dimension to this process. Senior managers will have to learn very quickly how to manage their 'knowledge workers', if they do not want to see them poached or lured away by their more astute European rivals.

Companies in the future will be much more value-driven than they are now. That phrase was used by the authors of *In Search of Excellence* (Peters and Waterman, 1982) to characterise the successful companies that they studied. They showed that the best companies were more motivated by visionary goals than by financial objectives. Such goals give meaning and purpose to those who work within organisations, and they also act as unifying agents where an organisation is highly diverse and geographically spread out. Companies which are now building a portfolio of operations in Europe will need at some stage to set out a philosophy of what their business is all about, both out of strategic necessity and in order to give their far-flung employees a sense of belonging to the same firm.

These are the changes that we will see in our business cultures, and they will generate several important issues for management at the highest levels.

Issues for top management

Manufacturing management in the future will face a number of specific challenges, including managing with information technology, managing cultural change and preparing managers for leadership.

The use of information technology in managerial decision-making has not yet been thought through. Inevitably the existence of new, powerful and easily accessible databases will provide a significant new tool for managers, but how should these new sources of information be used? In current management textbooks there is a lot of talk about how to use management science techniques to arrive at an optimum decision, but the difficulty is that in real life these clinical models of decision-making do not match practical problems. The development of advanced comprehensive databases will encourage many managers to think that they can rely on them completely when making important decisions. But I believe that this view is mistaken. We will need to find a way to integrate hard data with the 'fuzzy' data about people and values. So a key issue in the development of potential senior executives will be how to develop the ability to bring together both qualitative and quantitative factors, thereby arriving at a judgement. The art of judgement is sadly neglected these days, but in the future, when we have access to more data and more statistics, we will have to take this human function much more seriously.

If our European wealth-creating organisations are to survive, let alone prosper, during the transition to the post-industrial society and the single European Market, they will have to experience major culture change. So many of the accepted norms and practices of the past will have to be dropped. A sea change in business attitudes is coming upon us, because organisations are being subject to wave upon wave of changes – in technology, in markets, in the attitudes of those who work in organisations, and in the societies in which they operate. Organisations are going to be convulsed by massive cultural shifts as they seek to adapt to these changes, but it will be a painful process for most managers, having been schooled in an age quite different from the one they will be living in.

Cultural change in the past has often been seen as a soft issue but in the future the necessity for cultural change will be caused by structural, strategic, technological and financial imperatives which will have to be addressed. Otherwise, those organisations afflicted by seemingly intractable difficulties will crumble beneath the tide of change.

There remains a final issue for management development, that of preparing young people for leadership roles. Harold Leavitt (1983) has rightly pointed out that leadership is 'the orphan of Western management and management education'. Yet it is the mainspring for coping with the challenges that companies face. We need to develop models for strategic leadership that are not based on old-fashioned notions of leaders as omniscient heroes, but rather on new rationales founded on the idea of the leader as a pathfinder (to use Leavitt's description) who solves problems in a way that develops and draws on the competence of others. The new organisation structures and the new technologies that will go with them will force companies to rethink their leadership development programmes. There are few centres in the academic world which have really addressed the question of business leadership in tomorrow's company. Businesses will therefore have to be in the forefront cf the pioneering process themselves, collaborating with the best practitioners in management education.

Challenges for management education and future trends

These trends indicate that management education itself will have to adopt new techniques and new procedures. Far too much management education has been seen as irrelevant by the business community because it has not specifically addressed its needs. The answer therefore, increasingly, will be the forging of strong links between academic institutions and business organisations to arrive at jointly designed management-development programmes.

Co-operation between the academic and business worlds brings a number of benefits. Companies gain access to a high level of competence and experience in management development which they find difficult to develop internally, while the teaching institutions are exposed to new issues and concerns facing organisations.

Other results flow from this kind of co-operation. The qualifications issued by the academic bodies, in particular the Master of Business Administration (MBA), will be more inclined to mirror the practical needs of companies, demonstrating the attainment of competence rather than pure academic knowledge and linked to an individual's actual requirements. Also, by involving businesses in the design of management courses they will be introduced at an early stage to the new ideas and concepts that are taking root in the academic institutions, and because businesses will have been party to the creation of new programmes they will embrace the new ideas much more sympathetically. The design of management education will become a far more creative process. Not all academic institutions will take to this approach, and it will be up to the businesses themselves to search out those centres of learning excellence which do embrace this co-operative philosophy, and which have the skills to implement it.

An increasingly used approach to the development of managers at senior and general management levels is *issue-based learning*. The problems that general managers face bring together a number of disciplines that traditionally have been addressed separately by management educators. More and more in the future, programmes will be designed around issues and not around subjects. Managing structural change, quality assurance, introducing new values into organisations, exploiting new technology and addressing corporate strategy will be just some of the issues that management development will be concerned with. In responding to these needs management education teams will have to be equally multidisciplinary.

One implication of all this is that companies will have to become much more sophisticated in their use of management development programmes. They will need to plan their management development so that it relates much more clearly to their overall corporate objectives and to their corporate strategy. Thus, management development will become part of the forecasting process. Companies will have to anticipate the training they will need in advance of some of the strategic moves that they intend to make. The well-managed company will tend to see itself as a learning organisation, which needs continually to up-date itself and reinforce itself with new ideas and techniques, thereby being ready for any eventuality. If management development is to work, it must also be based on an accurate knowledge of individual managers. It will have to be founded not only upon a manager's needs but upon his or her potential. Assessing managers for management development has often been much too subjective. Individuals have been, and still are, frequently singled out for 'fast track' training programmes on the basis of personal bias or past performance, but these are faulty indicators of potential. Increasingly, organisations will use assessment centres to identify untapped managerial talent. As this becomes more common, organisations will be able to design management development programmes better suited to individual needs.

Companies will want to take special care in the development of those who show the greatest promise for top jobs. The question is how best to do this? More and more companies will develop people for senior management and for board positions with *action-centred learning*. This will particularly apply to those who are being groomed as future chief executives.

Action-centred learning is a technique whereby managers can experience working in new circumstances, exchange information with each other and learn from their mistakes. Ashridge Management College, for example, has developed 'action learning sets' for chief executives and 'board strategy seminars' for top managers. Both of these programmes enable the participants to share their ideas, expose real-life problems, talk about difficulties and receive counselling from experienced tutors. Years of experience are not enough to fit a person for senior responsibility, nor are academic concepts about organisations a recipe for understanding how to hold high office. When business life was slower than it is today it was possible to learn how to exercise power and leadership as one went along, but today that is no longer tenable. People are often asked to fill senior positions at times of crisis or to introduce substantial change. This puts added pressure upon the occupants of those positions to perform well. Professor Reg Revans was undoubtedly right when he argued that managers learn from doing, rather than by sitting in lecture theatres. Yet a newly appointed manager, director or chief executive cannot learn his or her new role and execute it at the same time; he or she needs time away from the business in which to cultivate the necessary skills in a supportive atmosphere.

Two things emerge from all this. One is that management education must be seen as a continuing process, if only because the pace of change is becoming much faster and managers need to be prepared for whatever lies ahead. The second is that management development must be combined with real life practice, it must contain active, action-based learning or it will just be forgotten. So many managers, especially in Britain, have rejected education and training because it has not seemed relevant to them. Maybe they have not asked enough from the providers of education. They have not always taken the trouble to spell out what their requirements are. Keeping the educational institutions at arm's length is certainly no answer. Business and academic organisations need to work together to achieve mutually harmonious results.

Philip Sadler

REFERENCES

Ackelsberg, R. and W. C. Harris (1989), 'How Danish companies plan', *Long Range Planning**, December.

Adair, John (1984), *The Skills of Leadership*, Gower.

Adriaans, W. and J. T. Hoogakker (1989), 'Planning for information system at Netherlands Gas', *Long Range Planning*, June.

Ajimal, K. S. (1985), 'Force field analysis: a framework for strategic thinking', *Long Range Planning*, October.

Allaire, Yvan and Mihaela Firsirotu (1990), 'Strategic plans as contracts', *Long Range Planning*, February.

Ansoff, H. Igor (1979), *Corporate Strategy*, 7th edn, Penguin.

Aram, John and Scott Cowan (1986), 'The directors' role in planning: what information do they need?', *Long Range Planning*, April.

Argenti, John (1989), *Practical Corporate Planning*, 2nd edn, Unwin Hyman.

Argyris, C. and D. A. Schon (1987), 'Organisational learning: a theory of action perspective', in D. S. Pugh (ed.) (1987) *Organisation Theory*, 2nd edn, Penguin.

Arrington Jun., C. B. and R. N. Sawaya (1984), 'Issues management in an uncertain environment', *Long Range Planning*, December.

Association of British Insurers (1990), 'Role and duties of directors', a discussion paper.

Attwood, Frank and Neil Stein (1986) *de Paula's Auditing*, 7th edn. Pitman.

Bamberger, Ingolf (1989), 'Developing competitive advantage in small and medium-sized firms', *Long Range Planning*, October.

Barham, Kevin and Clive Rassam (1989), *Shaping the Corporate Future*, Unwin Hyman.

Barron, R. J. (1989), 'The administrator as corporate strategist', *The Administrator*, March.

Bartlett and Ghoshal (1990), *Managing Across Borders*.

Bavley, Dan (1981), 'What is the board of directors good for?', *Long Range Planning*.

Beer, Professor Stafford (1979), *The Heart of Enterprise*, John Wiley & Sons.

Belbin, Meredith (1981), *Management Teams*, Heinemann.

Brightman, Harvey and Sidney Harris (1985), 'Is your information system mature enough for computerised planning?', *Long Range Planning*, October.

* *Long Range Planning* is the journal of the Strategic Planning Society.

Burns, T. (1987), 'Mechanistic and organisanic structures' in D. S. Pugh (ed.) (1987), *Organisation Theory*, 2nd edn, Penguin.

Burns, T. and G. M. Stalker (1966), *The Management of Innovation*, Tavistock.

Cadbury, Sir Adrian (1990), *The Company Chairman*, Director Books.

Caeldries, F. and R. van Dierdonck (1988), 'How Belgian businesses make strategic planning work', *Long Range Planning*, April.

Campbell, Andrew, Marion Devine and David Young (1990), *A Sense of Mission*, Economist/Hutchinson.

Carnall, Colin (1986), 'Managing strategic change: an integrated approach', *Long Range Planning*, December.

Carpenter, Michael (1986), 'Planning and strategy: which will win?', *Long Range Planning*, December.

Chandler, Alfred (1966), *Strategy and Structure*, 2nd edn, Anchor.

Chandler, John and Paul Cockle (1982), *Techniques of Scenario Planning*, McGraw-Hill.

Child, J. (1984), *Organisation: A guide to problems and practice*, Harper & Row.

Clarke, Christopher (1989), 'Acquisitions: techniques for measuring strategic fit', *Long Range Planning*, June.

David, Fred (1988), 'How companies define their mission', *Long Range Planning*, February.

Davis, Evan and John Kay (1990), 'Assessing corporate performance', *Business Strategy Review*, summer.

de Bono, Edward (1982), *Lateral Thinking for Management*, Penguin.

Demb, D. Chouet, T. Lossius and F. Neubauer (1989), 'Defining the role of the board', *Long Range Planning*, February.

Denning, Basil (1987), 'Strategic environmental appraisal', in John Fawn and Bernard Cox (1987), *Corporate Planning in Practice*, 2nd edn, Kogan Page.

Denning, Basil (1990), 'Strategy and Planning: definitions and hierarchies', a paper prepared for the Strategic Planning Society.

Derkinderen, Frans and Ray Crum (1984), 'Pitfalls of using portfolio techniques: assessing risk and potential', *Long Range Planning*, April.

Drucker, Peter (1954), *The Practice of Management*, Harper & Row.

Drucker, Peter (1958), 'Business objectives and survival needs', *Journal of Business*, April.

Drucker, Peter (1967), *Managing for Results*, Pan Piper.

Drucker, Peter (1973), *Management: Tasks, responsibilities and practices*, Harper & Row.

Drucker, Peter (1981), *The Bored Board*, an essay, Heinemann.

Drucker, Peter (1986), *Innovation and Entrepreneurship*, Heinemann.

Drucker, Peter (1989), 'What business can learn from non-profits', *Harvard Business Review*, July/August.

Drucker, Peter (1990), *The New Realities*, 2nd edn, Mandarin.

El-Namak, M. S. S. (1990), 'Small business: the myths and the reality ', *Long Range Planning*, August.

Engelow, J. L. and R. T. Lenz (1985), 'Whatever happened to environmental analysis?', *Long Range Planning*, April.

Ezra, Derek and David Oates (1989), *Advice From The Top*, David & Charles.

Fawn, John and Bernard Cox (1987), *Corporate Planning in Practice*, 2nd edn, Kogan Page.

Fisher, Anna B. (1990), 'Is long range planning worth it?', *Fortune*, 23 April.

Galbraith, J. K. (1967), *The New Industrial State*, Penguin.

Galbraith, J. K. (1989), Address to the Strategic Planning Society, March.

Gardner, John (1983a), *Morale*, Norton.

Gardner, John (1983b), *Self Renewal: The individual and the innovative society*, Norton.

Garratt, Bob (1987), *The Learning Organisation*, Fontana.

Ginn, Ron (1989), *Continuity Planning*, Elsevier Advanced Technology.

Ginter, Peter and Andrew Rucks (1984), 'Can business learn from wargames?', *Long Range Planning*, June.

Goold, Michael and Andrew Campbell (1988), 'Managing the diversified corporation', *Long Range Planning*, August.

Goold, Michael and Andrew Campbell (1989), a survey carried out for Ashridge Strategic Management Centre.

Goold, Michael and John Quinn (1990), *Strategic Control*, Hutchinson/Economist.

Grieve-Smith, John (1985), *Business Strategy: An introduction*, Basil Blackwell/Economist.

Haggerty, Patrick, (1980), 'Corporate self renewal', *Long Range Planning*.

Hamel, Gary, Yves Doz and C. K. Prahalad (1989), 'Collaborate with your competitors – and win', *Harvard Business Review*, January/February.

Handy, Charles (1985), *Understanding Organisations*, 3rd edn, Penguin.

Handy, Charles (1988), 'Careers for the 21st century', *Long Range Planning*, June.

Handy, Charles (1990), *The Age of Unreason*, 2nd edn, Arrow.

Hankinson, G. A. (1986), 'Energy scenarios: the Sizewell experience', *Long Range Planning*, October.

Harrison, Roger, quoted in Charles Handy (1985), *Understanding Organisations*, 3rd edn, Penguin.

Harvey-Jones, Sir John (1989), *Making it Happen*, 2nd edn, Fontana.

Heirs, Ben (1989), *The Professional Decision Thinker*, 2nd edn, Grafton.

Heller, Robert (1985), *The New Naked Manager*, Weidenfeld & Nicholson.

Hofer, Charles and Dan Schendel (1978), *Strategy Formulation: Analytical concepts*, West Publishing.

Holbrook, John and Terry Pritchard (1965), *Control of a Business*, Business Publications.

Huss, William and Edward Houton (1987), 'Scenario planning: what style should you use?', *Long Range Planning*, August.

Iacocca, Lee (1988), *Iacocca, An Autobiography*, Sidgwick & Jackson.

Institute of Directors (1984), *A New Agenda for Business*, 4th edn.

Institute of Directors (1985), *Guidelines for Directors*, 3rd edn.

Investors in Industry (1990), *Corporate Attitudes to Stock Market Valuations*, January.

James, Barry (1985), 'Alliance: the new strategic focus', *Long Range Planning*, June.

Jaques, Elliot (1990), 'In praise of hierarchy', *Harvard Business Review*, January/February, and based on E. Jaques (1989), *Requisite Organisation*, Cason Hall & Co.

Kanter, Rosabeth Moss (1989), *The Change Masters*, 4th edn, Unwin.

Kepner, Charles and Ben Tregoe (1976), *The Rational Manager*, 2nd edn, Kepner-Tregoe Inc.

Kono, T. and J. Stopford (1984), 'Long range planning in UK and Japanese corporations: a comparative study', *Long Range Planning*, April.

Kumar, Rakesh and Prem Vrat (1989), 'Using computer models in corporate planning', *Long Range Planning*, April.

Lauglaug, Antonio S. (1987), A framework for the strategic management of future tyre technology', *Long Range Planning*, October.

Lawrence, P. R. and J. N. Lorsch (1967), *Organisation and Environment*, Harvard University Press.

Leavitt, H. (1983), Stockton Lecture to the London Business School.

Leemhuis, Dr J. P. (1985), 'Using scenarios to develop strategies', *Long Range Planning*, April.

Lenz, R. T. (1985), 'Paralysis by analysis', *Long Range Planning*, August.

Levitt, Theodore 'Marketing myopia', *Harvard Business Review*.

Lindon-Travers, Ken (1990), *Non-Executive Directors*, Director Books.

Lloyd, Bruce (1989), *Entrepreneurship: Creating and managing new ventures*, Pergamon Press.

Lorenz, Christopher (1981), 'Pioneers: the anti-merger specialists', *The Financial Times*, 30 October.,

Lygo, Sir Raymond (1984), a paper presented to the 1984 Annual Conference of the Strategic Planning Society.

McCord, A. King (1962), 'Management by objectives', a paper to the Society for the Advancement of Management, 10 May.

McGregor, Douglas (1987), 'Theory X and theory Y', in D. S. Pugh (ed.) (1987), *Organisation Theory*, 2nd edn, Penguin.

McNamee, Patrick (1984), 'Competitive analysis using matrix displays', *Long Range Planning*, June.

Miesing, Dr Paul (1984), 'Integrating planning with management', *Long Range Planning*, October.

Millett, Dr Stephen (1988), 'How scenarios trigger strategic thinking', *Long Range Planning*, October.

Mills, Geoffrey (1981), *On The Board*, Gower/Institute of Directors.

Mills, Geoffrey (1989a), *Controlling Companies*, Unwin Hyman.

Mills, Geoffrey (1989b), 'Who controls the board?', *Long Range Planning*, June.

Mills, Roger (1988), 'Capital budgeting: the state of the art', *Long Range Planning*, August.

Minzburg, Henry (1987), *Harvard Business Review*, July/August.

Mitchell, Ewan (1978), *The Director's Lawyer and the Company Secretary's Legal Guide*, 4th edn, Business Books.

Mockler, Robert and D. G. Dologite (1988), 'Developing knowledge-based systems for strategic corporate planning', *Long Range Planning*, February.

Morse, Wesley (1986), 'The delusion of intrapreneurship', *Long Range Planning*, December.

Nagel, Arie (1984), 'Organising for strategic management', *Long Range Planning*, October.

Naisbitt, John (1984), *Megatrends*, Futura.

Narchal, Kittappa, and Bhattacharya (1987), 'An environmental scanning system for business planning', *Long Range Planning*, December.

Nolan, R. L. and C. G. Gibson (1974), 'Managing the four stages of EDP growth', *Harvard Business Review*.

Norburn, David (1989), 'The British boardroom: time for a revolution?', *Long Range Planning*, October.

Oakland, John (1989), *Total Quality Management*, Heinemann.

Ohmae, Kenichi (1983), *The Mind of the Strategist*, 2nd edn, Penguin.

Ohmae, Kenichi (1989), 'The global logic of strategic alliances', *Harvard Business Review*, March/April.

Palmer, Alfred (1953), *Company Secretarial Practice*, 8th edn, Longmans.

Peters, Tom (1989), *Thriving on Chaos*, 2nd edn, Pan.

Peters, Tom and Robert Waterman (1982), *In Search of Excellence*, Harper & Row.

Peters, Tom and Nancy Austin (1985), *A Passion for Excellence*, Collins.

Porter, Michael (1980), *Competitive Strategy*, Free Press.

Porter, Michael (1985), *Competitive Advantage*, Free Press.

Porter, Michael (1990a), 'The competitive advantage of nations', *Harvard Business Review*, March/April.

Porter, Michael (1990b), *The Competitive Advantages of Nations*, Free press.

PRONED (1989), *Non-Executive Directors: A survey of fees and related facts*, March.

Puckey, Sir Walter (1963), *Management Principles*, Hutchinson.

Richardson and Richardson (1989), *Business Planning: An approach to strategic management*, Pitman.

Robinson, S. J. Q. (1986), 'Paradoxes in planning', *Long Range Planning*, December.

Robinson, S. J. Q., R. E. Hitchins and D. P. Wade (1978), 'The directional policy matrix: tool for strategic planning', *Long Range Planning*, June.

Rostow, W. W. (1980), *Why the poor get richer and the rich slow down*, Macmillan.

Rowbotham and Bills, quoted in Charles Handy (1985), *Understanding Organisations*, 3rd edn, Penguin.

Sadler, Philip (1988), *Managerial Leadership in the Post-Industrial Society*, Gower.

Sallenave, Jean-Paul (1985), 'The uses and abuses of experience curves', *Long Range Planning*, February.

Sharp, J. D. (1990), 'A business strategy for the single European market', *Long Range Planning*, April.

Shurig, Russ (1984), 'Morphology: a tool for exploring new technology ', *Long Range Planning*, June.

Slatter, Stuart (1987), *Corporate Recovery*, Penguin.

Stacey, Ralph (1990), *Dynamic Strategic Management*, Kogan Page.

Stokke, P. R., W. K. Ralston, T. A. Boyce and I. M. Wilson (1990), 'Scenario planning for Norwegian oil and gas', *Long Range Planning*, April.

Taylor, Bernard (1988), *Strategic Planning: The chief executive and the board*, Pergamon Press.

Thomas, Dr Joe (1985), 'Force field analysis: a new way to evaluate your strategy', *Long Range Planning*, December.

Toffler, Alvin (1971), *Future Shock*, 2nd edn, Pan.

Tregoe, Benjamin and John Zimmerman (1980), *Top Management Strategy*, John Martin.

Vickers, Sir Geoffrey (1987), 'The art of judgement', in D. S. Pugh (ed.) (1987), *Organisation Theory*, 2nd edn, Penguin.

Wakerley, R. G. (1984), 'PIMS: a tool for developing competitive strategy', *Long Range Planning*, June.

Watson Jun., Thomas (1945), *A Business and its Beliefs: The ideas that helped build IBM*, McGraw-Hill.

Weber, M. (1987), 'Legitimate authority and bureaucracy' in D. S. Pugh (ed.) (1987), *Organisation Theory*, 2nd edn, Penguin.

Yoo, Sangjin and Lester Digman (1987), Decision support system: a new tool for strategic management', *Long Range Planning*, April.

INDEX